MW00378592

BUILDING ON RESILIENCE

BUILDING ON RESILIENCE

Models and Frameworks of Black Male Success Across the P–20 Pipeline

EDITED BY

Fred A. Bonner II

Foreword by Tim King
Afterword by Robert T. Palmer

STERLING, VIRGINIA

Published by Stylus Publishing, LLC
22883 Quicksilver Drive
Sterling, Virginia 20166-2102

Library of Congress Cataloging-in-Publication Data

Building on resilience : models and frameworks of Black male
success across the P-20 pipeline / edited by Fred A. Bonner II;
foreword by Tim King; afterword by Robert T. Palmer.
    pages cm
Includes bibliographical references and index.
ISBN 978-1-57922-961-0 (cloth : alk. paper)—
ISBN 978-1-57922-962-7 (pbk. : alk. paper)—
ISBN 978-1-57922-963-4 (library networkable e-edition)—
ISBN 978-1-57922-964-1 (consumer e-edition)
1. African American young men—Education. 2. African American
men—Education. 3. African American young men—Social
conditions. 4. African American men—Social conditions.
I. Bonner, Fred A.

LC2731.B85 2014
371.829'96073—dc23
                                                    2013047801

13-digit ISBN: 978-1-57922-961-0 (cloth)
13-digit ISBN: 978-1-57922-962-7 (paperback)
13-digit ISBN: 978-1-57922-963-4 (library networkable e-edition)
13-digit ISBN: 978-1-57922-964-1 (consumer e-edition)

Printed in the United States of America

All first editions printed on acid-free paper
that meets the American National Standards Institute
Z39-48 Standard.

Bulk Purchases

Quantity discounts are available for use in workshops and for
staff development.
Call 1-800-232-0223

First Edition, 2014

10   9   8   7   6   5   4   3   2   1

This book is dedicated to the strong and resilient Black men who have been an ever-present force in my life. Whether it was the "sage wisdom" of my godfather, the late Fred Lockett, or the "critical mentoring advice" advanced by Quintin Bullock, Jon Lofton, Gordon D. Morgan, Melvin C. Terrell, and Lonnie R. Williams, I have definitely been the beneficiary of their wise counsel. I also dedicate this volume to the Black man who will always serve as the "block" from which I was chipped—my father, "Coach 'Fred'" Arthur Bonner.

CONTENTS

PART TWO: POSTSECONDARY FRAMEWORKS AND MODELS

FOREWORD

To read any history of the twentieth century in American public education, one is inevitably struck by the fact that America's pundits, professors, and politicians have, for all their disagreements, always seemed to share one belief—the students of America's schools are in bad shape, and our Black boys are in the worst shape of all.

In Chicago, just 39% of African American male students graduate from high school. Black students make up 45% of the student body of Chicago public schools, yet they received 76% of the out-of-school suspensions. A University of Chicago Consortium on Chicago School Research study found that only 1 in 40 Black boys in Chicago public schools earns a four-year (bachelor's) college degree by the time he turns 25.

These statistics are startling and important for us to consider, but for too long we have allowed them to define perceptions of Black boys in our media, our politics, and even in our classrooms. Take for example the story of one of my former students. To these observers, Mr. Branch (at my school, Urban Prep Academy, we use surnames for all our students) is exhibit A of everything wrong with Black male high school students: low test scores, low income, low chance of success.

Mr. Branch was from a low-income, female-headed household located in one of the city's toughest neighborhoods. As a ninth-grader, he wasn't interested in being in an all-male school, he wasn't interested in being in school for two hours longer than students at other schools, he wasn't interested in wearing a jacket and necktie every day.

But rather than simply dwelling on what Mr. Branch lacked and what he didn't want to do, the teachers at Urban Prep focused on building positive relationships with him. These relationships empowered him to see in himself all the assets we saw in him from day one: drive, determination, loyalty, confidence, and resourcefulness.

Mr. Branch ultimately graduated from Urban Prep and went on to college where he is thriving today. His journey from a rocky start in high school to success in college is an increasingly common tale for the students at Urban Prep and young African American men across the country.

In some people's minds, deficits don't just simply put students like Mr. Branch at risk, they define a destiny. By showing us what is possible when we focus on the potential—in other words, the assets—of young Black boys and their communities rather than their deficits, Mr. Branch's story reveals that deficit-minded approaches are not only narrow minded, they are plainly inaccurate.

Like our school leaders and teachers, the researchers whose work is presented here have chosen to focus their energies not on an autopsy of a failed system, but rather on a close examination—and celebration—of what *works* for African American boys. The promising research and practical examples of strategies proven to drive success for African American boys should help reframe our conversations about failure and achievement for years to come. This vein of research will provide critical advancement of our ability to design effective interventions that will lead even greater numbers of African American boys to academic success.

I'm proud to be a part of this movement of educators developing practical, common-sense initiatives that lead more Black males to succeed in school. Urban Prep's graduates—all African American males, mostly from low-income families—have achieved what some think of as the impossible: a 100% college acceptance rate and the highest college enrollment rate of the city's public schools.

Mr. Branch is a part of that 100%—in fact, he was a member of our first graduating class. He and his classmates charted a path that forced politicians, school districts, and the news media to tell a different story about Black males, a story based on the assets of these young men, not their deficits; a story of success, not failure. This isn't to say that we should ignore or sugarcoat the issues facing Black males today. But instead of fixating on negative factors, we should foil these misperceptions with our own examples of young people who have successfully completed their education and earned degrees.

Forcing the country to take notice of the great things that Black male students are capable of is important because it will have a positive effect on students' identity and success for years to come. When the dominant presentation of Black males shows them dropping out of school and spending time in prison, Black male students who might already be unsure of their place in an educational environment feel further pressure to play down to the low level of expectations.

As more Black male students see more of their peers succeeding in school—and see those successes honored and celebrated on television and the Web—future generations will be apt to see themselves as likely to succeed. In turn, their schools and communities will establish higher expectations that are apt to help them do so.

Just as it is important for our students to see examples of their peers succeeding academically, it is vital for educators and education policymakers to develop awareness of the tremendous things that can happen when schools establish and meet high expectations. At Urban Prep, we have been greatly inspired and driven by research that established a framework of positive thinking about Black male academic success. Through the work of Shawn Dove of Open Society Foundations, Shaun Harper at the University of Pennsylvania, John Jackson of the Schott Foundation for Public Education, Pedro Noguera at New York University, Ivory Toldson at Howard University, and others, we learned of the great accomplishments of urban schools around the country. Their work defined an asset-driven approach to education that has been instrumental in enabling our teachers and staff to recognize the value and necessity of high expectations and building strong relationships with our students.

But in education, as in all things, the devil is in the details. It is not sufficient for us to simply say that we have established a framework of asset-based student empowerment and school improvement; we must unpack what that means for the daily work of leading a classroom and operating a school. We must push for greater clarity of how that framework can be implemented and for greater understanding of how we can better train teachers to replicate the strategies that work. The research compiled here does just that.

Great teachers always see the room for growth in even our most reluctant learners. As this research evinces, educators have been working diligently for decades to develop practical strategies that push students—and our nation—forward. Increasingly, we are seeing the fruits of our labors. Great progress in academic achievement for Black males has been made. Genuine breakthroughs for all students across the country are within reach.

Tim King
Founder and Chief Executive Officer
Urban Prep Academies

OPEN LETTER *(ABOUT BLACK MALES . . .)*

The birth of a child ignites within the imagination of a parent the possibility of a future not seen and redemption of a past that has been squandered. Every child born into this world is a shout from the Divine to humanity. *Your tomorrow is filled with hope, and you need not despair.*

This scenario is what all parents desire. But those who have been *kissed by nature's sun* and carry the invisible weight of a racialized past and tinted future are denied this joy. Black parents and Black children in this country are prescribed and offered a socially constructed fate where the future is rich with broken promises and deferred dreams. The legacy of systematic legal subjugation, policy formation designed to hinder movement and advancement, plus the psychosocial scars of genealogical purgatory have injured the forward momentum of Black boys.

In order for our community to deal with the crisis we face, we must confront several realities. We must first recognize the genius of our children. The industrial and Western model of education does not benefit a community with cultural roots in holistic learning and relational-based educational models. *Our children are brilliant.* Countless studies demonstrate the creative reasoning, abstract understanding, and pragmatic thinking of Black boys prior to their introduction to the fourth grade. The combination of early puberty, object-centered education, and de-emphasis of holistic learning shuts down the creative spark in many Black children, especially our boys. The school system's devotion to an industrial model of rote memorization and in-class rewards to the silent and least obtrusive students labels students who are gifted but nontraditional. Students with high oral and kinetic communication, intuitive problem-solving, and high abstract thinking skills are told through the educational structure, "You are not smart, worthy, or wanted." The reaction of many of our boys is twofold: disinterest on the one hand or acting out to get recognition from the teacher on the other.

The cruel aspect of education that is tripping up our children is the removal of relational-based learning in teacher training. Black boys soar in schools, on the field, in jobs when instructors demonstrate deep faith, commitment, and love for the student. When students understand that we care for them and their future, the behavior shifts quickly. Coaches, mentors, ministers, instructors, and teachers who demonstrate they are deeply committed to the student over and over witness students who were disruptive become stars of the class. Why? The reason is simple. African culture has a high relational pedagogy. In other words, the student cannot learn until he or she learns how much you care. When this simple technique and value is central, students go out of their way to perform and contribute to the classroom.

My own experience is a case study. I was labeled *learning disabled*. As a result, I spent several days a week in the basement of my elementary school. (I must note the irony of sending Black children to the basement, near the boiler, to motivate them to achieve.) At this point, based on statistics, I was destined to be low achieving. But two amazing teachers, Mrs. Burns and Mrs. Jaffe, came to my rescue. Mrs. Burns dealt with the so-called learning disabled, and Mrs. Jaffe was my fourth grade teacher. They both demonstrated a profound love for all students. Mrs. Burns made it clear that we did not belong in the basement, and it was her job to get us all out of the failing and bigoted learning disabled system. Mrs. Jaffe, a tough, loving woman, made it clear that she loved the students and demanded the best from them. Both of these women changed the trajectory of my life. They called my parents weekly saying, "Otis is incredibly smart, creative, and has a high IQ, but the tests are not designed to measure his gifts."

By the end of the fourth grade, my teachers discovered I had college-level vocabulary, reading comprehension, and abstract understanding of concepts, found through their commitment to relational and holistic learning, and their disdain for the old models of education, especially for Black boys.

All across the nation educators and institutions are throwing out the tired industrial models of learning and replacing them with dynamic relational models of education. The mantra of these schools is simple: Fit the curriculum to the child, not the child to the curriculum. When this takes place, the teacher seeks to inspire and illuminate, not test, test, and test again to compete for federal funds.

Schools such as the Urban Prep Academy in Chicago, an all-male and predominantly Black institution, have applied such a relational model in which students are the stars and the teachers are willing to invest in the student and creatively seek learning solutions to help the student thrive. All the students are seen as scholars, all are expected to graduate and attend college. As a result of this vision, 100% of all Urban Prep students graduate, and 100% are accepted to college. For those not familiar with Chicago, it should be noted Urban Prep is in the Englewood neighborhood, one of the poorest communities in the city with 40% of the residents at or near the poverty level. Urban Prep is all male and 99% African American.

Many find this amazing; I say it is not! This is the norm for Black boys and people of African descent when we shift how we teach and do not shy away from the brutal legacy of racism. *Black boys do not need extra help, they just need different assistance* to tap into the brilliance inherent in their DNA. Black boys are geniuses, and we must treat them as such if they are to realize their potential.

A dysfunctional love for the deficit model is apparent when speaking of Black Boys: *There is something wrong with them.* I say emphatically no; there is something wrong with the policymakers, curricula, and educators who refuse to throw out old models of education for children who have a unique history and an amazing future.

There is nothing wrong with Black boys, but a lot is wrong with adults. I pray that the book you hold in your hands will inspire and create a sense of righteous indignation to demand the best for and from our children. Our children deserve the best, and it is our responsibility as a village to protect and nurture the greatest of God's gifts to humanity, the gift of children.

Asking you to imagine a world where all Black boys are seen as brilliant, I remain

Rev. Otis Moss III

Senior Pastor

Trinity United Church of Christ

Chicago, IL

ACKNOWLEDGMENTS

I wish to acknowledge all of the special people who have believed in the work that I have accomplished in an effort to *move the needle* in a positive direction for Black males. There are too many of you to create an exhaustive list, but I will make an attempt to highlight a few: Aretha Marbley, Clement Price, Barbara Lofton, Cameron Harris, Jeremy Morris, Monica Moss, Pamela Garmon-Johnson, Anthony Nicotera, Dave Louis, Tommy Stevenson, Dorothy Bonner-Allen, Tommy Curry, Edrice Wyatt, Rosie Banda, Alonzo Flowers, Vicki Williams, Richard DeLisi, Earl Farrow, DeJuana Lozada, Timothy Proctor, Velma Banks, Penelope Lattimer, Petra Robinson, and William Campbell. I wish to extend a hearty thank-you to John von Knorring and the Stylus Publishing team for always providing the platform to transition my dream into a tangible product!

INTRODUCTION

Strengthening the Pipeline: A Need for Frameworks
and Models in Black Male Research

Fred A. Bonner II

The term *pipeline* has been applied metaphorically as a way to describe the conduit used by matriculates to flow through P–20 education systems. By extension, its application has been concomitantly associated with other descriptive terms such as *leaky* and *prison*. Thus, the dominant narrative that highlights the education pipeline for Black males in the United States concerns deficit framing and the attendant problems this population experiences in education contexts essentially from their earliest introduction to schools to their exit at the secondary and postsecondary end of the educational continuum. All too common are reports by scholars who suggest that the state of affairs for Black males in schools is at best concerning and at worst dire. According to Heilig and Reddick (2008), in speaking of their own emic experiences as Black males who have been involved in varying capacities with U.S. schools, "As educational researchers who are also Black males, we have personally and objectively observed evidence that the educational pipeline for young men of color is leaking rapidly. From witnessing our declining representation in high school honors courses, to college, and on to graduate school, we are used to being in a small minority " (para. 3).

Divining a solution that will address the problem of the pipeline will require the invocation of a bit of Stephen Covey's words of wisdom from *The Seven Habits of Highly Effective People*, namely, we should "begin with the end in mind" (1989, p. 95). Hence, the question then becomes, What is the end we seek for Black males in schooling contexts? Perhaps the knee-jerk response to this question is that we want all Black males to be successful. Yet, this prima facie retort begs further exploration through additional questions: What is our definition of *success*? Does our definition parallel, even remotely, how Black males define this term, particularly in light of their own lives and life circumstances? Additionally, what are the opportunity costs of being successful, especially academically successful in peer and school cohorts that could potentially view this form of achievement at best as abnormal and at worst as a threat? According to Noguera (2008), "We know less about the

1

specific nature of the perceptions and expectations that are held toward Black males and how these may in turn affect their performance within schools" (p. 18). Still other questions relate to identifying the multiple and competing factors that contribute to these males' success based on the definition we select as the most appropriate codification of the term *success*.

This book is grounded in the scholarship of several of the key researchers on Black male achievement in P–20 educational settings. Although success as an outcome variable can be viewed from different perspectives, the contributors to this volume galvanize around a definition of *success* in schools as characterized by Black males who achieve academic excellence through the typical indicators (e.g., good grades, positive matriculation, improving graduation rate, advanced or honors curricula participation). Although these scholars might not offer a unitary definition of *success* that holds true across the Black male diaspora, consistent across their scholarship are growth-producing discussions centered on the critical elements essential to implementing frameworks and models that can be sustained and that are empowering for Black males and those individuals who are committed to supporting their success. What is unique about this collection of frameworks and models is that each brings a perspective that advances strategies that are asset based (Bonner, 2000; Bonner & Bailey, 2006; Ford, 1992) as opposed to the deficit-oriented approaches that tend to ignore positive developmental accoutrements, such as *resilience*, that are essential to this population's learning, growth, and development. According to scholars (Alford, 2003; Bonner, 2000, 2001; Bonner & Bailey, 2006; Fashola, 2005; Ford, 1992, 1995, 2003; Grantham, 2004; Hébert, 2002; Hrabowski, Maton, & Greif, 1998; Whiting, 2006, 2010) this ideological positioning sets in place the frame of reference used to judge all Black males. The cycle is recapitulated and reinforced through a series of steps that move perceptions to perspectives and perspectives to positions and worldviews. Ultimately, with each movement and successive step, the individual becomes even more entrenched in his or her beliefs. For Black male populations and those who work with these men, if the point of initiation to begin the process of identity construction begins from a place of deficits, it is extremely difficult to change the course of the tide that has gained momentum flowing in that direction. Thus, as a means of changing the discourse about Black males, the previously mentioned researchers and the intellectual community members assembled in this book have committed to promote efforts at a grassroots level to challenge the status quo and advance contemporary and progressive counternarratives (Riessman, 1993; Rimstead, 1996) that begin with the end in mind. That is, we start with achievement and success by demanding that our P–12 schools and institutions of higher education start their journeys of colearning and educational achievement from a place that views these Black males not as damaged goods but as individuals with agency. The word *agency* is used here for a very specific purpose. It is highly important for those seeking to recast the narrative and truly begin from an end-in-mind place to recognize that these Black males are not just present, but they have agency. The distinction is that by merely considering their presence, the all-too-typical approach is to develop programming, fashion initiatives, and gather reams of assessment data. However, as a first step it is of paramount importance to recognize that these men are not only agents, but they have agency. When an individual has agency, he or she is not just a passive actor to be acted upon but is also capable of action.

Trying to identify a Black male prototype in the context of education and the education pipeline is a difficult task but is not to be discouraged. If this task is undertaken as a genuine effort to improve the life circumstances of these individuals, we as a nation and the world are also sure to be the beneficiaries, truly recalling the biblical words, "Whatever you did for one of the least of these" (Matthew 25: 31–46, New International Version) in a most profound way. In other words, the energy we put into supporting our marginalized and underserved populations in schools will not only advance these specific groups but will reap benefits for the country as a whole. Noguera (2008) refers to the work of Guinier and Torres (2002) in which these scholars state

> Those who are racially marginalized are like the miner's canary: their distress is the first sign of danger that threatens us all. It is easy enough to think that when we sacrifice this canary, the only harm done is to communities of color. Yet others ignore problems that converge around racial minorities at their own peril, for these problems are symptoms warning us that we are all at risk. (Guinier & Torres, 2002, pp. 11–12)

According to Jackson (2012) in *The Urgency of Now: The Schott 50 State Report on Public Education and Black Males*, the sobering reality of the current elementary and secondary landscape for this population indicates that

> academically only 10 percent of Black males in the United States are deemed proficient in 8th grade reading, and only 52% are graduating from high school in a four-year period. Thus the penal institutions remain populated with too many Black males and the classroom student rolls with too few. (para. 2)

Sadly, the postsecondary landscape does not yield statistics that are any more encouraging. According to a report in the *Journal of Blacks in Higher Education* (2005),

> In each of the three years from 1998 through 2000 there was a one percentage point decline in the graduation rate for black men. But for the past

four years the graduation rate for black men improved by one percentage point and now stands at 35 percent. Over the past 15 years black men have improved their graduation rate from 28 percent to 35 percent. ("Black Student College Graduation Rates Remain Low, but Modest Progress Begins to Show," 2005, p. 88)

These data represent the graduation rates of Black males in predominantly White institutions (PWIs); however, tracking the rates in our nation's historically Black colleges and universities (HBCUs), the numbers were not much different. Therefore, here we stand at the precipice of making a commitment to taking on the mantle of engaging in the arduous but critically important task of finding solutions and implementing strategies that will move the needle in a positive direction regarding the status of Black males and Black male education in the United States. One of the shortcomings of using a metaphor to describe complex situations is that it never fully captures the true context. Although the pipeline metaphor is used to frame each one of the chapters in this book, the authors attempt to provide as much of the backstory that will facilitate understanding how their models can be used in real time with real people in real situations. It is preferable for the reader who seeks plausible remedies to determine relevant limits and opportunities for the appropriate use of these models.

Building on Resilience: Models and Frameworks of Black Male Success Across the P–20 Pipeline is a seminal compendium offering in one volume the most critical contemporary scholars and their scholarship focused on Black males and their success in settings across the P–20 education continuum. While this book is not meant to focus on *gifted* Black male students, given the scope of several of the chapters, it would be a fair assessment to say that the experiences of Black males who are gifted and high achieving in some capacity across various contexts constitute a consistent theme. I have built my career conducting research that attempts to excogitate the experiences of academically gifted Black males in school settings across the P–20 education spectrum. This book is tailored for P–12 (parents, policymakers, principals, superintendents, and teachers) as well as for postsecondary (faculty, student affairs administrators) audiences. Chapter 1, by Sharon Michael-Chadwell, underscores the experiences of Black males in P–12 urban school settings. She deftly interweaves critical race theory, social cognitive theory, and social dominance theory to create a framework that can be used in and outside classroom contexts to illuminate the meaning and importance of interaction for Black male cohorts. In Chapter 2 H. Richard Milner IV, Quaylan Allen, and Ebony O. McGee foreground the often touchy subject of race. These authors urge teachers to engage in conversations about this topic as a critical first step in developing curricula and structuring instructional approaches supportive of Black male success. These authors offer a race talk framework that provides critical insight on how discussions about race can inform teacher practice. In discussing the importance of the advocacy process in Chapter 3, Tarek C. Grantham, Christopher O. Johnson, Angie C. Roberts-Dixon, and Eric M. Bridges pull back the curtain to reveal the primary actors who should always occupy center stage in these processes, focusing on the role of parent advocacy for Black males. Donna Y. Ford, L. Trenton Marsh, Jerell Blakeley, and Stanford O. Amos in Chapter 4 describe and interrogate the significant and indefensible absence of formally identified gifted Black male students in U.S. schools, with attention to access and recruitment barriers and the implications when access is denied. Four vignettes of gifted Black males are presented to stress the urgency of finding and serving these males however they use and demonstrate their gifts. In Chapter 5 Thomas P. Hébert brings out of the shadows the rural gifted Black male, who at best goes unnoticed and at worst remains unknown. Building on his article, "Jermaine: A Critical Case Study of a Gifted Child Living in Rural Poverty" (Hébert & Beardsley, 2001), he challenges those entrusted with the education of Black males to broaden their perspectives of this population who come from backgrounds of poverty to look beyond the confines of urban enclaves and to look at the challenges as well as the opportunities of these gifted males in bucolic settings. Hébert includes a visual model that is inclusive of the components found to be meaningful in the life of the young gifted Black male. Gilman Whiting's scholar identity model, discussed in Chapter 6, is one of the most referenced frameworks for addressing a major root cause for the lack of success Black males experience in school contexts. According to Whiting's model, it is important for these young men to first see themselves as scholars capable of being successful. In addition to these men, other key individuals such as administrators, parents, and teachers must also cosign on this newly formed identity. I offer Chapter 7 to fill the extant gap in the literature that addresses academically gifted Black males in postsecondary settings. It is based on my prior empirical work (Bonner, 2010) that uncovered six categories found to foster academic giftedness among African American males in HBCUs and PWIs.

Following in the vein of institutions of higher education, Alonzo M. Flowers in Chapter 8 extends the reach of the narrative on Black males in HBCUs and PWIs, particularly academically gifted Black males from poverty backgrounds who major in science, technology, engineering, and mathematics (STEM) fields. T. Elon Dancy II in Chapter 9 offers important insight into the fabric of his work *The Brother Code* (2012) in which he provides a comprehensive and compelling review of studies that treat Black boyhood and identity construction in schools. In constructing his narrative, he synthesizes the landscape of Black manhood and masculinities research in college. Dancy's model of manhood included in the chapter is quite innovative in that it seeks to inform thinking and practice about the role of these matters in educational settings. The chapter concludes with a comprehensive discussion of key implications for research and practice.

James L. Moore III, Lamont A. Flowers, and Lawrence O. Flowers discuss academic and career development for Black males in STEM fields in Chapter 10. Using qualitative data from an empirical investigation that included more than 30 individual and focus group interviews, these researchers share their framework that has the potential to inform the development of programs and services designed to promote academic and career self-efficacy among Black males in these fields. Several emergent themes are synthesized into a framework that has significant promise for helping Black males achieve success in STEM disciplines. Used in tandem with Alonzo M. Flowers's Chapter 8 on Black males from poverty backgrounds in STEM fields, this chapter offers a comprehensive perspective on how to promote change for this population in this area.

The community college serving as the institution of first choice for the majority of students of color in the nation is critical to the evolution of American higher education. Within these enclaves we see significant participation by Black students in general and Black males in particular. J. Luke Wood and Frank Harris III unpack the narrative that explains Black male engagement with the American community college in Chapter 11.

In an engaging commentary about intellect on the gridiron, Derrick L. Gragg presents his insights in Chapter 12. His powerful chapter uncovers the factors that affect academic persistence and graduation rates among academically talented Black males in athletics. Most inspiring about Gragg's chapter is the authenticity he brings to his narrative by including his own experiences as a scholar athlete at Vanderbilt University. His recommendations provide sage advice for research and practice to support Black male student athletes.

Serving as the capstone to this comprehensive volume is Chapter 13. One of the leading voices in the nation on issues affecting lesbian, gay, bisexual, and transgender communities of color in academe, particularly Black males, Terrell L. Strayhorn uses critical information from a number of his empirical studies that have explored the experiences of gay Black men on college and university campuses. Strayhorn offers a model that foregrounds college students' sense of belonging and the implications for Black gay male cohorts who grapple with finding their place in higher education contexts.

Robert T. Palmer pulls all the pieces together in his afterword, using Robert Frost's poem *The Road Not Taken* to impart to the reader the significance of the chapters and the work of the contributors in this book who stand at that fork in the road and are left with the decision of whether to pursue a line of inquiry that would put them in the academic mainstream. However, these scholars have chosen to take the pathway that is so often not taken; they have elected to pursue research that attempts to redirect and redefine the narratives that too frequently are consumed with documenting deficits as opposed to recognizing resilience. It is my hope that this book provides readers with road maps to assist in their journey down whatever pathway they choose, particularly if this trek involves providing needed support of Black males along the way.

The strength of *Building on Resilience: Models and Frameworks of Black Male Success Across the P–20 Pipeline* is its use of multiple lenses that bring a focus on Black males into a clearer view, especially those who are gifted and high achieving whether in academics or some other capacity. In the introduction of this volume, I use an example from Noguera (2008) in which he cites legal scholars Guinier and Torres who poignantly describe in their book *The Miner's Canary: Enlisting Race, Resisting Power, Transforming Democracy* how the status of affairs for marginalized populations in the country is much like the canary used by miners to warn of dangerous toxicity levels in the mining environment usually stemming from the presence of noxious gases. For Black male populations this is a powerful metaphor to spark critical thinking and engage discourse on the ways Black males respond in societal contexts, especially educational settings. Harkening back to my undergraduate experience as a chemistry major at the University of North Texas, I am reminded of the repeated admonishments meted out by the dutiful graduate student who taught my organic chemistry laboratory. As routine practice in the lab, we were often required to pour chemicals or a range of liquid substances into graduated cylinders, beakers, or some other vessel that would ultimately require us to take a measurement of the volume of the particular aqueous solution. I learned from these experiences that when measuring the amount of liquid in any of these containers the observer is required to get to an eye-level position to focus on the center of the *meniscus*, what scientists refer to as the phase boundary that becomes curved because of surface tension. In other words, the meniscus is the indentation, the lowest point in the curved middle portion of a liquid in a container. Most times, the curvature of the liquid is concave, but in the case of the element Mercury, the mensicus's curvature is convex. Whether concave or convex, the key lesson to be taken from this example is that unless the observer or scientist reports the volume of liquid contained in the vessel based on the center location of the meniscus, the measurements are inaccurate. This measurement process to determine liquid volume in many ways parallels how we should measure and subsequently structure our educational processes for Black males in general and gifted

Black males in particular. However, I am mindful of the lessons gained by reading the meniscus: at the center of the collection of molecules making up the liquid substance is the true reading of what the relevant volume is. How do we as a community inside and outside the schools find the meniscus? Who is at the center of this congeries of Black males in these multiple, layered, and competing contexts? Asking the question is typically easier than divining the solution. Yet, if we are truly to initiate change and support this cohort's success, we must channel our efforts to better prepare our parents, teachers, administrators, and Black males to not only create but also embrace empowering frameworks and models. Whether we are speaking in terms of canaries or menisci, the essential lesson here is that the good we do for Black males is the good we do for ourselves.

References

Alford, K. (2003). Cultural themes in rites of passage: Voices of young African American males. *Journal of African American Studies, 7*(1), 3–26.

Black student college graduation rates remain low, but modest progress begins to show. (2005). *The Journal of Blacks in Higher Education, 50,* 88–96. doi:10.2307/25073382

Bonner, F. A., II. (2000). African American giftedness. *Journal of Black Studies, 30,* 643–664.

Bonner, F. A., II. (2001). *Academically gifted African American male college students: A phenomenological study.* Storrs: National Research Center on the Gifted and Talented, University of Connecticut.

Bonner, F. A. II. (2010). *Academically gifted African American males in college.* Santa Barbara, CA: ABC-CLIO.

Bonner, F. A., II, & Bailey, K. (2006). Assessing the academic climate for African American men. In M. Cuyjet (Ed.), *African American men in college* (pp. 24–46). San Francisco, CA: Jossey-Bass.

Covey, S. R. (1989). *The seven habits of highly effective people.* New York, NY: Simon & Schuster.

Dancy, T. E. (2012). *The brother code: Manhood and masculinity among African American males in college.* Charlotte, NC: Information Age.

Fashola, O. (2005). *Educating African American males: Voices from the field.* New Thousand Oaks, CA: Corwin Press.

Ford, D. Y. (1992). Determinants of underachievement as perceived by gifted, above-average, and average Black students. *Roeper Review, 14*(3), 130–136. (Reprinted as a special issue of the *Mensa Research Journal*)

Ford, D. Y. (1995). Desegregating gifted education: A need unmet. *Journal of Negro Education, 64*(1), 52–62.

Ford, D. Y. (2003). Two other wrongs don't make a right: Sacrificing the needs of diverse students does not solve gifted education's unresolved problems. *Journal for the Education of the Gifted, 26,* 283–291.

Grantham, T. C. (2004). Rocky Jones: Case study of a high-achieving Black male's motivation to participate in gifted classes. *Roeper Review, 26,* 208–215.

Guinier, L., & Torres, G. (2002). *The miner's canary: Enlisting race, resisting power, transforming democracy.* Cambridge MA: Harvard University Press.

Hébert, T. P. (2002). Gifted males. In M. Neihart, S. M. Reis, N. M. Robinson, & S. M. Moon (Eds.), *The social and emotional development of gifted children: What do we know?* (pp. 137–144). Waco, TX: Prufrock Press.

Hébert, T. P., & Beardsley, T. M. (2001). Jermaine: A critical case study of a gifted Black child living in rural poverty. *Gifted Child Quarterly, 45,* 85–103.

Heilig, J. V, & Reddick, R. J. (2008). *Perspectives: Black males in the educational pipeline.* Retrieved from http://www.diverseeducation.com

Hrabowski, F. A., III, Maton, K. I., & Greif, G. L. (1998). *Beating the odds: Raising academically successful African American males.* Oxford, UK: Oxford University Press.

Jackson, J. H. (2012). *The urgency of now: The Schott 50 state report on public education and Black males.* Cambridge, MA: Schott Foundation for Public Education.

Noguera, P. A. (2008) *The trouble with black boys and other reflections on race, equity, and the future of public education.* San Francisco, CA: Jossey-Bass.

Riessman, C. K. (1993). *Narrative analysis.* Qualitative research methods series 30. Thousand Oaks, CA: Sage.

Rimstead, R. (1996). What Working-Class Intellectuals Claim to Know. *Race, Gender, & Class, 4*(1), 119–141.

Whiting, G. W. (2006). From at risk to at promise: Developing scholar identities among Black males. *Journal of Secondary Gifted Education, 17*(4), 222–229.

Whiting, G. (2010, November). *The Scholar Identity Model: GT coordinators and teachers working with young Black males.* Presentation at the National Association for Gifted Children Annual Convention, Atlanta, GA.

PART ONE

P–12 FRAMEWORKS AND MODELS

I

A FRAMEWORK FOR BLACK MALES IN P–12 URBAN SCHOOL DISTRICTS

Sharon Michael-Chadwell

In more than 16,000 school districts in the United States and since the 1980s, Black males in P–12 educational systems have been identified as being underachievers as well as linked to experiencing "higher rates of suspensions, expulsions, non-promotions, dropouts, special education placements, and the lowest rates of secondary school graduation" (Garibaldi, 2007, p. 324). Researchers (e.g., Hargrove & Seay, 2011; Michael-Chadwell, 2010; Michael-Chadwell, Bonner, & Lewis, 2009) have concluded that many Black males start schools as excited learners; by fourth or fifth grade, their excitement wanes because of an awareness of being treated unfairly by White teachers or being treated differently by other students as a result of negative imaging in the media. The social and economic implications related to the miseducation of Black males should be considered a significant phenomenon in the educational pipeline, which has become a foundation that threatens their abilities to achieve academically (Whiting, 2009).

Given the social significance and the milestones achieved in gifted and talented education, there is an imbalance in the history of the program and in the identification of Black and other historically underserved students for placement in these programs. Since the 50th anniversary of the 1954 Supreme Court case *Brown v. Board of Education*, gifted programs throughout the U.S. public school system may be facilitating a hidden segregation agenda, given the overrepresentation of White students in these programs at the expense of the underrepresentation of African American and other underserved gifted students (Staiger, 2004). While being classified as gifted is not guaranteed to equate with academic success, Whiting (2009) and I (Michael-Chadwell, 2008) concluded that Black males are at a greater risk of not achieving academic success in comparison with other student groups.

Meier, Kohn, Darling-Hammond, Sizer, and Wood (2004) stated, "Children of color and children of the poor still do not fare as well in school as their wealthier, White counterparts" (p. viii). Documented research indicated that the traditional means of identifying giftedness inadvertently negated the intellectual capacities of Black students and especially males, thereby minimizing opportunities for selection into gifted programs (Bonner, 2005; Ford & Moore, 2005; Michael-Chadwell, 2008; Villarreal, 2004). When examining the nature of gifted programs as well as the identification and selection of students, consideration of this phenomenon in the context of a theoretical framework is necessary to understand its manifestation in the public education system, especially for Black males in P–12 urban school districts. While much of the discussion in this chapter does lend itself to issues of underrepresentation of students of color in gifted and talented programs, there appears to be a parallel to the plight and education of Black males in school settings. Given this perspective, the following theories serve as an interwoven framework to understand this phenomenon as well as its implications on the interactions of Black males in the classroom and external environments: the social dominance theory (SDT), critical race theory (CRT), and social cognitive theory.

Social Dominance Theory

Understanding the premise of the SDT could explain the continued acceptance of the underrepresentation of minority students in relation to the nomination process used to identify potentially gifted students (Cross & Cross, 2005). The hypothesis associated with the SDT was that social stability maintenance occurs when subordinate groups believe that dominant groups are deserving of a large proportion of "positive social value" (p. 22). In postmodern American society, the male classified as high socioeconomic status (SES) represents the dominant group according to these researchers. Given the environmental challenges Black males face in urban settings, the application of the SDT signals an immediate imbalance in society's perceptions of race, readiness, and ability when compared with those of White males in higher SES income brackets.

When applying the context of the SDT to the public education system, certain dynamics affecting the relationship between the teacher and

Black students cannot be ignored. Harmon (2002) implemented a qualitative study and interviewed gifted African American students regarding their perceptions of effective versus ineffective teachers. Harmon noted that "these students were bused from their predominantly African American neighborhood to desegregate a predominantly White school and then returned to their predominantly African American neighborhood after busing was dismantled" (p. 68). The development of interview questions for Harmon's study focused on teacher efficacy in the following categories: teacher attitude, cultural competence, and student interactions. The implications of the study are that teachers will need to become more culturally competent as they work to meet the needs of African American students as well as diverse groups of students.

Obiakor (2004) contended that for the No Child Left Behind legislation to become successful, a "comprehensive support model [is required] that taps into the energies of students, families, schools, communities, and governments in the educational process" (p. 402). When considering the continuation of research on the disproportionate placement of Blacks in special and gifted programs in P–12 urban settings, Obiakor did not believe these children would become benefactors of this particular piece of legislation. Black males are overrepresented in special education programs, lose their motivation, and have a tendency to become disengaged from the educational process (Hargrove & Seay, 2011; Michael-Chadwell, 2008; Whiting, 2009). Although the rhetoric regarding the disproportionate placement of minorities in special and gifted programs continues, the deliberateness of enacting public policy to address these issues appears to go against the premise of the No Child Left Behind legislation (Obiakor, 2004). Similar to Obiakor's contentions, Robinson (2005) and Strange (2005) determined that perceptions of resegregation within the public school system would continue to persist with the overrepresentation and underrepresentation of minorities in special programs.

When examining the SDT in the context of the dynamics of race-ethnic identity, research has determined a relationship between the shortage of Black teachers and the academic success of Black students in public schools (Berry, 2005; Mabokela & Madsen, 2003; White, 2002). As schools desegregated, White (2002) argued that Black students were no longer being "challenged academically" (p. 272). Berry noted when prospective White teachers enter U.S. schools, colleges, and departments of education, their personal experiences and views of themselves as well as the world around them affect how they teach. Yet, Black educators contended that they understood their "own kind better and that there were certain kinds of knowledge that were more easily transmitted by Black teachers to Black children" (White, 2002, p. 272).

Lintner (2004) professed, "Teachers are a conduit for the interpretation and perpetuation of racial stereotyping in schools" (p. 29). For that reason, a manifestation of biases or stereotypes in the classroom might be a result of social, economic, and political privileges inherently given to Whites (Bond, 2004; Lawrence, 1997; Lintner, 2004). A relationship between teachers endorsing the values and beliefs of mainstream society and the dilemma of the misidentification of Black students is likely (Obiakor, 2004). In an earlier study on teacher perceptions of students in a culturally diverse class, Obiakor (1999) noted researchers' findings on the tendency of the teachers to respond more favorably to White students than to their culturally diverse counterparts. Obiakor, therefore, asserted that a continued misdiagnosis of the abilities and talents of Black students would have a diminishing effect on their self-esteem and self-efficacy. For Black males, there is a greater chance of this misdiagnosis, misidentification, and miseducation because of factors such as negative imaging and a lack of cultural understanding.

Teachers' perceptions of culture-related identities are relevant to the educational successes of students (Ladson-Billings, 2006; Neal, McCray, Webb-Johnson, & Bridgest, 2003). In particular, Neal et al. contended, "African American students . . . benefit from a culturally responsive pedagogy" (p. 49). In relation to non-Black students, Neal et al. emphasized that the probability of experiencing academic achievement among Black students increases when they perceive that their teachers are culturally sensitive in their instructional delivery. Ladson-Billings (2006) asserted that Black students might experience a cultural separation in relation to the schooling process when faced with a cultural incongruency between home, community, and school. Smith, Atkins, and Connell (2003) documented similar observations regarding cultural separation between the individualistic ethos related to academic achievement in the public education system and a strong adherence to a racial-ethnic ethos adopted by certain youths.

Neal et al. (2003) noted that the misperceptions of teachers as well as their negative reactions to culturally conditioned behaviors could contribute to academic and social failure among culturally diverse students. For example, stylized movements are characteristic and central to Black males' development, whereby these movements are an interchange of "movement, rhythm, percussion, music, and dance" (Neal et al., 2003, p. 50). Stereotypes associated with Black males' adoption of postures symbolic of masculinity, pride, strength, and control might affect teachers' expectations of their future behavior and academic successes; sometimes, teachers misconstrue these behaviors as related to emotional disturbance (Cullinan & Kauffman, 2005; Thomas, Townsend, & Belgrave, 2003).

Thomas et al. (2003) argued that Black males might resort to maintaining these stances either to hide feelings of rejection resulting from perceived and experienced injustices or to garner respect from teachers and peers. Similarly, Patten and Townsend (2001) reported that Black males remained vulnerable to ineffective instruction, underachievement, and being overrepresented in special programs for the learning challenged. Contingent on their use of Black English, teachers could either lower or raise their expectations of the academic abilities of these students (Neal et al., 2003), in particular regarding Black males.

Critical Race Theory

CRT addresses the historical suppression of Blacks, race and racism, and minimized self-empowerment (Gillborn, 2005; Hertzog, 2005; Saddler, 2005; Snipes & Waters, 2005); therefore, the theory postulates that the omnipresence of racism is a constant factor in the daily experiences of people of color (Hertzog, 2005). In the education environment, DeCuir and Dixson (2004) viewed CRT as a means of understanding social, assessment, power, discipline, and curriculum issues. Delpit (2003, 2006) argued issues of power become more prevalent as schools promote learning agendas based on the cultural constructs of White middle- and upper-class segments of society. Consequently, minority students might feel stereotypically threatened when challenged to demonstrate intellectual abilities that might confirm negative stereotypes, thereby hurting their academic performance (Lehrman, 2005).

Considerable discourse has occurred regarding the existence of achievement gaps between minority and White students in the U.S. public education system, with much of the attention focusing on the relationship between underrepresentation and underachievement (Snipes & Waters, 2005). If education leaders understood the premise of CRT, they could begin to develop praxis within their assigned learning communities to address issues of race and racism and the influences of such issues on how teachers view minority students' abilities and potential (Lynn, 2006; Stovall, 2004). Saddler (2005) claimed CRT offers a powerful framework for reexamining the state of affairs in the current public education system.

In an examination of germinal theories on intelligence, Morris (2002) suggested psychological research subjectively legitimized the perception that the intelligence of African Americans is inferior to that of Whites. Grounded in psychology, Morris said that remnants of this belief permeated the field of gifted education. Hence, the selection of individuals eligible for gifted programs is dependent on "enduring perceptions, whether conscious or unconscious, that African American people might be intellectually inferior to White people" (p. 59). Therefore, Morris suggested a need for more research on the significance of race and racism as variables in the nomination, assessment, and identification of students into gifted programs.

Studying the schooling of adolescent Black males, Duncan (2002) wrote:

> Although the standard education story explains the plight of young Black males as a persistent and troublesome, but random, outcome of a reasonably fair, *aracial* system; critical race theory holds that their situation is actually a manifestation of the racial politics that are intrinsic, even vital, to the day-to-day functions of U.S. society and social institutions such as schools. (p. 131)

Hence, within the framework of CRT, Duncan (2002) asserted that the exclusion and marginalization of Black males in school systems is a problem. Furthermore, marginalized populations such as Black males possess "values and attitudes that require explication and clarification because they are fundamentally different from those of the rest of society" (p. 133).

Noting arguments from critical race theorists such as Richard Delgado, Duncan concluded that because racism is an eminent feature of society, some believe that marginalized populations such as Black males possess values and attitudes fundamentally different from the perceived norms of mainstream society. Duncan suggested that in the school setting, the vulnerability and the marginalization of Black males translates into perceptions that this student population is too different, strange, and antagonistic when compared with other students. Hence, it is perceived that Black males will have difficulty in complying with schools' codes of conduct.

Duncan said there are social implications related to the marginalization of a group of people, the first of which is exclusion from society's economy and networks of care. Second, because of the persistence of marginalization and society's view of the existence of Black males as strange, Duncan asserted that this group might actually be adopting the belief they are an *estranged* population. In addition, Black males might view their "social and academic experiences as evidence of malevolence or neglect on the part of those in power, or else [as evidence of] basic defects in the social system of school" (Duncan, 2002, p. 133). In essence, this sentiment suggests a negative effect on Black males' abilities for academic achievement in schools and their inability to gain access to gifted programs available to other students. Linking this to the tenets of the social dominance theory, Duncan suggested that oppression and domination explain the exclusion and marginalization of Black males in school systems.

Social Cognitive Theory

In a study in which the focus was on the interactions of Black males in the classroom and their environments, Williams (2012) used the social cognitive theory as the foundation for the study's theoretical framework. Based on Albert Bandura's research, the premise of the theory suggests that behavior and knowledge is contingent on (a) environmental factors, (b) emotional capabilities, and (c) cognitive processing. For an individual to reach his or her full potential, all three capabilities must be in accord with each other according to Williams.

To understand the significance of the social cognitive theory on an individual's ability to learn, the following six constructs need explanation:

1. Reciprocal Determinism: the dynamic and reciprocal interaction of person (individual with a set of learned experiences), environment (external social context), and behavior (responses to stimuli to achieve goals);
2. Behavioral Capability: a person's actual ability to perform a behavior through essential knowledge and skills;
3. Observational Learning: A person's ability to observe and reproduce a behavior exhibited through modeling of the behavior;
4. Reinforcements: the internal or external responses to a person's behavior that affect the likelihood of continuing or discontinuing the behavior;
5. Expectations: the anticipated consequences of a person's behavior; and
6. Self-Efficacy: the level of a person's confidence in his or her ability to successfully perform a behavior. ("Behavioral Change Theory: The Social Cognitive Theory," 2013, para. 3)

In a social context, learning occurs based on interactions that are dynamic and reciprocal ("Behavioral Change Theory: The Social Cognitive Theory," 2013).

Swanson, Cunningham, and Spencer (2003) asserted that Black males were the most stigmatized and stereotyped group in the United States. In the framework of the social cognitive theory, concomitant images that depict stereotypical imaging of Black males include (a) the super athlete, (b) criminal or gangster, or (c) the hypersexed male. Given these stereotypes as well as economic, political, and social forces, Black males are at a greater risk of experiencing adverse outcomes and behaviors. Pajares (2002) suggested without positive role models, Black males born in poverty environments are more subject to adopting negative behaviors without understanding the codes of conduct necessary to function in society at large. According to Swanson et al. (2003), because of this type of environment, instances related to resilience and success as well as competence go unnoticed and unrecognized.

In the context and constructs of social cognitive theory, Moriearty and Carson (2012) said that Black males in the United States were experiencing a cognitive warfare. As individuals begin to map out perceptions into categories, inferences are drawn about encounters with others based on cognitive beliefs or stereotypes and affective feelings or prejudices. Moriearty and Carson concluded that a self-reinforcing feedback loop existed that changed the significance of the young Black male in "profound and intractable ways" (p. 1). The majority of U.S. society continues to harbor stereotypical notions related to Black males in terms of criminality and deviance while supporting the administration of policies that disproportionately suppresses them.

A Framework for Understanding the Plight of Black Males

The three theories described in this chapter represent an independent framework when examining factors related to the educational experiences of Black males in P–12 settings, especially those attending urban schools. The following Venn diagram depicts an interrelated relationship (Renzulli, 1999); in the context of Black males, this interrelated relationship consists of circumstances related to political, cultural, social, and academic factors that affect their abilities to achieve success. Hence, the creation of an interrelated framework is appropriate. Focusing on the interconnectivity of the three theories—SDT, CRT, and social cognitive theory—provides educational leaders with a more comprehensive framework to understand the needs of this population group in helping them become more successful in achieving academic and societal success. Figure 1.1 illustrates the interrelated relationship of the three theoretical frameworks in relation to the experiences of Black males.

Figure 1.1 Framework of Interrelated Constructs Influencing Black Males

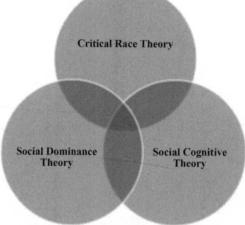

When examining the framework, the intersection of any two theories provides a better understanding when considering the needs of Black males to help them become more successful in P–12 schools such as those in urban settings. While each theory provides an explanation in understanding the plight of Black males, a collective understanding is necessary when considering the implications of the three theories, especially with the intention of reviewing P–12 program practices and barriers hindering Black males from accessing resources needed to improve their educational experience as well as recognizing their value in acquiring an education. To counter the ongoing cycles of underrepresentation of this cohort in academically rigorous as well as gifted and talented programming, it will become increasingly important for educators, parents, policymakers, and researchers to seek ways to improve their understanding of how this population is experiencing U.S. schooling (Michael-Chadwell, Bonner, & Louis, 2009).

Conclusion

Even though the U.S. population is becoming increasingly diverse in culture, the social implications are that in the public education system a continued misperception of Black males concerning race and ability remains. The reality is that gaps continue in their abilities to appreciate social, economical, academic, and political success in relation to others. Despite a prevailing acclamation of liberty and justice for all in the United States, a framework that interconnects the constructs that focus on Black males can become a foundation to understand their plight. In P–12 urban educational settings, the framework becomes the basis of implementing strategies needed to help those who "occupy the academic margins to become successful" (Michael-Chadwell et al., 2009, p. 244). Despite the images of the media, negative perceptions, and stereotypes, Black males want to be taken seriously as challengers for learning in the educational system and positive contributors to society.

References

Behavioral change theory: The social cognitive theory. (2013). Retrieved from http://sph.bu.edu/otlt/MPH-Modules/SB/SB721-Models/SB721-Models5.html

Berry, T. (2005). Black on Black education: Personally engaged pedagogy for/by African American pre-service teachers. *Urban Review, 37*(1), 31–48.

Bond, K. E. (2004). Diversity battles: Contending with look-good commitments, White women and Latinos. *Network Journal, 12*(1), 21. Retrieved from http://www.tnj.com/archives/2004/october2004/industry_focus.php

Bonner, F. A. (2005). Transitions in the development of giftedness. *Gifted Child Today*, *28*(2), 19–26.

Brown v. Board of Education, 347 U.S. 483 (1954).

Cross, J. R., & Cross, T. L. (2005). Social dominance, moral politics, and gifted education. *Roeper Review*, *28*(1), 21–30.

Cullinan, D., & Kauffman, J. M. (2005). Do race of student and race of teacher influence ratings of emotional and behavioral problem characteristics of students with emotional disturbance? *Behavioral Disorders, 30*(4), 393–402.

DeCuir, J. T., & Dixson, A. D. (2004, June/July). So when it comes out, they aren't that surprised that it is there. Using critical race theory as a tool of analysis of race and racism in education. *Educational Researcher, 33*(5), 26–32.

Delpit, L. (2003). The silenced dialogue: Power and pedagogy in educating other people's children. In S. Plaut & N. S. Sharkey (Eds.), *Education policy and practice: Bridging the divide* (Harvard Educational Review Reprints, 37; pp. 9–11). Cambridge, MA: Harvard Education Press.

Delpit, L. (2006). *Other people's children: Cultural conflict in the classroom* (2nd ed.). New York, NY: New York Press.

Duncan, G. A. (2002). Beyond love: A critical race ethnography of the schooling of adolescent Black males. *Equity & Excellence in Education, 35*(2), 131–143. Retrieved from http://principals.mpls.k12.mn.us/sites/ee869d27-88e5-478a-97e1-b5e41772b8f7/uploads/Duncan_Beyond_Love.pdf

Ford, D. Y., & Moore, J. L. (2005). This issue: Gifted education. *Theory into Practice, 44*(2), 77–79.

Garibaldi, A. M. (2007). The educational status of African American males in the 21st century. *Journal of Negro Education, 76*(3), 324–333.

Gillborn, D. (2005). Education policy as an act of White supremacy: Whiteness, critical race theory and education reform. *Journal of Education Policy, 20*(4), 485–505.

Hargrove, B., & Seay, S. (2011). School teachers perceptions of barriers that limit the participation of African American males in public school gifted programs. *Journal of the Education of the Gifted, 34*(3), 434–467.

Harmon, D. (2002). They won't teach me: The voices of gifted African-American inner-city students. *Roeper Review, 24*(2), 68–76.

Hertzog, N. B. (2005). Equity and access: Creating general education classrooms responsive to potential giftedness. *Journal for the Education of the Gifted, 29*(2), 213–259.

Ladson-Billings, G. (2006). It's not the culture of poverty, it's the poverty of culture: The problem with teacher education. *Anthropology and Education Quarterly, 37*(2), 104–110.

Lawrence, S. (1997). Beyond race awareness: White racial identity and multicultural teaching. *Journal of Teacher Education, 48*(2), 108–118.

Lehrman, S. (2005). Performance without anxiety. *Scientific American, 292*(2), 36–37.

Lintner, T. (2004). The savage and the slave: Critical race theory, racial stereotyping, and the teaching of American history. *Journal of Social Studies Research, 28(1),* 27–32.

Lynn, M. (2006). Race, culture, and the education of African Americans. *Educational Theory, 56*(1), 107–120.

Mabokela, R. O., & Madsen, J. A. (2003). Crossing boundaries: African American teachers in suburban schools. *Comparative Education Review, 47*(1), 90–112.

Meier, D., Kohn, A., Darling-Hammond, L., Sizer, T., & Wood, G. (2004). *Many children left behind*. Boston, MA: Beacon Press.

Michael-Chadwell, S. (2008). *Teachers' and parents' perceptions concerning the underrepresentation of gifted African-American students: A phenomenological study* (Doctoral dissertation). Available from ProQuest Dissertations and Theses database. (UMI No. 3348677)

Michael-Chadwell, S. (2010). Examining the underrepresentation of underserved students in gifted programs from a transformational leadership vantage point. *Journal for the Education of the Gifted, 34*(1), 99–130.

Michael-Chadwell, S., Bonner, F., & Louis, D. (2009). African American high school males' perceptions of academically rigorous programs, identity, and spirituality. *The National Journal of Urban Education & Practice, 3*(1), 230–246.

Moriearty, P., & Carson, W. (2012). *Cognitive warfare and young Black males in America: A social cognition theory*. Retrieved from Race, Racism and the Law website: http://racism.org/index.php?option=com_content&view=article&id=1491: cognitivewar&catid=139&Itemid=155&showall=&limitstart=5

Morris, J. E. (2002). African American students and gifted education. *Roeper Review, 24*(2), 59–62. Retrieved from http://www.tandfonline.com/doi/abs/10.1080/02 783190209554130#preview

Neal, L. I., McCray, A. D., Webb-Johnson, G., & Bridgest, S. T. (2003). The effects of African American movement styles on teachers' perceptions and reactions. *The Journal of Special Education, 37*(1), 49–57.

Obiakor, F. E. (1999). Teacher expectations of minority exceptional learners: Impact on "accuracy" of self-concepts. *Exceptional Children, 66*(1), 39–53.

Obiakor, F. E. (2004). Educating African American urban learners: Brown in context. *Western Journal of Black Studies, 28*(3), 399–407.

Pajares, F. (2002). *Overview of social cognitive theory and of self-efficacy*. Retrieved from http://www.uky.edu/~eushe2/Pajares/eff.html

Patten, J. M., & Townsend, B. I. (2001). Teacher education leadership and disciplinary practices: Exploring ethics, power, and privilege in the education of exceptional African American learners. *Teacher Education and Special Education, 24*(1), 1–2.

Renzulli, J. S. (1999). What is this thing called giftedness, and how do we develop it? A twenty-five-year perspective. *Journal for the Education of the Gifted, 23*(1), 3–54.

Robinson, M. W. (2005, Fall). Brown: Why we must remember. *Marquette Law Review, 89*(1), 53–73.

Saddler, C. A. (2005). The impact of Brown on African American students: A critical race theoretical perspective. *Educational Studies, 37*(1), 41–55.

Smith, E. P., Atkins, J., & Connell, C. M. (2003). Family, school, and community factors and relationships to racial-ethnic attitudes and academic achievement. *American Journal of Community Psychology, 32*(1/2), 159–173.

Snipes, V. T., & Waters, R. D. (2005). The mathematics education of African Americans in North Carolina: From the Brown decision to No Child Left Behind. *Negro Educational Review, 56*(2/3), 107–126.

Staiger, A. (2004). Whiteness as giftedness: Racial formation at an urban high school. *Social Problems, 51*(2), 161–182.

Stovall, D. (2004). School leader as negotiator: Critical race theory, praxis, and the creation of productive space. *Multicultural Education, 12*(2), 8–13.

Strange, C. (2005, August). *Perceptions and practices that influence the identification of gifted students from low socioeconomic backgrounds* (Unpublished doctoral dissertation). Baylor University, Waco, TX.

Swanson, D., Cunningham, M., & Spencer, M. (2003). Black males' structural conditions, achievement patterns, normative needs, and opportunities. *Urban Education, 38*(5), 608–633. Retrieved from http://clients.ikodum.com/changes/pdfs/8-BLACK%20MALES'%20STRUCTURAL.pdf

Thomas, D. E., Townsend, T. G., & Belgrave, F. Z. (2003). The influence of cultural and racial identification on the psychosocial adjustment of inner-city African American children in school. *American Journal of Community Psychology, 32*(3/4), 217–228.

Villarreal, B. J. (2004). *The neglected of the neglected of the neglected: A case study of gifted English learners in two Austin elementary schools* (Doctoral dissertation). Available from Proquest Dissertations and Theses database. (UMI No. 3150938)

White, M. A. (2002). Paradise lost? Teachers' perspective on the use of cultural capital in the segregated schools of New Orleans, Louisiana. *The Journal of African American History, 87,* 269–281.

Whiting, G. (2009). Gifted Black males: Understanding and decreasing barriers to achievement and identity. *Roper Review, 31*(4), 224–233.

Williams, K. (2012). *A phenomenological study: African-American males in the educational profession* (Doctoral dissertation). Available from ProQuest Dissertations and Theses database. (UMI No. 3494879)

2

A FRAMEWORK FOR THINKING AND TALKING ABOUT RACE WITH TEACHERS

H. Richard Milner IV, Quaylan Allen, and Ebony O. McGee

Black males continue to be underserved in the educational system from prekindergarten through postsecondary education (Howard, 2008). Although there are Black male students who succeed in spite of inadequate and inequitable learning environments (Graham & Anderson, 2008; Harper, 2012; Wright, 2011), too many Black males are placed on the margins of teaching and learning, which can make it difficult for them to succeed (Milner, 2007). In this chapter, we argue that educators—and teachers in particular—in P–12 educational settings often struggle to develop curriculum and instructional practices that meet the needs of Black male students. In particular, we focus on an aspect of Black students' experiences that teachers often overlook: race. Our emphasis on race is grounded in the following realities that can have a direct influence on Black male students:

- overrepresentation of students of color including Black males in special education (Artiles, Klingner, & Tate, 2006; Blanchett, 2006; O'Connor & Fernandez, 2006);
- over-referral of African American students to the administrator's office for disciplinary actions and consequences (Davis & Jordan, 1994; Skiba, Michael, Nardo, & Peterson, 2002);

- under-referral of African American students to gifted education and advanced courses (Ford, 2010);
- an overwhelming number of African American and Latino American students expelled or suspended (Monroe, 2006; Noguera, 2003); and
- underrepresentation of students of color in schoolwide clubs, organizations, and in other prestigious arenas, such as the school's homecoming court and student government (Milner, 2010a).

These contemporary school-based realities seem to be products of a long and troubled history of race, discriminatory policies and practices, and racial representation of Black men. Popular discourse on Black males, emanating from social anxiety and fear, (Foucault, 1979; Hall, Critcher, Jefferson, Clarke, & Robert, 1978; Marriott, 1996), has portrayed Black men as lazy, uneducable, sexually superior, dangerous, subhuman, and exemplary of an inferior race (Gibbs, 1988; Jackson & Moore III, 2006; Majors & Billson, 1992; Staples, 1982). Disproportionately high incarceration rates, suspensions from school, and over-referral for discipline seem to bear out negative views of Black male identity (Alexander, 2010; Mauer, 1999; J. M. Wallace, Goodkind, Wallace, & Bachman, 2008).

Currently, dominant discourse on Black males describes them as deviant, violent, intellectually inferior, and as Howard et al. (2012) wrote, a "menace to society" (p. 89). These views of Black men have influenced school practice and policy. For example, teacher perceptions of Black males are often influenced by racist discourse about Black masculine performance in which teachers regularly interpret the behaviors of Black boys as aggressive, defiant, and intimidating (Davis, 2003; Ferguson, 2000; Monroe, 2005; Neal, McCray, Webb-Johnson, & Bridgest, 2003; Weinstein, Curran, & Tomlinson-Clarke, 2004). The misguided interpretation of these behaviors and assumption of deviance results in Black males' encountering disciplinary policies at higher rates while also experiencing discipline that is often unnecessary and in many cases harsher than what their White counterparts experience for committing the same offense (Allen, 2013b; Bushway & Piehl, 2001; Ferguson, 2000; Monroe, 2005; Skiba, 2001).

Teacher practices and school policies thus act as tools of identity regulation where Black boys are constructed as "different" through normalizing judgments (Foucault, 1979; Haywood & Mac an Ghaill, 1996). To succeed in schools, then, Black boys must prove they are normal by self-consciously regulating their every action in ways that prove conformity to institutionally generated norms. In essence, they must assuage the fears and preconceived notions their teachers may have of them. We argue that race has a particular impact on Black boys because, as Ferguson (2000) pointed out in her discussion of the "good Schoolboys" and the "bad Troublemakers,"

> As African American males, Schoolboys were always on the brink of being redefined into the Troublemaker category by the school. The pressures and dilemmas this group faced around race and gender identities from adults and peers were always palpable forces working against their maintaining a commitment to the school project. (p. 10)

Under these circumstances, even well-behaved, academically successful Black boys can still be relabeled as troublemakers if their behaviors confirm preconceived racist notions of Black male identity (Allen, 2013a). Considering the power teachers hold as academic gatekeepers and normalizers of appropriate behavior, it is important then to examine what teachers believe about their Black male students as well as how they think about race in their own work as educators.

Educational researchers have revealed several important considerations regarding social messages about African American males vis-à-vis schooling, including race-conscious teacher, self, and societal perceptions on the journey toward completing K–12 education; racialized definitions of group membership; and social, teacher, and self-constructions of what it means to be a Black male in the context of learning and participation in school (Gay & Howard, 2000; Howard, 2010; Milner, 2010b; Zumwalt & Craig, 2005). Thus, teachers should be conscious of these considerations in their planning and implementation of learning opportunities for students (Milner, 2010a). As the teaching force is overwhelmingly White (Coopersmith, 2009; Milner, 2010a) this focus on racial consciousness is important, as many teachers may consider that addressing race in their work is irrelevant and inconsequential. Teachers may also believe that focusing on race may be unnecessary, as they adjudge their own life experiences have not been shaped by structural or individual forms of race or racism (Milner, 2010a).

In the context of education, racism and stereotyping among the predominantly White teaching population is one of the reasons for African American students' high rate of failure (Kailin, 1999). Tyler, Boykin, and Walton (2006) studied 62 White elementary teachers at two predominantly Black low-income schools and discovered grading rubrics that were lowered for students who exhibited more communal and collaborative behaviors and higher for students who demonstrated competitive and individualistic behaviors. In Ferguson's (2000) ethnographic study of one elementary school, negative teacher-student interactions were observed to be driven by White teachers' overreacting and relying on stereotypes and deficit ideologies to interpret their Black students' language and forms of self-expression. Lack of preparation to teach students whose racial/ethnic backgrounds are different from the teachers' own may also affect increasing rates of teacher turnover for White teachers (Milner, 2010b).

Although we realize additional identity markers such as gender, sexual orientation, religion, and socioeconomic status shape the lives of Black males, we are focusing on race because it is a constant thread across the other identity spaces. Of course, additional attention should be focused on the other areas, but we have found that race remains one of the most important aspects of teachers' work that needs to be addressed in order to improve their practices with Black male students.

Accordingly, teachers may adopt color-blind approaches to their work with Black male students when, in essence, teachers should focus on developing and enacting race-congruent curricula. In this chapter, we present an evolving framework to help teachers talk about race, which we believe will ultimately inform their thinking and consequently their practices with Black male students. Before describing the framework, we define what we mean by *race*.

Defining *Race*

According to many scholars, race is physically, socially, legally, and historically constructed. The meanings, messages, results, and consequences of race are developed and constructed by human beings, not by some predetermined set of scientific laws or genetics (Baker, 1998; Hernandez, 2003; Omi & Winant, 2004). Genetically and biologically, individuals are more the same than they are different. Nakkula and Toshalis (2006) make this point by stating,

> There is no biologically sustainable reason for establishing "races" as distinct subgroups within the human species. . . . Race is a concept created in the modern era as a way of drawing distinctions between people such that some might benefit at the expense of others. (p. 123)

Our analysis of empirical research and policy will not allow us to accept a eugenics perspective in which there is a "biological basis for [some people's perception that there is a] . . . superiority of Whites" (Howard, 2010, p. 28). In the simplest and plainest of terms, White people are not biologically or genetically superior to other groups in terms of intelligence, cognitive ability, aptitude, or skill.

Thus, race is

- *Physically constructed*: Based on skin color, people in society construct ideas, characteristics, and belief systems about themselves and others

(Monroe, 2013). These physical constructions are sometimes inaccurate, but the constructions remain. It is important to note that physical constructions of race vary from one society to the next. For instance, constructions of race in continents such as Africa or Asia are different from constructions of race based on phenotype in North America.

- *Socially constructed*: Based on a range of societal information and messages, people construct and categorize themselves and others. These social constructions are linked to how groups of people perform, for instance.
- *Legally constructed*: Laws in U.S. society, for example, help us const what race is. Landmark cases and legal policies such as th Naturalization Law, *Plessy v. Ferguson* (1896), *Takao Ozawa 1 States* (1922), *Brown v. Board of Education* (1954), and, subsequently, *Brown v. Board of Education* (1955) all influence our constructions and definitions of race in U.S. society.
- *Historically constructed*: Historical realties related to how people have been treated and how people have fared in a society also shape the construction of race. In U.S. society, for instance, a history of Jim Crow laws, slavery, and racial discrimination force us to construct and think about race in particular ways.

A holistic understanding of the definitions and constructions of race can assist in explorations of how race operates in and beyond the classroom in ways that can leave Black male students feeling simultaneously invisible and hypervisible, as their experiences are omitted, distorted, and stereotyped. Schools are part of a complex network of discriminatory and biased cultural and social practices that actively subordinate the culture and language, along with the social, economic, and political positions, of African American males and other students of color. Teachers should be armed with tools to understand how racism operates in a variety of educational settings, including subtle microaggressions that systematically marginalize Black males; they should also interrogate their own beliefs regarding deficit and negative labeling of this vulnerable student population. We turn now to a discussion of the framework we present about race for teachers.

A Race Talk Framework

Although it may seem trivial to suggest that teachers need a framework for thinking and talking about race, research is clear that some teachers struggle to have open and honest dialogues about race (Lewis, 2001; Milner,

2010a; Tucker, Dixon, & Griddine, 2010). Our purpose is to provide guiding questions to help teachers think through and address four important components: researching the self, researching the self in relation to others, shifting from self to system, and understanding curriculum and instruction.

Researching the Self

Although it is essential for teachers to think and talk about the fact that some of their students are Black and what this means for their students and their life experiences inside and outside the classroom, it is also essential for teachers, as a precursor to understanding others, to understand themselves as racial beings. The idea here is that teachers should think about how their own lives are affected by race. Indeed, Cornel West (1993) explained that it is difficult to work for emancipation on behalf of others (and to work to solve problems with and on behalf of others) until people (in this case, teachers) are emancipated themselves. This is relevant for all teachers, including those sharing similar racial backgrounds with their students. As we know, teacher-student racial similarities do not always equate with racial congruence (Morris, 2005). Thus, even teachers of color should reflect on the role race plays in their lives and how it shapes their self-understanding. Several interrelated questions should be considered in researching the self to talk about race in this framework:

- What is my racial heritage? How do I know?
- In what ways does my racial background influence how I experience the world, what I emphasize in my classroom, and how I evaluate and interpret others and their experiences? How do I know?
- How do I negotiate and balance my race in society and in my classroom with my Black male students? How do I know? Are my fears of African American male students impeding their educational experience to receive equitable pedagogical treatment in relation to other students in my classroom?
- What do I believe about race in society, and how do I attend to my own convictions and beliefs about race in my classroom with my Black male students? Why? How do I know?
- How does the social context (where I teach and where my Black male students live) influence my understanding of self and my Black male students as racial beings? How do I know?
- How have my beliefs about learning and pedagogy changed as a result of having African American male students in my classrooms?

Indeed, we are suggesting that the first feature of the framework is for teachers to examine themselves before thinking deeply about others. Admittedly, teachers and teacher education programs tend to provide few opportunities for self-reflection and introspection with a race focus. Teachers should be encouraged to ask critical questions, not only about their teaching techniques and skills, but to pursue inquiries that offer a self-conscious consideration that can lead them to an enhanced understanding of themselves and their students, with particular consideration for understanding their Black male students.

Researching the Self in Relation to Others

A second feature of this framework is researching the self in relation to others. Ladson-Billings (2009) explained how essential it is for teachers to think about themselves and how their own life experiences have intersected with and diverged from the students they taught. The idea here is to have teachers think about the multiple layers of differences and similarities that exist between themselves and their Black male students. We agree that such reflection would importantly require an understanding of intersectionality analysis (Crenshaw, 1993), as race, class, and gender may intersect in ways that create varied experiences and understandings of the world. This means that the intersection of race, class, and gender for a White middle-class female teacher may produce realities that are similar to or different from that of a Black working-class male student. However, our point is that race remains a salient frontrunner in this intersectionality. When teachers research the self in relation to others by examining the intersections of identity, they can name these similarities or differences and identify the opportunities and barriers to creating successful working relationships with their Black male students.

Another aspect to researching the self in relation to others involves proactively understanding the distinctive backgrounds and lived experiences of Black male students. This includes teachers learning who their students are, where they come from, and how their racial histories and material realities may influence their understanding of society. To further avoid essentialist views of Black males, teachers should strive to learn from and about Black males in the community context where their students live. This may also allow teachers to identify the strengths and assets Black males bring into the school, including forms of cultural wealth such as resiliency and high academic aspirations (Allen, 2013a; Grantham, 2004; Yosso, 2006). Identifying Black male strengths and assets also disrupts dominant deficit-oriented discourse on Black males.

Questions that should be considered in the second feature of the framework include:

- In what ways do my Black male students' racial backgrounds influence how they experience the world and the classroom? How do I know?
- Do I bring additional stress upon myself as a result of racialized misunderstandings and stereotypical interpretations of my African American male students? If so, how can I decrease or eliminate it?
- What do my Black male students believe about race in society, and how do they and I attend to the tensions inherent in my and their convictions and beliefs about race? Why? How do I know?
- How do I negotiate and balance my own interests with those of my Black male students, which may be inconsistent with or diverge from mine? How do I know?
- What are and have been some social, political, historical, and contextual nuances and realities that have shaped my Black male students' racial ways or systems of knowing, past and present? How do race (and perhaps gender) shape the realities of my Black male students in similar or different ways from my Black female students or White male students? How consistent and inconsistent are these realties with mine? How do I know?

We believe it is essential for teachers to move from thinking and talking about themselves historically and in the present to doing so in ways that are grounded in questions about their students. These questions could force teachers to examine what they know about their Black male students and suggest what teachers need to learn in areas where their knowledge is limited to best or better meet the needs of their Black male students. This means teachers may also have to learn about the communities in which their students live as well as deepen their knowledge and understanding about Black male students' family members.

Shifting From Self to System

A third feature of this framework is for teachers to think and talk about how systems influence and shape Black male students' experiences. Lopez (2003) wrote that "racism is perceived as an individual or irrational act in a world that is otherwise neutral, rational, and just. . . . It positions racism at the individual level and ignores other ways in which it functions in society" (p. 69). Teachers may find it irrelevant to think and talk about race because they do not believe they have been racist themselves or because they think they do not know anyone who is racist. However, thinking about race on an individual level can leave too many unanswered questions about how Black males experience race and racism in society and schools through structures and systems.

For example, the Schott Foundation for Public Education (2012), which has tracked graduation rates of Black males from public schools since 2004, reported that 52% of Black males who entered ninth grade in the 2009–10 school year graduated in four years. This statistic of Black male high school graduation rates is often compared with 78% of White non-Latino male students and 58% of Latino male students. The chief executive officer of the Schott Foundation determined that at the current rate, it would take nearly 50 years for Black males to graduate at the same rate as White males (Schott Foundation for Public Education, 2012). What is more devastating is what happens to almost a quarter of those Black male students who drop out of high school. Nearly 23% of all young Black men ages 16 to 24 who have dropped out of high school are in jail, prison, or a juvenile justice institution in America (Sum, Khatiwada, & McLaughlin, 2009), highlighting the dismal economic and social consequences of Black males not graduating from high school. Several researchers have suggested that the low expectations held by White teachers for Black male students (Lynn, Bacon, Totten, Bridges, & Jennings, 2010), the lack of the teacher being an effective learning agent (Bell, 2010), and the lack of cultural congruity between White teachers and Black male students (Rothon, Arephin, Klineberg, Cattel, & Standfield, 2011), contribute to the dropout rates. These are the types of structures teachers may seek to analyze in addition to understanding racism on an individual level. Shifting from the self to the system requires teachers to move beyond thinking and talking solely about themselves and their students to include examinations of race at a systemic and institutionalized level.

Several questions can prove helpful as teachers shift from the individual level of thinking and talking about race to the systemic level:

- In what ways do popular discourse and Black male representation influence social and school policies and practices? How do I know?
- How might race have an impact on systems in school that place Black males at a disadvantage? How do I know?
- What systemic and organizational barriers and structures shape Black male experiences locally and more broadly? How do I know?
- How do or might teachers unknowingly or inadvertently contribute to individual and structural forms of racism that can have an influence on student opportunities to learn? How do I know?

- What school policies or practices intentionally or unintentionally reproduce inequitable outcomes for my Black male students? How do I know?
- In what ways do popular discourse and Black male representation influence social and school policies and practices? How do I know?

We believe it is important that teachers understand racism as more than just individual bias or prejudiced behavior but also as a systemic reality that reproduces inequalities for Black males. Teachers should understand the pervasiveness of race and racism in social and school policies, even those policies claiming to be neutral, objective, or color blind (Delgado, 1991; Ladson-Billings & Tate, 2006). Furthermore, when teachers raise their racial consciousness, they can act as agents to contest and disrupt the racially reproductive nature of school policies and practices.

Understanding Curriculum and Instruction

The final feature of this framework focuses on teachers' thinking and talking about curriculum and instruction. Taken together, the collective framework is designed to help teachers think and talk about the sociology of the classroom as well as the curriculum and instruction in those environments. The fourth dimension of the framework requires that teachers make explicit links between race and the curriculum as well as how they teach.[1] The point here is that race can inform what teachers teach, how they teach it, and how they assess what has been taught. For example, when educators do not include curriculum content related to Black males in a social studies class (e.g., the four Black male U.S. senators in American history from 1870 to 2008, the slave rebellions led by Nat Turner in the United States and Toussaint L'Ouverture in Haiti), students are actually learning something about Black males through the absence of the content in the curriculum (McCutcheon, 2002).

Perhaps unknowingly, educators who avoid infusing Black experiences into the curriculum may deny Black students the right to recognize their race's contributions to society. Very often students learn about cultural hegemony from a curriculum dominated by White contributions and White norms to the exclusion of those from other racial, ethnic, and cultural groups (Banks, 2001; Gay, 2010).

Several questions are featured in this component of the framework:

- In what ways does or should the curriculum incorporate Black male students? How do I know?

- What can I do to ensure that Black males see themselves reflected in the curriculum? How do I know?
- How do my instructional practices relate to and are responsive to the lived experiences of my Black male students? How do I know?
- How can I rework my curriculum and instructional practices to ensure that Black males are well represented in the curriculum and how I teach it?
- How can I support my students by drawing upon what my Black male students already know and experience in their everyday lives to make sense of what is being taught in my curriculum?
- How can I transform the Common Core standards and other standards to ensure they address the complex needs of Black male students?

Indeed, we are arguing that emphases on the first three features should ultimately transform what teachers teach and how they teach the curriculum. Attempting to better understand themselves, others (their Black students), and systems of racism and discrimination are only part of the challenge of the framework. We hope teachers will think and talk seriously about how they rework their curricula and teach in ways that honor and place value on the multiple strengths that Black male students bring into the classroom.

Figure 2.1 provides a visual representation of the cyclical and interrelated nature of the framework we propose. It is important to note that the

Figure 2.1 A Race Talk Framework

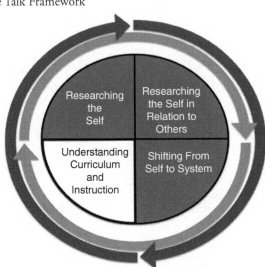

framework is not linear, and that ultimately we hope teachers' curricula and instructional practices are transformed. After presenting the framework, in the final sections of this chapter, we outline implications for research then practice.

Implications for Research

Considering the changing racial demographics of the U.S. student population compared with the relatively homogenous nature of the teaching workforce (Coopersmith, 2009), we suggest that future research examine teachers and their Black male students. Regarding teachers, it may be useful to examine how they undertake and operationalize the elements of our proposed framework. Research may focus on how teachers understand the self as it pertains to their own racial identities, as well as the self in relation to other identity categories. In particular, research may examine how teachers see the intersection of their own identities as similar to or different from those of their students, as well as the resulting opportunities and barriers these similarities or differences may present. Other studies may look at the extent to which teachers have knowledge of or understand how race pervades structures and systems, and how they view their own roles in maintaining the status quo or creating change. Finally, it would be helpful to know more about how teachers actually transform their curricula and instructional practices to meet the needs of Black male students. The previously presented questions in the framework could prove useful to researchers as they work to examine teachers' thinking and discourse about race.

In addition to using the framework to study teachers, it may be equally important to study Black male students, including their own views of the self, the self in relation to others, knowledge of institutionalized racism, and curriculum and instruction. The voice of Black male students is often absent from popular discourse as well as from discussions pertaining to their academic achievement. However, the Black male experience is unique because of the intersection of race and gender. For example, Black male students often face a gendered racism where being a Black *man* is often a position of subordination. The race-gendered microaggression of racial profiling, in and out of school, illustrates how Black men are targeted because they are Black *men* and not simply because they are Black or because they are male (Allen, 2013b; Mutua, 2006). For this reason, researchers, teachers, and educators must understand the particular experiences and needs of Black men at the intersection of their identities. Multiple insights from the Black male perspective may provide useful implications for practice.

Implications for Practice

In practice, it takes considerable humility for teachers to be able to reflect within the framework presented here. Teachers may find it difficult to engage in this type of reflection, especially those who historically have adopted color-blind ideologies, beliefs, and practices in their past work. But we are resolute in our recommendations because research has demonstrated that it is critical that educators recognize their own and their students' racial backgrounds in order to plan for, work with, and teach complete rather than fragmented, disconnected students (Irvine, 2003; Ladson-Billings, 2009; Obidah & Teel, 2001).

As we have argued, many teachers of Black male students adopt a color-blind approach to teaching, believing that this will allow them to be fair or neutral. This thinking may ignore the reality that Black males do experience race in every meaningful aspect of their lives. We argue that to assume color blindness not only limits teachers' ability to connect with their students but also camouflages their own biases toward and against students of color.

Finally, we understand that factors outside race (such as gender, socioeconomic status, sexual orientation, and religion) are critical aspects for teachers to understand to address and be responsive to the needs of Black male students. Indeed, teachers must understand how race and these intersectional qualities influence the lives of Black boys and men. Educators must understand the history of Black masculine construction, current representations of Black male identity, and their implications for their Black male students. However, what remains constant among the different identity characteristics of these students is race. Moreover, we have found that race remains a constant struggle for teachers to understand and should thus be addressed in teachers' thinking and discourse to improve the experiences and outcomes of Black male students (Milner, 2010a).

Note

1. The *curriculum* can be defined as what students have the opportunity to learn in schools (Eisner, 1994; McCutcheon, 2002). Curriculum theorist Elliott Eisner proposed several important forms of the curriculum: (a) the explicit curriculum concerns student-learning opportunities that are overtly taught and stated or printed in documents, policies, and guidelines, such as in course syllabi or on school websites; (b) the implicit curriculum is intended or unintended, but it is not stated or written down but actually inherent to what students have the opportunity to learn; (c) a third form of curriculum, the null curriculum, deals with what students do not

have the opportunity to learn. Thus, information and knowledge that are not available for student learning are also a form of the curriculum because *students are actually learning something based on what is not emphasized, covered, or taught.* What students do not experience in the curriculum becomes messages for them. For example, if educators are not taught to question, critique, or critically examine power structures, the students are learning something—possibly that it may not be essential for them to critique the world in order to improve it. From Eisner's perspective, what is *absent* is essentially *present* in student learning opportunities.

References

Alexander, M. (2010). *The new Jim Crow: Mass incarceration in the age of colorblindness.* New York, NY: New Press.

Allen, Q. (2013a). Balancing school and cool: Tactics of resistance and accommodation among Black middle-class males. *Race Ethnicity and Education, 16*(2), 203–224.

Allen, Q. (2013b). "They think minority means lesser than": Black middle-class sons and fathers resisting microaggressions in the school. *Urban Education, 48*(2),171–197.

Artiles, A. J., Klingner, J. K., & Tate, W. F. (2006). Representation of minority students in special education: Complicating traditional explanations. *Educational Researcher, 35*(6), 3–5.

Baker, L. D. (1998). *From savage to Negro: Anthropology and the construction of race, 1896–1954.* Berkeley: University of California Press.

Banks, J. A. (2001). Citizenship education and diversity: Implications for teacher education. *Journal of Teacher Education, 52*(1), 5–16.

Bell, E. E. (2010). *Understanding African American males.* Retrieved from ERIC database. (ED511010)

Blanchett, W. J. (2006). Disproportionate representation of African Americans in special education: Acknowledging the role of White privilege and racism. *Educational Researcher, 35*(6), 24–28.

Brown v. Board of Education, 347 U.S. 483 (1954).

Brown v. Board of Education, 349 U.S. 294 (1955).

Bushway, S. D., & Piehl, A. M. (2001). Judging judicial discretion: Legal factors and racial discrimination in sentencing. *Law & Society Review, 35*(4), 733–764.

Coopersmith, J. (2009). *Characteristics of public, private, and Bureau of Indian Education elementary and secondary school teachers in the United States: Results from the 2007–08 schools and staffing survey* (NCES 2009324). Washington, DC: National Center for Education Statistics.

Crenshaw, K. (1993). Demarginalizing the intersection of race and sex: A Black feminist critique of antidiscrimination doctrine, feminist theory, and antiracist politics. In D. K. Weisberg (Ed.), *Feminist legal theory* (pp. 383–395). Philadelphia, PA: Temple University Press.

Davis, J. E. (2003). Early schooling and academic achievement of African American males. *Urban Education, 38*(5), 515–537.

Davis, J. E., & Jordan, W. J. (1994). The effects of school context, structure, and experiences on African American males in middle and high school. *Journal of Negro Education, 63*(4), 570–587.

Delgado, R. (1991). Brewer's plea: Critical thoughts on common cause. *Vanderbilt Law Review, 44*(11), 1–13.

Eisner, E. W. (1994). *The educational imagination: On the design and evaluation of school programs.* New York, NY: MacMillan.

Ferguson, A. A. (2000). *Bad boys: Public schools in the making of Black masculinity.* Ann Arbor: University of Michigan Press.

Ford, D. Y. (2010). *Reversing underachievement among gifted Black students.* Waco, TX: Prufrock Press.

Foucault, M. (1979). *Discipline and punish* (A. Sheridan, Trans.). New York, NY: Vintage.

Gay, G. (2010). *Culturally responsive teaching: Theory, research, and practice.* (2nd ed.). New York, NY: Teachers College Press.

Gay, G., & Howard, T. (2000). Multicultural teacher education for the 21st century. *The Teacher Educator, 36*(1), 1–16.

Gibbs, J. T. (1988). *Young, Black, and male in America.* New York, NY: Auburn House.

Graham, A., & Anderson, K. A. (2008). "I have to be three steps ahead": Academically gifted African American male students in an urban high school on the tension between an ethnic identity and academic identity. *Urban Review, 40*(5), 472–499.

Grantham, T. C. (2004). Rocky Jones: Case study of a high-achieving Black male's motivation to participate in gifted classes. *Roeper Review, 26*(4), 208–215.

Hall, S., Critcher, C., Jefferson, T., Clarke, J., & Robert, B. (1978). *Policing the crisis: Mugging, the state and law and order.* London, UK: Macmillan.

Harper, S. R. (2012). *Black male student success in higher education: A report from the national Black male college achievement study.* Philadelphia: University of Pennsylvania, Center for the Study of Race and Equity in Education.

Haywood, C., & Mac an Ghaill, M. (1996). Schooling masculinities. In M. Mac an Ghaill (Ed.), *Understanding masculinities* (pp. 50–60). Buckingham, UK: Open University Press.

Hernandez, T. K. (2003). "Multiracial" discourse: Racial classifications in an era of color-blind jurisprudence. In J. F. Perea, R. Delgado, A. P. Harris, & S. M. Wildman (Eds.), *Race and races: Cases and resources for a diverse America* (pp. 69–77). St. Paul, MN: West Group.

Howard, T. C. (2008). "Who really cares?" The disenfranchisement of African American males in preK–12 schools: A critical race theory perspective. *Teachers College Record, 110*(5), 954–985.

Howard, T. C. (2010). *Why race and culture matter in schools: Closing the achievement gap in America's classrooms.* New York, NY: Teachers College Press.

Howard, T. C., Flennaugh, T. K., & Terry, C. L., Sr. (2012). Black males, social imagery and the disruption of pathological identities: Implications for research and teaching. *Educational Foundation, 26*(2), 85–102.

Irvine, J. J. (2003). *Educating teachers for diversity: Seeing with a cultural eye.* New York, NY: Teachers College Press.

Jackson, J. F. L., & Moore, J. L., III. (2006). African American males in education: Endangered or ignored? *Teachers College Record, 108*(2), 201–205.

Kailin, J. (1999). How white teachers perceive the problem of racism in their schools: A case study in "liberal" Lakeview. *The Teachers College Record, 100*(4), 724–750.

Ladson-Billings, G. (2009). *The dreamkeepers: Successful teachers of African American children* (2nd ed.). San Francisco, CA: Jossey-Bass.

Ladson-Billings, G., & Tate, W. F., IV. (2006). Toward a critical race theory of education. In A. D. Dixson & C. K. Rousseau (Eds.), *Critical race theoy in education: All God's children got a song* (pp. 11–30). New York, NY: Routledge.

Lewis, A. E. (2001). There is no "race" in the schoolyard: Colorblind ideology in an (almost) all White school. *American Educational Research Journal, 38*(4), 781–811.

Lopez, G. R. (2003). The (racially neutral) politics of education: A critical race theory perspective. *Educational Administration Quarterly, 39*(1), 68–94.

Lynn, M., Bacon, J. N., Totten, T. L., Bridges, T. L., III, & Jennings, M. E. (2010). Examining teachers' beliefs about African-American male students in a low-performing high school in an African American school district. *Teachers College Record, 112*(1), 289–330.

Majors, R., & Billson, J. M. (1992). *Cool pose: The dilemmas of Black manhood in America.* New York, NY: Touchstone.

Marriott, D. (1996). Reading Black masculinities. In M. Mac an Ghaill (Ed.), *Understanding masculinities: Social relations and cultural arenas* (pp. 185–201). Buckingham, UK: Open University Press.

Mauer, M. (1999). *Crisis of the young African American male and the criminal justice system.* Washington, DC: Sentencing Project. Retrieved from http://www.sentencingproject.org/doc/publications/rd_crisisoftheyoung.pdf

McCutcheon, G. (2002). *Developing the curriculum: Solo and group deliberation.* Troy, NY: Educators' Press International.

Milner, H. R. (2007). Race, culture, and researcher positionality: Working through dangers seen, unseen, and unforeseen. *Educational Researcher, 36*(7), 388–400.

Milner, H. R. (2010a). *Start where you are, but don't stay there: Understanding diversity, opportunity gaps, and teaching in today's classrooms.* Cambridge, MA: Harvard Education Press.

Milner, H. R. (2010b). What does teacher education have to do with teaching? Implications for diversity studies. *Journal of Teacher Education, 61*(1/2), 118–131.

Monroe, C. R. (2005). Why are "bad boys" always Black? Causes of disproportionality in school discipline and recommendations for change. *The Clearing House, 79*(1), 45–50.

Monroe, C. R. (2006). Misbehavior or misinterpretation? Closing the discipline gap through cultural synchronization. *Kappa Delta Pi Record, 42*(4), 161–165.

Monroe, C. R. (2013). Colorizing educational research: African American life and schooling as an exemplar. *Educational Researcher, 42*(1), 9–19.

Morris, E. W. (2005). From "middle-class" to "trailer trash": Teachers' perceptions of White students in a predominantly minority school. *Sociology of Education, 78*(2), 99–121.

Mutua, A. D. (2006). Theorizing progressive Black masculinities. In A. D. Mutua (Ed.), *Progressive Black masculinities* (pp. 3–42). New York, NY: Routledge.

Nakkula, M. J., & Toshalis, E. (2006). *Understanding youth: Adolescent development for educators*. Cambridge, MA: Harvard Education Press.

Neal, L. V. I., McCray, A. D., Webb-Johnson, G., & Bridgest, S. T. (2003). The effects of African American movement styles on teacher's perceptions and reactions. *The Journal of Special Education, 37*(1), 49–57.

Noguera, P. A. (2003). Schools, prisons, and social implications of punishment: Rethinking disciplinary practices. *Theory into Practice, 42*(4), 341–350.

Obidah, J. E., & Teel, K. M. (2001). *Because of the kids: Facing racial and cultural differences in schools*. New York, NY: Teachers College Press.

O'Connor, C., & Fernandez, S. D. (2006). Race, class, and disproportionality: Reevaluating the relationship, poverty and special education placement. *Educational Researcher, 35*(6), 6–11.

Omi, M., & Winant, H. (2004). Racial formations. In P. S. Rothenberg (Ed.), *Race, class, and gender in the United States* (Vol. 7, pp. 13–22). New York, NY: Worth.

Plessy v. Ferguson, 163 U.S. 537 (1896).

Rothon, C., Arephin, M., Klineberg, E., Cattel, V., & Standfield, S. (2011). Structural and sociopsychological influences on adolescents' educational aspirations and subsequent academic achievement. *Social Psychological Education, 14*(2), 209–231. doi: 10.1007/s11218-010-9140- 0

Schott Foundation for Public Education. (2012). *Yes we can: The Schott 50 state report on public education and Black Males 2010*. Retrieved from http://www .blackboysreport.org/bbreport.pdf

Skiba, R. (2001). When is disproportionality discrimination? The overrepresentation of Black students in school suspension. In W. Ayers, B. Dohrn, & R. Ayers (Eds.), *Zero tolerance: Resisting the drive for punishment in our schools* (pp. 176–187). New York, NY: New Press.

Skiba, R. J., Michael, R. S., Nardo, A. C., & Peterson, R. L. (2002). The color of discipline: Sources of racial and gender disproportionality in school punishment. *Urban Review, 34*(4), 317–342.

Staples, R. (1982). *Black masculinity: The Black male's role in American society*. San Francisco, CA: Black Scholar Press.

Sum, A., Khatiwada, I., & McLaughlin, J. (2009). *The consequences of dropping out of high school: Joblessness and jailing for high school dropouts and the high cost for taxpayers*. Retrieved from http://iris.lib.neu.edu/clms_pub/23/

Takao Ozawa v. U.S., 260 U.S. 178 (1922).

Terry, C. L., Sr. & McGee, E. O. (2012). "I've come too far, I've worked too hard!" Reinforcement of support structures among Black male mathematics students. *Journal of Mathematics Education at Teachers College, 3*(2), 73–85.

Tucker, C., Dixon, A., & Griddine, K. S. (2010). Academically successful African American male urban high school students' experiences of mattering to others at school. *Professional School Counseling, 14*(2), 135–145.

Tyler, K. M., Boykin, A. W., & Walton, T. R. (2006). Cultural considerations in teachers' perceptions of student classroom behavior and achievement. *Teaching and Teacher Education, 22*(8), 998–1005.

Wallace, J. M., Jr., Goodkind, S., Wallace, C. M., & Bachman, J. G. (2008). Racial, ethnic, and gender differences in school discipline among U.S. high school students: 1991–2005. *Negro Educational Review, 59*(1/2), 47–62.

Watson, D. (2011). "Urban, but not too urban": Unpacking teachers' desires to teach urban students. *Journal of Teacher Education, 62*(1), 23–34.

Weinstein, C. S., Curran, M., & Tomlinson-Clarke, S. (2004). Toward a conception of culturally responsive classroom management. *Journal of Teacher Education, 55*(1), 25–38.

West, C. (1993). *Race matters*. Boston, MA: Beacon Press.

Wright, B. L. (2011). I know who I am, do you? Identity and academic achievement of successful African American male adolescents in an urban pilot high school in the United States. *Urban Education, 46*(4), 611–638.

Yosso, T. J. (2006). Whose culture has capital? A critical race theory discussion of community cultural wealth. In A. D. Dixson & C. K. Rousseau (Eds.), *Critical race theoy in education: All God's children got a song* (pp. 167–189). New York, NY: Routledge.

Zumwalt, K., & Craig, E. (2005). Teachers' characteristics: Research on the demographic profile. In M. Cochran-Smith & K. M. Zeichner (Eds.), *Studying teacher education: The report of the AERA panel on research and teacher education*, (pp. 111–156). Mahwah, NJ: Erlbaum.

3

PARENT ADVOCACY FOR BLACK MALES IN GIFTED AND ADVANCED PROGRAMS

Tarek C. Grantham, Christopher O. Johnson,
Angie C. Roberts-Dixon, and Eric M. Bridges

If you are in a situation where you believe the schools are unresponsive to the needs of your child,
and if indeed you have firm evidence of your child's exceptional characteristics beyond your own
subjective prejudice, you can help the schools to make the necessary changes. . . . School leaders
and teachers need your help and companionship in serving the needs of your child. (Marland,
1981)

Marland's (1981) charge is particularly relevant to parents of Black males in today's public schools because of the declining status of Black male achievement in schools (Schott Foundation for Public Education, 2012). Educators are not effectively meeting a large number of Black males' academic needs. In addition, parents are struggling to meet their needs at home. Neither parents nor educators should function as silos and bear the challenge of educating Black males alone. President Barack Obama's Executive Order 13621 (2012), "White House Initiative on Educational Excellence for African Americans," calls for "enhancing the educational and life opportunities of African Americans by fostering positive family and community engagement in education" (p. 546). The president and his administration called for schools to work more proactively with parents of Black students to reduce racial isolation and resegregation of elementary and secondary schools. This urgency stems in part from Black student underachievement and their inequitable enrollment in gifted and advanced programs (Ford, 2011). These sentiments for increased parent engagement and advocacy resound even more for Black males given the paucity of their enrollment in K–12 gifted and advanced educational programs and in college (Bonner, 2010; Hilton, Wood, & Lewis, 2012). For example, Black males represent 36.6% of the male student population in Georgia, and their enrollment in gifted program services is 15.6%, as shown in Table 3.1 (Georgia Department of Education, 2012). This percentage is glaringly below the equity index or threshold that is recommended for educators and parents to use when determining equitable representation in gifted programs (Ford, in press).

When parents of gifted Black males are informed about these report cards and are actively engaged in the educational policy and practices related to gifted education programs, they are in a better position to advocate on their children's behalf and to proactively address enrollment disparities and other issues of equity and excellence (Baldwin, 1987; Ford, 2011; Ford & Grantham, 2003; Frasier, 1991, 1997; Mitchell, 1981), and to conscientiously recruit mentors who can help them (Grantham, 2004; Grantham, Trotman Scott, & Harmon, 2013). The purpose of this chapter is to provide guidance for such parents and for educators of Black males with high academic potential to become more effective coadvocates who can reverse patterns of underrepresentation and underachievement by redressing inadequacies in gifted education program policy and practice.

Effective Advocacy in Gifted Education

A national study conducted by the National Association of Gifted Children Task Force on Advocacy provided a view of advocacy efforts at the local and state levels (Robinson & Moon, 2003). A cross-case analysis conducted by Robinson and Moon of six case studies examined successful advocacy events on behalf of gifted and talented children as well as factors that facilitated positive outcomes for advocacy efforts at the state and local levels.

One characteristic from the case studies that contributed to advocacy event success was leadership. The strength of leadership emerged from professional educators and advocacy organizations working with parents, as well as local parent groups. Robinson and Moon (2003) referred to leaders in these cases as *champions* who generated positive outcomes for gifted programs. Common traits of these champion advocates included (a) motivation, strong persistence and commitment related to creating change; (b) self-education in pursuit of knowledge of best practices in gifted education, tacit knowledge of the advocacy context, and practical knowledge of advocacy strategies; and

TABLE 3.1
Comparison of 2011–2012 Male Student Enrollment in Georgia Public Schools and Gifted Programs by Race/Ethnicity Using an Equity Index of 20%

Race/Ethnicity	Male Student Enrollments in Georgia				Representation[a]			
	Public Schools	Percentage	Gifted Programs	Percentage	Equity Index	Minimum	Maximum	Outcome
American Indian	1,753	0.2%	184	0.2%	0.04	0.16%	0.24%	W
Asian	28,697	3.4%	7,665	8.3%	0.68	2.72%	4.08%	O
Black	301,970	36.6%	14,388	15.6%	7.32	29.28%	43.92%	U
Hispanic	101,132	12.2%	5,747	6.2%	2.44	9.76%	14.64%	U
Pacific Islander	834	0.1%	66	0.1%	0.02	0.08%	0.12%	W
White	366,594	44.4%	61,065	66.4%	8.88	35.52%	53.28%	O
Two+ Races	24,060	2.9%	2,934	3.2%	0.58	2.32%	3.48%	W
Total	825,040	100%	92,049	100%	—	—	—	—

Note. Georgia Department of Education 2011–2012.

[a] *Representation Outcome:* U = underrepresented, O = over-represented, or W = within range. To determine the outcome of equitable representation in gifted programs among male students in Georgia, an equity index (EI) is used. The EI is a percentage used to calculate the acceptable range for a group's representation to be equitable. Based on the Office of Civil Rights 20% threshold rule, Ford (in press) recommended that an EI is based on the following calculation: EI = percentage of male enrollment in public school × 20% threshold. To create the acceptable percentage male enrollment in gifted programs range using the EI, the following calculation was used: minimum acceptable percentage male enrollment in gifted programs = (percentage of male enrollment in public school – EI); maximum percentage acceptable male enrollment in gifted programs = (percentage of male enrollment in public school + EI). If the percentage male enrollment in gifted programs falls outside the acceptable percentage range (minimum to maximum) using the EI, then Ford indicates that the enrollment is beyond statistical chance, and human or systemic factors are operating (e.g., potentially discriminatory attitudes, biased or inappropriate tests, instruments, policies, and procedures).

(c) skills in leadership, problem solving, communication, and public relations. Four other characteristics that emerged in these case studies centered on advocacy strategies, including planning, collaboration, communication, and program development. To more fully understand how some of these characteristics are situated in the advocacy process aimed to address equity among students who are underrepresented in gifted education programs, Grantham's (2003) gifted program advocacy model (G-PAM) can be applied.

An Advocacy Model for Underrepresented Gifted Ethnic Minority Students

Grantham's (2003) G-PAM was developed to study Arkansas's Pulaski County Special School District's efforts to increase Black student enrollment in gifted programs. The G-PAM offers teachers of underrepresented gifted ethnic minority students (GEMS) a framework that can be used to guide parents in their advocacy efforts. The problems of underrepresentation among GEMS in gifted programs require parents to become upstander parents for equity and excellence. Grantham (2011) defined *upstander parents* as those who recognize the crisis in educational attainment among underrepresented GEMS and who engage in conscientious, deliberate, and immediate responses to aid. At the heart of upstanding is simply *taking a stand and adopting proactive roles to address injustices*. Upstander parents are critical for any advocacy effort to be effective, and they are key players in the G-PAM four-phase advocacy process, including conducting a needs assessment, developing an advocacy plan, implementing and taking action, and systemically following up and evaluating efforts (see Figure 3.1).

In the G-PAM, these phases can promote effective advocacy and influence positive gifted program outcomes for underrepresented GEMS, and specifically gifted Black males for the purposes of this discussion. In Phase I, upstander parents conduct a needs assessment to understand what is going on and what needs to happen in gifted education related to gifted Black males. In Phase II, upstander parents collaborate with school personnel to develop an advocacy plan to address concerns identified in the needs assessment, focusing on what advocates want to accomplish on behalf of gifted Black males and how they plan to achieve it. Phase III, implementation, emphasizes the manner in which upstander parents as advocates will take action to execute the advocacy plan. Phase IV consists of follow-up and evaluation of advocacy efforts undertaken by upstander parents. These four phases provide a framework that can inform advocacy efforts and generate positive outcomes for Black males in gifted programs. Embedded in each

Figure 3.1 G-PAM Model

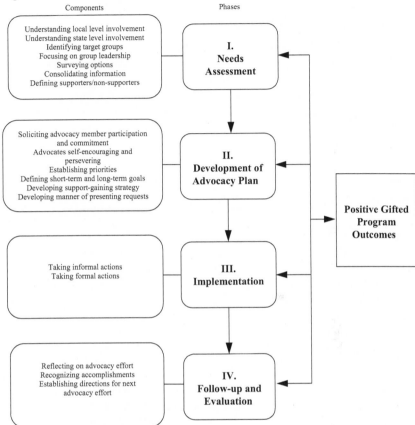

Note. From "Increasing Black Student Enrollment in Gifted Programs: An Exploration of the Pulaski County Special School District's Advocacy Efforts," by T. C. Grantham, 2003, *Gifted Child Quarterly*, *47*(1), 46–65. Copyright 2003 by Sage Publications.

phase are specific tasks or domains of advocacy that relate to each of the four phases of the G-PAM (see Figure 3.1).

Phase I: Needs assessment. When engaging in effective needs assessment efforts, gifted program personnel are working with upstander parents, helping them gain an understanding of local- and state-level involvement in gifted education. They identify target groups that can have significant influences on gifted programs and services for underrepresented GEMS. After target groups have been identified, advocacy members determine who the leaders are and survey opinions relative to gifted education for underrepresented GEMS. An important aspect of the needs assessment for upstander parents is to recognize who's who, what they think of equity issues in gifted education, and on which side of the fence they stand. This is the result of consolidating information and defining supporters and nonsupporters of balancing under-representation in gifted education. Table 3.2 contains an Advocate's Guide for Assessment of Equity in Gifted Programs to assist upstander parents in the needs assessment process to better understand the status of underrepresented GEMS. The issues in the guide, while not exhaustive, are complex and require the support of conscientious gifted program personnel to effectively collect and interpret the information. It is important that efforts are made to dissect data by gender and race so that upstander parents can identify the trends for Black males in gifted and advanced programs.

TABLE 3.2
Advocate's Guide for Assessment of Equity in Gifted Programs

Equity Domain to Assess	Questions to Pursue by Advocates

Statistical analysis of district and gifted enrollment by demographic variables	• What is the composition of the district's student enrollment by demographic variables, including race/ethnicity, language, gender, and socioeconomic status?
	• What is the composition of the student population receiving gifted services by demographic variables, including race/ethnicity, language, gender, and socioeconomic status?
	• Determine if Black students are statistically underrepresented in gifted programs. A statistically significant underrepresentation of Black students warrants a further school-by-school inquiry including statistical data/analyses regarding
	  ○ number (%) of students by demographic variable referred for evaluation of gifted eligibility,
	  ○ number (%) of students by demographic variable determined eligible for gifted services, and
	  ○ number (%) of students by demographic variable withdrawing from, or otherwise discontinuing participation in, gifted programs/services.

Gifted program notice	• Is the notice of the gifted program, with respect to both content and method of dissemination, effective? • Does the notice clearly explain the purpose of the program, referral/screening procedures, eligibility criteria, and identifies the district's contact person? • Is the notice provided annually to students, parents, and guardians, in a manner designed to reach all segments of the school community?

TABLE 3.2
Advocate's Guide for Assessment of Equity in Gifted Programs (Continued)

Equity Domain to Assess	Questions to Pursue by Advocates
Gifted program referral/screening of students	• Are multiple referral sources (e.g., teachers, parents, etc.,) used and are accessible to and used by all segments of the school community? • Have teachers and other district staff involved in the referral process been trained or provided guidance regarding the characteristics of giftedness in general, and their manifestation in Black students? • Are the referral/screening criteria applied in a nondiscriminatory manner? • Are all referral/screening criteria/guidelines directly related to the purpose of the gifted program? • Are the standardized tests and cutoff scores appropriate (valid and reliable) for the purpose of screening Black students for the gifted program?
Evaluation and placement of students in the gifted program	• Are the eligibility criteria applied in a nondiscriminatory manner? • Are the eligibility criteria consistent with the purpose and implementation of the gifted program? • Are assessment instruments/measures and cutoff scores appropriate (valid and reliable) for the purpose of identifying students for gifted services? • To the extent that subjective assessment criteria are used, have those individuals conducting the assessments been provided guidelines and training to ensure proper evaluations? • Are alternative assessment instruments used in appropriate circumstances?
Gifted program student participation	• Are continued eligibility standards/criteria and procedures applied in a nondiscriminatory manner, and do they ensure equal access for all qualified students? • Are continued eligibility standards/criteria applied in a nondiscriminatory manner? • Are continued eligibility standards/criteria consistent with the purpose and implementation of the gifted program?

Note. Adapted from Grantham, Frasier, Roberts, & Bridges, (2005). Parent advocacy for culturally diverse students. *Theory into Practice, 44*(2), 138–147.

Phase II: Development of advocacy plan. Once a needs assessment has been conducted and upstander parents know what is happening (and needs to happen) to address the needs of underrepresented GEMS, an advocacy plan is developed. Effective advocacy efforts to develop an advocacy plan occur when upstander parents solicit increased participation and commitment from other advocates. In addition, upstander parents provide group encouragement and perseverance to strengthen their efforts within the community and school (Walker, 2002). When parents establish priorities, and their short- and long-term goals related to equity and excellence are well-defined, then advocacy efforts are likely to have greater success. The parent advocacy plan also includes the development of support-gaining strategies for underrepresented GEMS. Specifically, in a case study of effective advocacy that increased Black student enrollment in Pulaski County Special School District's gifted program, Grantham (2003) found that proactive policies designed to desegregate the gifted program were used as part of an advocacy plan. Three goals were to monitor nominations to see that minorities are included, monitor the number of students involved in the special activities of the gifted program to see that minorities are included, and plan to conduct parent meetings and conferences. Goals such as this that promote equity through accountability provided a framework for the action to be taken that resulted in increased representation. Upstander parents can borrow from school districts whose advocacy plans have included initiatives that address equity and excellence.

Phase III: Implementation. This phase consists primarily of parent advocates taking action in an informal or formal manner. Informal actions may occur, for example, during passing conversation with teachers in the school or community when upstander parents express their interest in seeing more Black males in gifted and advanced programs. Formal actions may relate to upstander parents' organizing (or collaborating with school administrators to organize) a presentation by an expert in gifted education on characteristics of gifted students and barriers to equitable representation among GEMS in gifted programs. The underlying goal of the parent advocacy plan that warrants this type of action may be to revise the local gifted program identification policies and procedures. Grantham (2003) found that these types of informal and formal actions taken by parents who worked with a gifted program coordinator generated positive outcomes in the representation of gifted programs. For starters, upstander parents can address the following three action areas prior to taking other formal actions.

1. Gifted program time lines. Contact the school to find out who is eligible to make referrals for the gifted program, when and how school personnel assess students for gifted education services, when forms are due, and so

on. Many school districts allow parents to make referrals for assessment leading to placement in gifted education programs. Upstander parents who observe their Black male children demonstrating exceptional abilities and performance at home can share their observations with school personnel through an assessment referral of their child for gifted education services. Being aware of time lines is critically important; not adhering to deadlines diminishes opportunity.

2. General test preparation. Consult with gifted program personnel to understand what tests are administered as part of the gifted program assessment process and if there are parent manuals to help parents know how to prepare. Search the test publisher's website for online practice tests or sample items to get an understanding of the content knowledge, skills, and abilities that are targeted. In addition, identify parents and older successful Black students who took the test for information about their experience in taking it. These efforts can help reduce test anxiety among Black males and counter poor performance from stereotype threat. When negative stereotypes about Blacks' abilities are emphasized by test administrators and internalized by Black males, this can cause them to perform poorly (Perry, Steele, & Hilliard, 2003). Upstander parents must recognize that Black males' test preparation cannot be left to chance or the goodwill of school personnel.

3. Gifted program policies and procedures. Contact the local district gifted program coordinator or the state department for information on the identification procedure for gifted programs, the appeals process, and general information on the type of program experiences parents should expect for children should they be eligible for services. Most states have policies that govern how local school districts design and implement the criteria that make students eligible for gifted services, the type of services to be provided at various educational levels (e.g., elementary, middle, and high school), and the requirements for continuation from year to year.

Phase IV: Follow-up and evaluation. Once action has been taken to advance an advocacy plan, efforts to follow up and evaluate the outcomes are necessary. In this phase, upstander parents work with school personnel to reflect on their efforts and determine levels of effectiveness in various areas, such as recognizing accomplishments related to Black male students' progress (e.g., referrals for assessment, placement in programs, achievement, program retention between advanced courses and between grade level), and establishing new directions to work toward other goals that promote equity *and* excellence in gifted education. It is worth noting that the National Parent Teacher Association (NPTA,

2009), promotes six national standards for quality family and school partnerships. The themes undergirding these standards (communication, connection, success, voice, power, and collaboration) inform the G-PAM and can be used to guide areas of evaluation related to the parent advocacy group's functionality. Effective school-initiated gifted program parent advocacy, with the goal of promoting equity *and* excellence for Black males in gifted education programs, may be characterized and evaluated based on the following areas.

1. Communicating effectively about Black male issues is the foundation for a solid partnership between Black males' families and schools, where two-way communication is regular and meaningful related to the needs and experiences of Black males in gifted and advanced programs.
2. Connecting positively with parents of Black males emphasizes the reality that parents are the most important support system in the lives of gifted Black male students and that teachers value their advocacy by making parents feel welcome and by building trusting relationships that support learning in school and at home.
3. Promoting success among Black male students depends on parents' role in the process of helping gifted Black males at home and valuing their sons' school achievement.
4. Voicing concerns for Black males in the gifted and advanced program is a critical area of advocacy that teachers must empower parents to do. Parents should be encouraged to take the responsibility to monitor and ensure that gifted Black males are treated fairly and have access to learning opportunities that will support their success. When the teachers do not, parents should speak up and not be silenced or silence themselves.
5. Sharing decision-making power relates to parents being full partners in gifted program policies and practices that affect gifted Black males and their families; ideally, parents and educators are interdependent in sharing authority in decision making to promote balanced quality programs, parental trust, public confidence, and mutual support of each other's efforts in helping gifted Black males succeed.
6. Collaborating effectively within Black communities stresses the use of resources within and beyond Black male students' communities to strengthen schools, families, and student learning.

Advocating for Gifted Black Males: First Steps

To fully understand their role as advocates, upstander parents of Black males must be knowledgeable and informed. Secured or armed with data, upstander parents of Black male students can better appreciate the magnitude of the issues surrounding equity and excellence in school settings and gifted and talented programs. At least five types of information are foundational for families of Black male students as they seek to address and redress concerns: underrepresentation of Black males in advanced programs, patterns of underachievement, bystander teachers, and core attributes of giftedness.

Awareness of underrepresentation among gifted Black male students. One of the first steps for upstander parents is to understand inhibiting barriers to the identification of Black male students in gifted and advanced programs. The use of ineffective and inappropriate traditional definitions of *giftedness* and inhibiting identification policies and procedures is historically cited as one of the most egregious barriers (Ford, 2011; Frasier & Passow, 1994; Hilliard, 1987). Parents should be aware of federal policy that argued against barriers created by traditional approaches in gifted education. "Schools must eliminate barriers to participation of economically disadvantaged and minority students with outstanding talents" and "must develop strategies to serve students from under-represented groups" (U.S. Department of Education, Office of Educational Research and Improvement [USDE], 1993, p. 28). The term *gifted* has evolved to reflect current knowledge and thinking in the area of gifted education and is defined as children with outstanding talent. If used, this nontraditional definition offers parents of Black male students some policy assurance to reduce barriers in the identification process. According to the federal definition,

> Children and youth with outstanding talent perform or show the potential for performing at remarkably high levels of accomplishment when *compared with others of their age, experience, or environment* [emphasis added]. These children and youth exhibit high performance capability in intellectual, creative, and/or artistic areas, possess an unusual leadership capacity, or excel in specific academic fields. They require services or activities not ordinarily provided by the schools. Outstanding talents are present in children and youth *from all cultural groups, across all economic strata* [emphasis added], and in all areas of human endeavor. (USDE, 1993, p. 27)

With this understanding, it is important to question the extent to which the state definition and the local school district's gifted education identification policies and educational programming reflect the spirit of this definition. For example, are local norms on standardized tests used for assessment of students, or do they only rely on national norms that may not reflect a child's experience or environment?

Recognizing patterns of underachievement. Upstander parents should realize that historically many educators in mainstream society perceived underachievement among Black male students to be the result of intellectual inferiority (Herrnstein & Murray, 1994; Jensen, 1980). Upstander parents must also realize that they are key people who can raise issues to change misconceptions of how underachievement manifests itself in school contexts. For example, a grandparent of a Head Start student in rural Louisiana raised an underachievement-related issue in this way: "If the corn doesn't grow, nobody asks what's wrong with the corn" (Perry et al., 2003). The implication here is that when Black males underachieve it is because something is wrong with them; it's not the school, or in the grandparent's case, the farmer who failed to provide adequate nutrients or water for the corn to grow. While research does indicate that reasons for underachievement can be student related (e.g., negative attitude, perfectionism, low academic self-esteem; Ford, 2011), upstander parents of Black male students must also understand how systemic issues influence underachievement.

Hilliard (1991) asked teachers: "Do we have the will to educate all children?" Underachievement among Black males may be because of the negative beliefs that teachers have of their ability to achieve and learn, and their accompanying motivation to educate Black students. As advocates, upstander parents of gifted Black males need to recognize when some teachers misinterpret differences as deficits (Grantham, 2013; Torrance, 1974). In such cases, parents should feel empowered to challenge negative beliefs and assumptions through discussion with their child's teacher, and if necessary, the administration. Because many gifted classes tend to be overrepresented with gifted students who are White and middle class, parents of Black male students should not overlook the direct or indirect negative expectations they inherently know exist. Early in their children's education, upstander parents can start to work with educators to recognize negative systemic patterns as well as proactively address underachievement before it becomes a debilitating issue among gifted Black students.

Recognizing bystander teachers, promoting upstanders. Grantham (2011, 2013) suggested that schools have too many bystander teachers. Bystanders are those who fail to respond to students in an educational crisis. For example, if something academically egregious or controversial is happening to a student in school, educators are more likely to stand by or pass by than to intervene. Disturbingly, when the student or victim is Black, White educators are less likely to intervene. More specifically, when the gifted student in crisis is Black and male, teachers may be less likely to intervene (Ford, 2011). The lack of culturally responsive educators is one of the primary reasons gifted Black students, particularly males, underachieve and fail to reach their full academic potential in school. Unresponsive teachers stand by and fail to look for gifted behaviors in culturally relevant ways. Researchers have found that the lack of teacher referrals is a critical barrier for Black students to gain access to gifted and advanced programs (Elhoweris, Alsheikh, & Holloway, 2005), leaving them stuck in classes that fail to challenge their minds. Upstander parents must understand bystander behavior, which Grantham (2011) said has five major categories:

1. *Self-preservation*: natural instincts or learned dispositions to remove one-self from harm or situate oneself to seek or sustain benefits in the midst of a crisis
2. *Perceived inability*: belief that one lacks skills, competence, or resources to address a crisis
3. *Situation ambiguity*: unclear understanding of circumstances surrounding the evolution or the urgency of the crisis
4. *Diffusion of responsibility*: disassociating oneself with roles and duties in a crisis situation
5. *Pluralistic ignorance*: using or misinterpreting the surrounding group's response to justify one's avoidance-related feelings, beliefs, and actions about a crisis

Upstander parents must understand and confront bystander teacher behaviors (see Table 3.3) and encourage bystanders to become upstander teachers (see Grantham 2011 for a more detailed discussion), *take a stand*, and proactively work to meet the needs of gifted Black males.

Understanding core attributes of giftedness. To more fully understand and appreciate a construct of giftedness and children with outstanding talent, upstander parents of Black males must be aware of core attributes of giftedness. Frasier's (1994) Talent Assessment Profile (F-TAP) is an assessment system that facilitates the collection and display of data from multiple test and nontest sources so teams of educators, including upstander parents, have information easily available to make recommendations about a student's needs for gifted program services. Ten core attributes of giftedness provide the foundation for the F-TAP model and for upstander parents to make a referral based on traits, aptitudes, and behaviors (TABs) associated with giftedness or children with outstanding talent. Frasier's TABs and their definitions are

1. *Motivation*: evidence of desire to learn
2. *Interests*: a feeling of intentness, passion, concern, or curiosity about something
3. *Communication skills*: highly expressive and effective use of words, numbers, symbols, and so on

TABLE 3.3
Example Bystander Teachers and Problems

Causes of Bystander Effect	Bystander Teachers' Attitudes and Behaviors	Problems
1. Self-Preservation	• "The rigor in my gifted class will be watered down and that will affect my reputation with parents as a teacher of the gifted."	• The teacher of the gifted is not concerned about his/her reputation among Black parents of males who deserve to be in the gifted program.
2. Perceived Inability	• "My gifted classes are predominantly White, and Black males are convinced that being in the gifted classes is trying to act White. So, I do not pressure them to enroll."	• By not acknowledging one's understanding of this pressure with Black males and their parents and finding ways to help them overcome it, teachers perpetuate the misconception that enrollment in gifted programs is acting White.
3. Situation Ambiguity	• "I didn't notice any race discrepancies in the gifted program; I see all students the same."	• A color-blind philosophy in viewing Black males in gifted programs creates a false reality that negative stereotypes do not exist.
4. Diffusion of Responsibility	• "Not me. His reading teacher should make the referral."	• Not capitalizing on shared responsibility with teacher colleagues denies Black males the benefit of proactive support or a safety net.

5. *Pluralistic Ignorance*	• "As a Black teacher in our predominantly Black school, I know that if a serious problem of Black male representation existed in our two advanced classes, then Black parents, Black teachers, Black administrators, Black school board members, or Black community leaders . . . somebody would have said or done something. We have had these classes for years and have professed raising the achievement levels of all children in school, not just gifted students who don't need any help."	• Pride in only two advanced options can make the Black community of educators and parents become complacent as this pales in comparison with the multiple options available in many predominantly White and/or affluent schools. Unawareness of complacency in academic course offerings or of Black males' needs in them can perpetuate perceptions of inferior Black schools and incompetent educators because of a lack of understanding of the social and emotional needs of gifted students.

4. *Problem-solving ability*: effective, often inventive, strategies for recognizing and solving problems
5. *Memory*: large storehouse of information on school or nonschool topics
6. *Inquiry*: questions, experiments, explores
7. *Insight*: quickly grasps new concepts and makes connections, senses deeper meanings
8. *Reasoning*: logical approaches to figuring out solutions
9. *Imagination/creativity*: produces many ideas, highly original
10. *Humor*: bringing together two or more heretofore unrelated ideas or planes of thought in a recognized relationship

Upstander parents of Black male students need to carefully study the TABs and observe behaviors in the child's performance at home that indicate unusual potential. Using the TABs, upstander parents can develop and maintain a record-keeping system for future referral purposes. Frasier (1994) recommended that this system does not have to be elaborate but may be initiated by simply designating a box, file, or drawer where parents retain work samples. By keeping records of things children do at home and by initiating or responding to requests for referrals, upstander parents can effectively participate in advocating for their children.

Benefits of Parental Advocacy to Schools

It is important to acknowledge that although gifted Black males and their families appear to be the ones who profit the most from parental advocacy efforts, schools receive substantial benefits when culturally diverse parents become involved in their children's education (Friesen & Huff, 1990). These benefits include the following:

Helping teachers understand diverse students. Educators struggle to know how they can best meet the social and cultural needs of Black males, particularly when their backgrounds differ in terms of race and gender. Upstander teachers can successfully use parent advocates as resources to help them discover creative ways of addressing and including a variety of cultural perspectives in the curriculum and program planning.

Consistency of expectations. Cooperation and collaboration between upstander parents and upstander school personnel increase the likelihood of consistency in academic and social expectations of Black males in home and school settings. When values are shared and reinforced in the home and in school, gifted Black male students are more likely to display achievement-oriented attitudes and behaviors across contexts. In addition, they will be more strongly encouraged to reach their full potential.

More complete understanding of gifted behaviors. When schools include upstander parents of Black students in the gifted program identification and placement decision-making processes, they stand a greater chance of not being overlooked. Upstander educators will be led by and with upstander parents to gain a more complete understanding of the gifted behaviors of Black male students inside and outside school. Upstander parents may help to raise important questions regarding how gifted Black male students think, feel, and behave, particularly when noticing or anticipating a pattern of underachievement.

Parents as nonpartisan stakeholders. Parental efforts are more likely to be viewed as purely seeking to benefit the students in contrast to other educational stakeholders (e.g., elected educational officials, educational consultants) who may, by their efforts, be viewed as acting in their own political or professional interests. Along this line, upstander parents are often free of the institutional and legal constraints that may limit the ability of other stakeholders to advocate for causes that would most benefit gifted Black students. As nonpartisan advocates, upstander parents' role in school initiatives to address programmatic needs and changes (e.g., policy development, curriculum design and implementation, and program evaluation) can provide the support to make grassroots as well as large-scale school improvements.

Summary

To reverse underrepresentation among Black male students in gifted and advanced programs, the role of upstander parents as advocates is critical. Black male underachievement and underenrollment in gifted and advanced programs is an educational crisis. A critical goal of advocacy for the needs of gifted Black males is to hold schools accountable for administering gifted program policies and services that promote excellence and equity. This chapter presents a gifted program advocacy model with recommendations for upstander parents to engage in different types of advocacy. When upstander parents challenge bystander teachers to become upstander educators and take an active role in the educational trajectory of Black males in gifted and advanced programs, everyone wins.

References

Baldwin, A. Y. (1987). Undiscovered diamonds: The minority gifted child. *Journal for the Education of the Gifted, 10*(4), 271–285.

Bonner, F. A. (2010). *Academically gifted African American male college students.* Santa Barbara, CA: Praeger.

Elhoweris, M. K. Alsheikh, N., & Holloway, P. (2005). Effect of children's ethnicity on teachers' referral and recommendation decisions in gifted and talented programs. *Remedial and Special Education, 26*(1), 25–31.

Exec. Order No. 13621, 3 C.F.R. 545-547 (2012).

Ford, D. Y. (2011). *Reversing underachievement among gifted Black students* (2nd ed.). Waco, TX: Prufrock Press.

Ford, D. Y. (in press). Under-representation of African American and Hispanic students in gifted education: Impact of social inequality, elitism, and colorblindness. *Roeper Review.*

Ford, D. Y., & Grantham, T. C. (2003). Parenting gifted culturally diverse children: A focus on education-related issues and needs. *Understanding Our Gifted, 15*(4), 12–17.

Frasier, M. M. (1991). *Minority parents' role in the education of their gifted and talented children.* Retrieved from ERIC database. (ED350801)

Frasier, M. M. (1994). *A manual for implementing the Frasier Talent Assessment Profile (F-TAP): A multiple criteria model for the identification and education of gifted students.* Athens: Georgia Southern Press.

Frasier, M. M. (1997). Gifted minority students: Reframing approaches to their identification and education. In N. Colangelo & G. B. Davis (Eds.), *Handbook of gifted education* (pp. 498–515). Boston, MA: Allyn & Bacon.

Frasier, M. M., & Passow, A. H. (1994). *Towards a new paradigm for identifying talent potential* (Research Monograph 94112). Storrs: National Research Center on the Gifted Talented, University of Connecticut.

Friesen, B. J., & Huff, B. (1990). Parents and professionals as advocacy partners. *Preventing School Failure, 34*(3), 31–36.

Georgia Department of Education. (2012). *K–12 gifted student eligible vs. served comparison: School year 2011–12 student record data collection.* Atlanta, GA: Author.

Grantham, T. C. (2003). Increasing Black student enrollment in gifted programs: An exploration of the Pulaski County Special School District's advocacy efforts. *Gifted Child Quarterly, 47*(1), 46–65.

Grantham, T. C. (2004). Multicultural mentoring to increase Black male representation in gifted programs. *Gifted Child Quarterly, 48*(3), 232–245.

Grantham, T. C. (2011). New directions for gifted Black males suffering from bystander effects: A call for upstanders. *Roeper Review, 33*(4), 263–272.

Grantham, T. C. (2012). *Comparison of 2011–2012 male student enrollment in Georgia public schools and gifted programs by race/ethnicity using an equity index of 20%.* Athens, GA: Diversity and Equity in Advanced Programs Research Group, The University of Georgia.

Grantham, T. C. (2013). Creativity and equity: The legacy of E. Paul Torrance as an upstander for gifted Black males. *Urban Review, 45*(4), 518–538.

Grantham, T. C., Frasier, M. M., Roberts, A. C., & Bridges, E. M. (2005). Parent advocacy for culturally diverse students. *Theory into Practice, 44*(2), 138–147.

Grantham, T. C., Trotman Scott, M., & Harmon, D. (Eds.). (2013). *Young, triumphant, and Black: Overcoming segregated minds in desegregated schools.* Waco, TX: Prufrock Press

Herrnstein, R., & Murray, C. (1994). *The bell curve: Intelligence and class structure in American life*. New York, NY: The Free Press.

Hilliard, A. G., III. (1987). The ideology of intelligence and I.Q. magic in education. *Negro Educational Review, 38*(2/3), 136–145.

Hilliard, A. G., III (1991). Do we have the will to educate all children? *Educational Leadership, 49*(1), 31–36.

Hilton, A. A., Wood, J. L., & Lewis, C. W. (2012). *Black males in postsecondary education: Examining their experiences in diverse institutional contexts*. Charlotte, NC: Information Age.

Jensen, A. R. (1980). *Bias in mental testing*. New York, NY: The Free Press

Marland, S., Jr. (1981). Parent role in changing schools. In B. S. Miller & M. Price, (Ed.), *The gifted child, the family, and the community* (pp. 159–161). New York, NY: Walker.

Mitchell, P. B. (Ed.). (1981). *An advocate's guide to building support for gifted and talented education*. Washington, DC: National Association of State Boards of Education.

National Parent Teacher Association. (2009). *PTA national standards for family-school partnerships: An implementation guide*. Alexandria, VA: Author.

Perry, T., Steele, C., & Hilliard, A. (2003). *Young, gifted, and Black: Promoting high achievement among African American students*. Boston, MA: Beacon Press.

Robinson, A., & Moon, S. M. (2003). A national study of local and state advocacy in gifted education. *Gifted Child Quarterly, 47*(1), 8–25.

Schott Foundation for Public Education. (2012). *The urgency of now: The Schott 50 state report on public education and Black males*. Cambridge, MA: Author.

Torrance, E. P. (1974). Differences are not deficits. *Teachers College Record, 75*(4), 471–487.

U.S. Department of Education, Office of Educational Research and Improvement. (1993). *National excellence: A case for developing America's talent*. Washington, DC: U.S. Government Printing Office.

Walker, S. Y. (2002). *The survival guide for parents of gifted kids: How to understand, live with, and stick up for your gifted child*. Minneapolis, MN: Free Spirit Publishing.

4

MISSING IN ACTION

African American Males in Gifted Education

Donna Y. Ford, L. Trenton Marsh, Jerell Blakeley, and Stanford O. Amos

For numerous reasons, African American males disproportionately experience poor and negative educational, social, and economic outcomes; the most common are *unreasonably* (a) high dropout rates, (b) low graduation rates, (c) low test scores, (d) low grade point averages, (e) low representation in gifted education and advanced placement classes, (f) high participation rates in special education, and (g) high suspension and expulsion rates (Donovan & Cross, 2002; Ford, 2010, 2013a; Losen, 2011; Schott Foundation, 2012; U.S. Department of Education, Office for Civil Rights, 2009, 2012). And we cannot ignore or be surprised that these negative school outcomes are accompanied by high apathy, low self-efficacy, low academic motivation, disengagement, and disinterest among too many African American (which we use interchangeably with Black) males at all academic levels, even in the primary grades. As Upchurch (1997) noted, our Black males are convicted in the womb. That is, deficit thinking threatens and effectively takes a toll on their lives (Valencia, 2010).

The *achievement gap* has many faces, comes in many forms, and is couched in several terms—*opportunity gap, experience gap, language gap, technology gap, resource gap, expectation gap*, and *teacher quality gap*, to name but a few. For ages, laypeople, researchers, policymakers, school leaders, and organizations have sought to understand and address the complicated and deep-seated issues of African American males' pervasive and appalling academic and social outcomes and trajectory. Less common or sparser is advocacy for and scholarship on *gifted* African American males. In this chapter, which shares the concerns of the editor and most if not all the contributors to this book, we shed some light on this emptiness by shining the proverbial light on this specific underestimated and underserved group of Black students. Our Black males are diamonds in various stages—undiscovered, underestimated, undervalued, and depreciated—based on their experiences, expectations held of them, and academic identity.

One logical starting point is to discuss the achievement gap(s) whereby Black males are performing below White students—the litmus test of success. It is noteworthy that African American males are performing, on average, below Black females and all other groups. It is unacceptable that information on the gaps is rarely tailored to gifted Black males specifically (Ford, 2010). However, it is more than reasonable to make inferences from the general population of Black males to gifted Black males.

No one variable or correlate is responsible for the unclosed and widespread achievement gaps between African American students and White students, and between Black males and Black females. Differential educational performance and outcomes must be dissected and digested using social, cultural/familial, school, and individual contexts (Ford, 2010; Moore, Henfield, & Owens, 2008; Moore & Lewis, 2012; Vega et al., 2012). There are no band-aids or easy fixes, and not attending to all contexts collectively is a recipe for stagnation and neither narrows nor closes the gap(s). Poor achievement, be it temporary, situational, or long term (e.g., moving to a new school, parental/caregiver divorce, personal or family illness, teacher disinterest, etc.), is a function of knotty, interwoven factors that affect the achievement of African American students (Barton & Coley, 2009; Cohen & Lotan, 2004), including those who are gifted. Being gifted does not seem to help gifted Black males weather storms; in fact, being gifted may include additional pressures that some find difficult to cope with (e.g., using peers as a case in point, this includes social isolation from White classmates and cultural isolation from Black friends and classmates (e.g., Ford, 2010, 2013a; Ford, Moore, Whiting, & Grantham, 2008; Moore & Lewis, 2012).

While this chapter focuses on disconsolate issues that are or seem difficult for many educators and decision makers to discuss, admit to, digest, and share responsibility for, it is also optimistic in that narrowing and, ideally, eliminating the achievement gaps is possible; efforts must neither decrease nor cease. Equitable change requires political, professional, and personal will, along with demonstrated commitment from adults—educators (e.g., teachers, school counselors, psychologists, administrators, etc.) and African American families. And it may be necessary to couple this commitment to increase gifted education access with legislative backing, such as that provided by the

Office for Civil Rights (see Ford, 2013a; Ford & Frazier Trotman, 2000). It is, therefore, critical that educators and professionals work individually and collectively to improve gifted African American males' achievement and outcomes. A much-needed but neglected step in the right direction is to desegregate gifted education. With this assertion guiding our work, we begin with vignettes of four gifted Black males who have had different experiences in school (more detailed discussions appear in Ford, 2013a).

Gifted Black Males: Easy and Not So Easy to Identify

Black males are underrepresented in gifted education by over 55%. When converted to numbers, more than 150,000 Black males are unidentified and underrepresented in gifted education yearly (see Ford, 1998, 2010, 2013a).

This section contains vignettes on four Black males from different backgrounds. Given page limitations, we cannot use case studies that certainly have depth and fill in many blanks. Thus, we urge readers to delve into the lives of these young Black males and to use them in classes, workshops, and professional development using Ford (2011), the Internet, books, and other sources (e.g., social media). Each story is informative and can inform underrepresentation barriers and solutions. Every vignette ought to remind readers of the varied experiences of students, and that opportunity, experience, and expectation gaps are quite influential. With the additional support of educators as advocates, we can positively change the destiny of Black males. Be mindful that these young males are not homogeneous; on critical sociodemographic characteristics, the four do not share the same income or socioeconomic status (family education, occupation, etc.), family structure, social and cultural capital, or academic identity. These scenarios are adapted from Ford (2013a).

- Farrah Gray. Raised in the economically impoverished south side of Chicago, at 14 Farrah Gray became a self-made millionaire after creating a food company selling syrups he concocted after watching his grandmother cook. Farrah began his business career as a 6-year-old, selling hand-painted rocks and homemade lotions door-to-door. He carried business cards with "21st-Century CEO" printed on them at age 7, and started the Urban Neighborhood Enterprise Economic Club a year later. Farrah later had a role on a talk show for teens, an office on Wall Street, and a series of books about business. Farrah received an honorary doctorate at age 21 and, by the age of 28, was placed on a variety of lists of top businesspeople in the United States.

- Tony Hansberry. He was identified as a child prodigy after developing an innovative suture method at age 14 that decreases hospital stays and increases efficiency during operations for hysterectomies. Tony's mother is a nurse, and his father is a pastor. As an eighth grader he teamed up with an administrator at Shands Hospital in Gainesville, Florida, to create the innovative surgical procedure. The technique was a success, revered by the medical profession for increased ease, increased safety, and decreased surgical time. Tony is humble. "People think I'm a genius. It's not that at all, I just like medicine" (Ford, 2013a). Tony continued his education in the field that caught his interest as a child. In 2012 he was a freshman majoring in biomedical engineering at Florida A&M University.
- Stephen Stafford. At 13 years of age Stephen was earning credits toward his premed, computer science, and mathematics degrees at Morehouse College. Stephan is middle class, lives with both parents, and has been homeschooled for a few years. Stephan has given some credit to his older sister for teaching and supporting him before he entered school. Stephen indicated that literature is his most difficult subject, not because it is difficult for him but that he dislikes reading. In talking about testing and intelligence, Stephen noted, "The whole IQ thing, it's a number. . . . No matter what your IQ is, it's always about what you do with it rather than I have this number telling me I'm smart. You can be smart without a number. It's what you do and who you think you are" (see Ford, 2013a).
- Semaj Booker. On January 14, 2007, 9-year-old Semaj Booker stole a neighbor's vehicle and led police on a chase at speeds upward of 80 miles per hour before blowing the car's transmission on a highway exit and coasting into a tree. Semaj was being raised by his unmarried mother, Sakinah, who has three other sons. According to her and the police, this was Semaj's third stolen car in the past month. Sakinah believes her son learned to drive by playing arcade and video games such as *Grand Theft Auto*; she noted that her son was often smart enough to play an entire video game in one night within a couple of hours of receiving the game. A few hours after being caught and turned back over to his mother, Semaj disappeared again, this time making his way to the airport where he managed to convince a ticket agent that a lost ticket that had been reported belonged to him (Burbank, 2007). Semaj managed to sneak out of his house and travel about 50 miles to Seattle-Tacoma International Airport. Police speculate that he hitched a ride or stole another car. His mother reported him missing at 7:30 a.m. the same day. She later told reporters that Semaj loathes his life

in Washington state, has tried to run away nine times since moving to the region less than a year ago, and is seeking a strong male figure. According to his mother, Semaj does not like their neighborhood and is afraid of a sex offender who lives nearby. At the Seattle-Tacoma Airport, Semaj did not have a reservation, nor did he have a means of buying a ticket. But he single-handedly conned a representative of Southwest Airlines and the Transportation Security Administration into allowing him to board a flight to San Antonio via Phoenix.

Given their accomplishments, no one reading the stories of Farrah, Tony, and Stephen would or should be surprised if they were formally identified as gifted. However, given the magnitude of underrepresentation among Black males in gifted education, the probability of their being formally recruited and retained in gifted education is questionable. In fact, an interview with Stephen and his mother reveals that he was *not* identified as gifted because of a C in one class and because he stated he does not test well (Ford, 2013a).

Semaj's story is a classic case of a student who is obviously gifted but whose abilities and potential have gone unrecognized and are not used to his or society's advantage. Of the four young men, Semaj is least likely to be recognized, referred to, and identified as gifted, even though he is *also* a critical thinker and problem solver, perhaps not in school but undeniably in the real world. His street smarts or social intelligence (Sternberg, 1983) are unlikely to be appreciated and valued by teachers, many of whom adhere to stereotypical and traditional notions of gifted being grounded in intelligence test scores and academic performance (achievement tests and grades). As so with over 150,000 Black males, Semaj is missing in action—a gifted Black male who would benefit from having his intelligence channeled into academics and service.

Unapologetically and unwaveringly, we declare that Semaj (and many thousands of Black males like him) must be—not just should be—served in gifted education. He is intelligent, intellectually gifted. We have no data on his achievement scores and grades. Semaj may even have been average on tests and grades or even failed in school then and now. Sadly, this is another gifted underachieving Black male caught in the achievement gap trap (Ford, 2010). We see this young gifted Black male as one more opportunity to channel and redirect intelligence, to redirect and save a life, and to contribute to society in productive ways. This is also what Upchurch (1997) needed and wanted: an end to the school-prison pipeline that is all too familiar and commonplace in our nation. We can and must save our sons (see www.sosconsulting4bm.com).

Recommendations for Change: Saving Our Sons

To proactively and equitably tackle and eliminate underrepresentation, to ensure equity for gifted Black males—students like Semaj, Stephen, Farrah, and Tony—we offer the following assertions and associated recommendations to effect real, equity-based, and long overdue changes. We assert that increasing access to gifted education for Black males will happen more likely with teachers—the vast majority of whom are White (85%)—being trained in gifted education, but not in a color-blind way. The most effective training focuses on cultural and gender differences, with attention to income and socioeconomic status. Given the magnitude of Black male underrepresentation, it cannot be assumed or concluded that middle-class Black males are equitably represented in gifted education. It cannot even be assumed that Black males with high grades, high test scores, or both will be equitably identified and served in gifted education. Subjectivity by teachers and decision makers has trumped objective and less subjective information as summarized by Ford et al. (2008) regarding teacher referrals and checklists. Deficit thinking (Valencia, 2010) is a powerful, effective, dangerous, and damaging mindset that renders educators blind or resistant to the gifts that are evident and promising in Black males.

It is worth noting that deficit thinking, intentional or unintentional, has the same impact: access denied for Black males. Relying on Merton's prejudice-discrimination, Ford (2013b) described his 2 × 2 model and provided extensive implications for gifted education.

Prejudice is the thought/belief while discrimination is the behavior/action. Unsurprisingly, and perhaps expectedly, one (in this case, an educator/decision maker) can be prejudiced and discriminate. Conversely, and ideally, one can be *unprejudiced and not discriminate*. This must be our overarching goal.

However, there are two other belief-behavior realities. One can be *unprejudiced yet discriminate*. One of many examples is school personnel who believe that Blacks are as intelligent and capable as Whites, and they want to diversify gifted education; however, contrary to their beliefs and values, school personnel use instruments and follow policies and procedures that are barriers for Black males in accessing gifted education. Unfortunately, and all too frequently and pervasively, these educators are bystanders who cater to social pressures (e.g., from supervisors and the status quo); they compromise and fail to stand by their beliefs, and they fail to advocate for Black males. Social pressure undermines their advocacy and actions. The final example is educators who are *prejudiced but do not discriminate or act on their beliefs*. This is where legal sanctions and recourses come into play. Should the federal government or another antidiscrimination organization get involved (or be a looming threat), they will not act on their racially prejudiced beliefs. This may be the only support or advocacy for some Black families given civil rights legislation. With this said, we now summarize a few premises and recommendations to set gifted education on the right course.

1. Underrepresentation among Black males has existed for as long as local, district, state, and federal data have been collected (locally, districtwide, statewide, and nationwide).
   - Past and present policies and procedures have been ineffective and inequitable. Stephen was not identified as gifted because he had a C in one class. And although he also reports being a poor test taker, he is a *prodigy* by every definition of the word. New policies and procedures for identifying gifted students are needed at every level.
   - Past and present tests and instruments have been ineffective and inequitable. New tests and instruments are needed. Semaj is clearly intelligent (e.g., problem solver, critical thinker). This may not be evident on a traditional intelligence or achievement test. High-stakes testing seldom improves educational access and outcomes for Black students, and Black males in particular.
   - Past and present mind-sets have been ineffective and inequitable; new mind-sets are needed. Deficit thinking has compromised and continues to strangle the educational and social experiences and successes of Black males, regardless of income, socioeconomic status, family structure, and potential. Being middle class is no guarantee, as often predicted, of success for Black males. We are thankful that Stephen and Tony are at least two exceptions. There are no excuses for middle-class Black males (living with one or both parents) to be denied access to gifted education. Yet, it happens. The underrepresentation numbers and percentages speak volumes, with over two decades of national data demonstrating that Black males remain missing in action in gifted education.
2. When underrepresentation exists, it is inequitable, lacking in accountability, and culturally irresponsible and irresponsive to not err on the side of inclusion.
   - There are too many false negatives among African American males (and too many false positives among White males and females) identified as gifted. Of the four young males featured, Semaj appears to have the least support in the home, community, and school, followed by Farrah.

- When Black males are underrepresented in gifted education, it is equitable to hold decision makers and their attitudes, instruments, policies, and procedures accountable rather than students. Black males under the age of 18 are children, not adults; they are students, not professionals.

- There may be more African American males who are gifted but do not fit traditional White middle-class characteristics than those who do (e.g., Semaj Booker and, to some extent, Stephen Stafford). Yet, even when Black males do perform high intellectually and academically, this still fails to guarantee access to gifted education, as described extensively in Ford (2013a). Color blindness and deficit thinking among educators and decision makers are significant barriers. Efforts must be proactive and ongoing relative to recruiting and retaining Black males overall (Ford, Moore, & Trotman Scott, 2011), with attention to those who do not fit traditional characteristics of gifted (high scores/high achievers) like Tony Hansberry and Farrah Gray, as well as students like Stephen Stafford (low scores/high achiever).

Summary

Recruiting and retaining Black males in gifted education is essential. Recognizing, supporting, and educating our missing-in-action students dictates opening doors to gifted education for Black males who display nontraditional characteristics of achievement, intelligence or behavior (e.g., high test scores/low grades, low test scores/high grades, high performance/poor behaviors).

Underrepresentation is undeniably influenced by deficit thinking (Valencia, 2010) about Black males. Deficit thinking (e.g., stereotypes, biases, low and negative expectations) compromises referrals, how nomination forms and checklists are completed, the selection of tests and instruments, the specific cutoff score, and the ultimate placement criteria and decision (Ford, Harris, Tyson, & Frazier Trotman, 2002).

There is no quick fix or panacea for reversing underachievement and low achievement among gifted African American males, and narrowing or closing the achievement gap has been (unnecessarily) challenging but not impossible. Educators must be vigilant about the omnibus goal of improving the participation of these Black male students in gifted programs despite challenges and past efforts that have yet to be effective, and irrespective of entrenched low expectations of African American males educationally and socially. Low expectations often beget low performance and poor outcomes.

One key recommendation lies in the nonnegotiable need to directly, aggressively, and consistently address any factor or factors that hinders or comprises the identification and support of gifted Black males. In other words, the comprehensive strategies (e.g., prevention and intervention) should match the problems and needs specific to Black males. And the problems should not be thought to reside exclusively within the Black male student, his family, and his community. Underrepresentation does not exist in a vacuum.

Ensuring that African American males reach their potential and are challenged requires a social justice philosophy whereby school leaders and educators (P–12) advocate for the needs and rights of African American males—without excuses. A social justice stance is guided by the belief that all students are entitled to a free, appropriate, equitable, and culturally responsive education. It is a sad reality that racism is unlikely to decrease or disappear in the near future. Racism is present and pervasive in all types of school settings; schools are social institutions and, thus, not exempt from the social ills common in the larger society. Nonetheless, with substantive preparation in Black culture combined with knowledge of gifted characteristics (see Ford, 2011), teachers and other school personnel from all racial backgrounds must become more aware of and self-reflective about their own views about Black males. This culturally responsive preparation (across and within racial groups) must include discussions about theories and research on expectations, prejudice, stereotypes, racial identity, and White privilege, along with attention to attendant discriminatory behaviors, policies, and practices. Summaries of such theories or frameworks by Allport, Merton, Sue, Cross, and McIntosh, to name a few, are summarized by Ford (2011, 2013a, 2013b).

In higher education, it is essential that professors restructure their curricula and programs so that preservice and in-service educators (e.g., teachers, counselors, psychologists, and administrators) graduate from their undergraduate and graduate programs as culturally competent, that is, interested in and prepared to work with African American males. Knowledge, dispositions, and skills in culture and cultural differences render educators effective and efficacious at working with Black males, our consistently lowest performing and underestimated students.

School personnel must also effectively work with, support, and advocate for African American families (Moore et al., 2008). When African American families are supported, informed, and empowered, they have a positive influence on their African American sons. Clearly, a collaborative partnership between school personnel and families or caregivers is likely to recruit and retain more African American males.

From a social and cultural perspective, educators and families must adopt and implement strategies and supports to help gifted African American males cope with negative peer pressures. An antiachievement ethic is commonly a problem among Black students (Ford, 2010; Ford et al., 2011). Therefore, schools and homes must set a nonnegotiable, stubborn standard of high expectations and stand ready to support African American males who are contending with unsupportive peers. School personnel need to implement initiatives that build on Black males' academic and motivational assets and strengths. Tutoring, study skills, test taking skills, and time management and organizational skills are necessary skills. Also, mentoring and role modeling are essential for increasing coping skills among this student group that must come to grips with being (unnecessarily) an anomaly: gifted, Black, and male.

A Final Word

A few guiding philosophies inform this chapter. The first central premiseis that poor achievement (whether the achievement gap, underachievement, or low achievement) among African American males can be reversed. Poor achievement is learned, and it can (and must) be unlearned (Ford, 1996, 2010). African American males are not born underachieving or low achieving.

A second premise is that giftedness exists in all racial, cultural, gender, and economic groups. Thus, African American males' underrepresentation in gifted education, and their underachievement and low achievement, should not exist to the degree witnessed in our schools. Clearly, a mind is a terrible thing to waste and erase (Ford, 2010, 2013a).

A third premise is that low achievement among gifted Black males is a function of what occurs in schools relative to attitudes, policies, and practices (e.g., attitudes grounded in low educator expectations, deficit or negative thinking, and racism; culturally incompetent educators; sexism; classism; irrelevant and color-blind curricula; and few or no human and fiscal resources, etc.).

A fourth premise is that the term *Black male* is loaded and riddled with negative connotations and low expectations. The term often invokes concepts of poverty, anger or rage, crime and violence, hypermasculinity, and a litany of other entrenched and debilitating stereotypical beliefs that African American males (including gifted ones) have a disregard or disdain for self-improvement or self-advancement. When this deficit-oriented view is adopted among school personnel (Valencia, 2010), it is almost impossible for these specific students to muster up the commitment, energy, and resources to challenge decision makers and naysayers, and be resilient.

A final premise guiding this chapter is that educators need to adopt and practice a social justice or civil rights policy and stance (see Ladson-Billings, 2006, 2009) to help ensure that gifted African American males receive the education they are legally and ethically entitled to in terms of desegregation mandates (see *Brown v. Board of Education*, 1954; Civil Rights Act of 1964; *Green v. County School Board*, 1968; *Swann v. Charlotte-Mecklenburg Board of Education*, 1971). When the federal government mandated desegregated schools, those rules were also for (and are still for) gifted classes as well.

African American males in all school levels (e.g., elementary, secondary, and postsecondary) and settings (urban, suburban, rural) can excel academically but rarely achieve as highly as other student populations (e.g., White males, White females, African American females, etc.). Too many are underachievers and low achievers, and too many are not expected to perform at high or higher levels by teachers, peers, and sometimes family members (see Ford, 2010). More than any other group, these males face entrenched, unrelenting deficit thinking in educational and social settings. This is a complex, multifaceted conundrum, one that begs for understanding and solutions. Academic, social, familial, and cultural factors work independently and interactively to contribute to these problems. They can also work to contribute positively to solutions.

Despite the poor or negative outcomes of these otherwise capable African American males, this admittedly widespread situation is neither permanent, unchangeable, nor hopeless. Black males are certainly capable of high and higher levels of achievement; so many more can and must excel in academic settings. Such higher achievement is possible when educators are culturally competent; when families are supportive, supported, and empowered; and when there are tenacious, unyielding efforts, strategies, and mind-sets to increase and expand the academic potential and identities of gifted Black males.

References

Barton, P. E., & Coley, R. J. (2009). *Parsing the achievement gap II*. Princeton, NJ: Policy Information Center, Educational Testing Service.

Brown v. Board of Education, 347 U.S. 483 (1954).

Burbank, L. (2007). Young airline stowaway faces charges. *NPR*. Retrieved from http://www.npr.org/templates/story/story.php?storyId=7549118

Civil Rights Act of 1964, Pub.L. 88-352, 78 Stat. 241 (1964).

Cohen, E. G., & Lotan, R. A. (2004). Equity in heterogeneous classrooms. In J. A. Banks & C. A. M. Banks (Eds.), *Handbook of research on multicultural education* (2nd ed., pp. 736–750). San Francisco, CA: Jossey-Bass.

Donovan, M. S., & Cross, C. T. (Eds.). (2002). *Minority students in special and gifted education*. Washington, DC: National Academy Press.

Ford, D. Y. (1996). *Reversing underachievement among gifted Black students: Promising practices and programs*. New York, NY: Teachers College Press.

Ford, D. Y. (1998). The underrepresentation of minority students in gifted education: Problems and promises in recruitment and retention. *The Journal of Special Education, 32*(1), 4–14.

Ford, D. Y. (2010). *Reversing underachievement among gifted Black students* (2nd ed.). Waco, TX: Prufrock Press.

Ford, D. Y. (2011). *Multicultural gifted education* (2nd ed.). Waco, TX: Prufrock Press.

Ford, D. Y. (2013a). *Recruiting and retaining culturally different students in gifted education*. Waco, TX: Prufrock Press.

Ford, D. Y. (2013b). Multicultural issues: Gifted underrepresentation and prejudice—Learning from Allport and Merton. *Gifted Child Today, 36*(1), 62–67.

Ford, D. Y., & Frazier Trotman, M. (2000). The Office for Civil Rights and nondiscriminatory testing, policies, and procedures: Implications for gifted education. *Roeper Review, 23*(2), 109–112.

Ford, D. Y., Harris, J. J., III, Tyson, C. A., & Frazier Trotman, M. (2002). Beyond deficit thinking: Providing access for gifted African American students. *Roeper Review, 24*(2), 52–58.

Ford, D. Y., Moore, J. L., III, & Trotman Scott, M. (2011). Key theories and frameworks for improving recruitment and retention of African American students in gifted education. *The Journal of Negro Education, 80*, 239–253.

Ford, D. Y., Moore, J. L., III, Whiting, G. W., & Grantham, T. C. (2008). Conducting cross-cultural research: Controversy, cautions, concerns, and considerations. *Roeper Review, 30*(2), 82–92.

Green v. County School Board, 391 U.S. 430 (1968).

Ladson-Billings, G. J. (2006, October). *From the achievement gap to the education debt: Understanding achievement in U.S. Schools*. Presidential address at a meeting of the American Educational Research Association, San Francisco, CA.

Ladson-Billings, G. J. (2009). *The dreamkeepers: Successful teachers for African-American children* (2nd ed.). San Francisco, CA: Jossey-Bass.

Losen, D. (2011). *Discipline policies, successful schools, and racial justice*. Los Angeles, CA: The Civil Rights Project/Proyecto Derechos Civiles.

Moore, J. L., III, Henfield, M. S., & Owens, D. (2008). African American males in special education: Their attitudes and perceptions toward high school counselors and school counseling services. *American Behavioral Scientist, 51*(7), 907–927.

Moore, J. L., III, & Lewis, C. W. (Eds.). (2012). *African American students in urban schools: Critical issues and solutions for achievement*. New York, NY: Peter Lang.

Schott Foundation for Public Education. (2012). *The urgency of now: The Schott 50 state report on Black males and public education*. Boston, MA: Author.

Sternberg, R. J. (1983). Components of human intelligence. *Cognition, 15*(1), 1–48.

Swann v. Charlotte-Mecklenburg Board of Education, 402 U.S. 1 (1971).

Upchurch, C. (1997). *Convicted in the womb*. New York, NY: Bantam.

U.S. Department of Education. (2009, 2012). Office for Civil Rights Data Collection. Retrieved both years from http://ocrdata.ed.gov/

Valencia, R. R. (2010). *Dismantling contemporary deficit thinking: Educational thought and practice*. New York, NY: Routledge.

Vega, D., & Moore, J. L., III, Baker, C. A., Bowen, N. V., Hines, E. M., & O'Neal, B. O. (2012). Salient factors affecting urban African American students' achievement: Recommendations for teachers, school counselors, and school psychologists. In J. L. Moore III & C. W. Lewis (Eds.), *African American students in urban schools: Critical issues and solutions for achievement* (pp. 113–140). New York, NY: Peter Lang.

5

AN EXAMINATION OF THE LIVED EXPERIENCE OF A GIFTED BLACK CHILD IN RURAL POVERTY

Thomas P. Hébert

M y four-year journey as an assistant professor at the University of Alabama was coming to a close, and I was planning the next chapter of my professional career. I had decided to move on to another university, and before leaving Tuscaloosa, I chose to begin a research study that altered my professional career and enriched my life significantly.[1] Over several years I had come to know a classroom teacher named Teresa Beardsley, who was enrolled in a graduate degree program in gifted education. Teresa traveled to campus from the most economically impoverished county in the state and often enlightened me with stories that were troubling. She described school conditions that were appalling and the difficult challenges she and her colleagues faced. Moreover, Teresa shared vivid stories of the young children in her classroom and expressed her concern for their well-being. A passionate educator, Teresa remained tireless in her efforts to improve education for children in Pine Grove, Alabama.[2]

Teresa and her husband, James, had been living in Pine Grove since 1972, when they arrived in the community with Volunteers in Service to America (VISTA) following the civil rights movement. Following their work as VISTA volunteers, they were hired as teachers by the county school board and dedicated 36 years to teaching the children of Pine Grove. Since 1972,

Teresa, James, and their two children have been the only Caucasian citizens in this rural Black community. Recently Teresa and James retired as educators and continue to enjoy life in Pine Grove.

As Teresa shared stories of her students with me, I was especially intrigued with her experiences working with a highly creative Black child named Jermaine. She said that since having Jermaine as a student, she continued to provide after-school enrichment experiences for him and two other students. Teresa described Jermaine as a vivacious child who was not only lively and animated but also humorous. She reported that in kindergarten he was discovered standing on his head in his chair while the teacher was presenting a lesson. When his teacher posed a question, Jermaine answered correctly and elaborated in great detail. The teacher announced to the class, "If you can do that and still give me the answers, then you can act like Jermaine" (Hébert & Beardsley, 2001, p. 93). Fortunately, Jermaine's kindergarten teacher appreciated his antics; however, Teresa said that his creative behaviors were not always appreciated by others. The assistant principal knew him as "that bad little boy I have to keep my eye on," while another teacher who had observed Jermaine during bus duty reported, "That boy is just too bad to handle" (p. 93).

Although adults in his elementary school may have been bewildered by his behavior, they had to acknowledge his abilities. Jermaine's scores on the Otis-Lennon School Ability Test ranged from 118 to 120. Vocabulary and language expression were his most prominent strengths. His achievement scores ranged from the 86th to the 99th national percentiles in language arts and reading. His scores in math were in the average range. According to Teresa, when Jermaine's scores were compared with the above-average students in his class who scored in the 40th and 50th percentiles, his performance was considered remarkable.

Teresa reported that when Jermaine first arrived at the elementary school, his clothes were ill fitting, and on cold winter days he came to school without a coat or sweater. She said that although the majority of children in Pine Grove were poor, Jermaine knew he had less than others. While some students had expensive sneakers, Jermaine's mother purchased his at a discount store in Selma. Jermaine's "bargain-town" Nikes were noticed right away, and he suffered the ridicule of his peers. Moreover, Jermaine's family lived in a modest cabin with a cinder block foundation. The home was heated with a woodstove and cooled by opening windows and doors. In Jermaine's front yard were nonfunctioning automobiles and a satellite dish providing television service.

Teresa had saved a portfolio of Jermaine's work in her first grade classroom and continued to preserve examples of his creative writing and the art he produced during their after-school enrichment sessions. She showed them to me, and I was struck by Jermaine's love of language and the creative expression evident in his work. A first grader, he decided to write his autobiography. The following paragraph is the introduction to his life story:

> I was tumbling through my mother's stomach—BOOM . . . BOOM . . . BOOM. I came out crying. Everybody comes out crying. Someone was holding me, and I wanted my momma. I was named Jermaine after my granddaddy. He didn't have a nickname or a middle name, so I don't either. He was my momma's daddy. (Hébert & Beardsley, 2001, p. 93)

Following several intriguing conversations about Jermaine, Teresa invited me to visit her community. I spent a day travelling throughout Milledge County with Teresa visiting Pine Grove and several surrounding towns. Later that day, Jermaine joined us in Teresa's SUV as we traveled throughout the rural community. I enjoyed visiting with Jermaine, and we ended our afternoon together enjoying ice cream at Teresa's dining room table. As I prepared to leave I explained to Jermaine my interest in understanding highly creative children, and he smiled as he agreed to become involved in my research study.

Context of the Study

I conducted the research in Milledge County, which played a critical role in understanding the way of life in Pine Grove and Jermaine's experiences. Less than 30 miles away in Selma, historically significant events had taken place that continued to influence life in Pine Grove. On March 7, 1965, over 600 civil rights marchers were stopped at the Edmund Pettus Bridge in Selma and were driven back by state and local lawmen who brutally attacked them with billy clubs and tear gas. Several days later, Martin Luther King Jr. led another symbolic march to the bridge. Freedom marchers did not rest. Later that month, over 3,000 citizens walked in quiet protest from Selma to the state capital in Montgomery. Shortly after, President Lyndon Johnson signed the Voting Rights Act of 1965. The memories of those horrendous times remained vivid in the minds of the residents of Pine Grove. Several community members had been with King and shared with me how they hoped their grandchildren appreciated the suffering they had endured during that troubling period in America's history.

At the time of the study, the estimated population of Milledge County was 13,468. Documented as the poorest county in the state of Alabama, the per-capita personal income reported was $10,759, with 45.2% of the county's population falling below the poverty level (Hébert & Beardsley, 2001,

p. 90). A small manufacturer of corrugated cardboard was the sole industry in this rural county and employed only a few people from Pine Grove. The majority of people living in Milledge County were forced to rely on public assistance to survive. Those with access to transportation commuted 30 to 40 miles beyond the county lines to work in catfish processing plants (Hébert & Beardsley, 2001, p. 90).

Teachers faced serious challenges in Pine Grove. School buildings constructed in the late 1940s remained in great disrepair, and resources were severely limited. Milledge County schools had annually been on a list of school districts threatened to be taken over by the Alabama Department of Education if achievement scores did not improve substantially. These challenges the schools faced also affected special education programs. Although the state legislature in Alabama mandated identification and programming for gifted students in 1972, Milledge County had not complied with the law since its inception (Hébert & Beardsley, 2001, p. 91).

Conducting the Study

For several summers, Teresa and James acquired funding from the local manufacturing company to provide a summer tutorial reading and science program for the children. During this three-week experience known as Rocket Readers, local high school students worked as tutors with elementary school children in remedial drill activities designed to improve reading comprehension and build vocabulary. As a science teacher James delighted in teaching a curriculum unit on crustaceans to train the children in scientific methodology. With community members carpooling the children, about 50 students arrived at the small country church in Pine Grove every morning for a four-hour academic program combined with some time for softball during a physical education period. Teresa and James said their rationale for offering Rocket Readers each summer was to help children with reading as well as provide them time for socialization during the summer when they tended to become removed from each other, living miles apart in isolated areas.

I learned that Jermaine had attended the Rocket Readers program the previous summer, and the experience had not been productive. Although they realized that the tutorial work was inappropriate for him, Teresa and James encouraged Jermaine to participate simply for social interaction, thinking that Jermaine would enjoy being with others. Jermaine quickly became bored and a discipline problem for his high-school-age tutor. Having learned from that experience, Teresa and I agreed that the three weeks of Rocket Readers would be an ideal time for me to work with Jermaine in creative writing. Throughout the three-week summer experience, I traveled from

Tuscaloosa to Pine Grove and spent the mornings working with Jermaine on the front steps of the country church. It was the ideal opportunity to conduct my research with Jermaine as I observed him with his peer group during the softball games, interviewed him regarding his life experiences, and provided him some quality time to pursue his creative writing.

As I concluded my work with Jermaine that summer, I told him that I wanted to continue working with him during the school year by corresponding with him. During his fourth-grade school year, I mailed him children's novels that I thought he would enjoy. I selected Newbury Award–winning novels that featured African American children as main characters and other material I thought might appeal to his creativity. I continued phone conversations with Teresa concerning his response to the books and his progress in school. I maintained delivery of high-quality novels the following year, and that summer I returned to Pine Grove to conduct an in-depth interview with Jermaine, then a fifth grader preparing to make the transition to middle school.[3]

Findings

Through in-depth case study research, I gained an understanding of the lived experiences of Jermaine, a gifted Black child living in rural poverty. The model in Figure 5.1 serves to represent the findings of this research and is designed to illustrate Jermaine's story.

Figure 5.1 A Graphic Representation of Jermaine's Experience

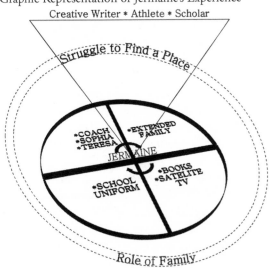

A Struggle to Find a Place in the Community

Jermaine lived with his mother, his older brother and sister, and an aunt. According to his teachers, Jermaine and his 16-year-old sister were frequently responsible for his elderly aunt, who was physically handicapped and intellectually disabled. Teresa said that residents in the community often spoke of Jermaine's mother's absence from the home. She was part of a group of adults who sat in the front of an abandoned country store for long periods of the day and evening hours. Jermaine's older brother, a high school junior, received services from the county's program for students with intellectual disabilities.

According to Teresa and other residents, the small rural community of Pine Grove determined a ranking for its members. Like many small towns, families in Pine Grove had roles according to their perceived place in the community. Jermaine's family fell into the lowest rank. Considered outcasts and largely ignored, they were spoken of in derogatory terms. The family was viewed as being inclined to odd behavior, and adults would refer to the "crazy" factor, often mentioning Jermaine's handicapped aunt and older brother. Moreover, Jermaine's family's property was next door to a cemetery, and residents remarked that "no one in their right mind" would live near a cemetery (Hébert & Beardsley, 2001, p. 92).

Teresa said that in Pine Grove, like in many small rural towns, the heart of the community was the church. The social life of the community revolved around the church and provided residents with time to spend together, which helped develop understanding and tolerance. Few families could maintain high status in the community without being affiliated with the church. Jermaine's family did not attend church, and the support systems the church offered did not touch Jermaine's life.

The Role of Family in Jermaine's Life

His family, disparaged by others in Pine Grove, remained very important to Jermaine. Jermaine loved and respected his mother but did not make demands of her. He was accustomed to her frequent absences. Jermaine's extended family was also very important to him. He pointed out the influence his family had on his creative abilities. He claimed that he inherited his storytelling ability from his grandfather who entertained the family with really good campfire stories. He also spoke fondly of two of his mother's brothers, Walter and McKinley, who lived in Detroit and visited Pine Grove regularly. He looked forward to their arrival during the holiday season. These two favorite uncles often appeared as important characters in Jermaine's creative writing.

Jermaine's Creativity

Jermaine's portfolio of creative writing provided strong evidence of his love of language. His creative expression was remarkable for such a young child and evident in every piece of work that Teresa had saved. One of my favorite examples of Jermaine's creativity is evident in his first grade story titled, "How the Sun Got Hot."

> Once upon a time, there lived a humongous sun and a smaller moon. They were very cold indeed. They lived in a dark, shivery sky. They kept warm by holding onto each other. One time, millions of years after time began, moon let go of sun, he was tired of holding onto his humongous friend. The sun fell from the sky. It fell to earth and landed in the hottest volcano there was. Moon tried to reach his friend, but he couldn't reach into the hot volcano. Moon cried. Thunder and rain came to earth. The enormous sun sank to the deepest part of the volcano. It turned so red from heat, it exploded from the volcano. The sun was on fire as it shot back into the sky. When the moon saw the sun coming home, he ran to his friend. Moon said, "SUN! What happened to you?" Sun said, "I fell into a warm place and I won't ever be cold again." The moon had to move far away from the ball of fire that was his friend. And Moon missed holding his friend, Sun. Sometimes he still cries. When you hear thunder and feel rain, you will know that moon is crying for his lost friend. (Hébert & Beardsley, 2001, p. 93)

As I worked with Jermaine during the summer reading program, I spent mornings with him brainstorming ideas for additional creative stories he wanted to publish. I agreed to serve as his secretary, taking dictation as he tilted his head back, closed his eyes, and crafted his imaginative stories. During those morning sessions I learned how he obtained his creative ideas and incorporated them in his writing. At one point in the story in which he described a mollusk-shaped "virgin black candle," he opened his eyes in midsentence and asked me, "Do you know where I got that idea?" When I encouraged him to explain, he pointed out that he had seen a virgin black candle in one of his favorite television shows on a satellite TV station. Later that morning he smiled as he said, "That triton [virgin black candle] I just used I got that idea from *Hocus Pocus*. It's one of my favorite shows" (Hébert & Beardsley, 2001, p. 93). These conversations with Jermaine enabled me to understand the significant role the satellite dishes throughout Pine Grove played in the lives of children living in rural isolation. Satellite television was for many the only connection to a world beyond Milledge County, and for Jermaine, satellite television apparently served as a consistent source of inspiration for his creative work.

Another source of inspiration for the young author was his fascination with animals. Many of the stories Jermaine dictated to me were tales about salamanders, catfish, and animals found in south Alabama. The first story he enjoyed writing for me was titled "The Odd Couple: Charley and Grant," an adventurous tale about two baby iguanas who survived a severe winter blizzard together. When I questioned him about his fascination with animals that lived in rural Alabama, he explained that although he spent hours watching satellite TV shows, his favorite programs were "*National Geographic* shows on wildlife animals, and not *The Jerry Springer Show!*" (Hébert & Beardsley, 2001, p. 94).

Throughout our writing sessions on the front steps of the country church, we often discussed the beauty of the surrounding countryside. One morning we were engaged in a rather sophisticated conversation about solitude and whether the quiet of country living would help children become more creative. Jermaine said that the quiet of the Alabama countryside helped to inspire his ideas, and through his daydreaming he was able to nurture his creative thinking process. He described how the chirping of crickets inspired him, and he daydreamed about what a day in the life of a cricket would involve. He pointed out that often his daydreams took place at night as he enjoyed a sunset or became mesmerized by the little glow of lights from fireflies. He referred to this as his "thinking in the dark time" when he would reflect on some of the movies he had watched and think of ideas for movies he dreamed of writing someday.

I learned later that Jermaine's creative writing also appeared to be inspired by the books I mailed him. I had sent a copy of Todd Strasser's *Help! I'm Trapped in My Gym Teacher's Body*, a rather whimsical story about a young boy who undergoes a magical transformation and resides in the muscular physique of the physical education teacher while the gym teacher simultaneously becomes trapped in the young boy's body. Shortly after Jermaine received the book, I got a phone call from Teresa. She reported that his fifth grade teacher came to her exclaiming, "I don't know where he gets all of these ideas, but today, he wrote a story about metamorphosis! Where could he be getting these words?" (Hébert & Beardsley, 2001, p. 94). Apparently Todd Strasser's book had served as the inspiration for a clever story and a vocabulary booster.

Extrafamilial Support

Along with the emotional support Jermaine received from his extended family, he made important connections with supportive individuals beyond his family. A relationship with a classmate became significant to Jermaine during his early years in school. A young boy named Cedric befriended Jermaine in kindergarten, and they were assigned to the same classroom from then on. Cedric was a popular boy and the grandson of the school's cook, Sister Sophia. Teresa pointed out that Sister Sophia was always empathetic to children who entered her lunchroom and noticed those who needed encouragement or extra food on their tray. She became more familiar with Jermaine through his friendship with her grandson. When she learned of a story Jermaine had written or a good grade he had earned, she showered him with encouragement. Cedric's mother, a teacher's aide, also took notice of Jermaine and provided support. Eventually Cedric asked and found out that his mother and grandmother were willing to have Jermaine as a guest on weekends. Later Sister Sophia reported to Teresa that Jermaine was invited to spend Thanksgiving with her family so "he could get a good meal like everybody ought to have" (Hébert & Beardsley, 2001, p. 95).

Jermaine also found support within Teresa's family. Teresa, James, and their two children had been an important source of extrafamilial support for Jermaine since he was a student in Teresa's first grade classroom. Jermaine visited their home occasionally to play computer games with Teresa's son and share his creative stories with her daughter. The family had appreciated Jermaine's intelligence and celebrated his creativity since he was young. Teresa served as a strong advocate for Jermaine throughout his years in elementary school. She struggled hard during his primary grade years to help other teachers understand his lively behavior and appreciate his remarkable abilities. Jermaine felt strongly about his relationship with "Miss Teresa," as he pointed out that she was always available to help him, and whenever he had a problem he knew that he could go to her and she would help him solve it.

When Jermaine reached fifth grade, another significant person in his life emerged.

Mr. Cooper, a gentleman from Detroit, Michigan, returned to Pine Grove to retire. Needing something to occupy his time, he formed athletic teams for the children in the community to compete against teams from surrounding towns. Coach Cooper played an important role for Jermaine. He recognized Jermaine's intelligence and chose him to be the quarterback for the new football team. Jermaine explained why he was selected for the prestigious position: "Coach Cooper saw that I really knew my plays, and I knew how to call them. That's what it takes to be a quarterback. Coach said he chose me to play quarterback because I'm smart and fast. Because I'm the quarterback, I'm getting new respect. A lot of kids who didn't used to like me now wave to me in school and say, 'What's up?'" (Hébert & Beardsley, 2001, p. 95).

The Emergence of Jermaine's Self-Identity

During the three years I collected data on Jermaine, I saw evidence of an emerging self-identity in this gifted and creative child. The little boy known for standing on his head in his kindergarten chair appeared to be a confident 10-year-old. His fifth grade school year included several significant events that brought about important changes for him.

One critical factor that influenced Jermaine's fifth grade year was the school district's decision to require a school uniform. The uniform became an important socioeconomic equalizer that enabled Jermaine to come to school looking like everyone else. Jermaine's uncles provided his mother with the funds she needed to purchase the khaki pants, hunter green polo shirt, and what Teresa referred to as "tie-up Sunday dress shoes" being sold in stores in Selma. Teresa said this change helped create a sense of school community. She noted how it influenced Jermaine's situation, pointing out that fifth graders who were so much more aware of brand-name clothing no longer could ridicule him for wearing secondhand clothing that was ill fitting.

Jermaine also presented a confident view of himself in his creative writing. He had earned a positive reputation as the community's elementary school quarterback, and he had a new following of friends. The books Jermaine received in the mail apparently also helped to increase his social status. They did more than serve as inspiration for writing creative stories. Teresa reported that when Jermaine was finished reading the books he shared them with three new best friends who had joined him in the top fifth grade reading group. Jermaine's small personal library earned him important social capital, and he became more highly respected by his peers.

As they enjoyed new books together, Jermaine's new friends collaborated with him as partners for the fifth grade science fair, winning first place in a countywide competition. This same group also captured an award for a Black History Month project on the life of Harriet Tubman. This consistent success as a team supported Jermaine in maintaining healthy friendships with others who understood him. He had negotiated a place for himself in the community and discovered a small group of students who appreciated his creativity and intelligence, and he was happy to compete with them academically. With the exception of a B in math, Jermaine earned straight As in fifth grade. His identity was emerging as he saw himself becoming a scholar, creative writer, and athlete.

Jermaine's emerging self-identity and the positive view he had of himself was also evident in a story he wrote as part of a fifth grade essay contest sponsored by the county teacher's association. The guidelines for the students were to craft a creative essay about themselves tackling problems of crime and misguided youth in Milledge County. Jermaine decided to address the community problem by transforming himself into a superhero. The following is the introduction to his composition, titled *The Adventures of Turbo Man*:

> I live two lives. The first one is when I am Courtney Davis, a well-respected lawyer. My other life is as Turbo Man. That is my name when I help people who are in trouble. I wear a red suit of hard steel. I can bend metal with

my bare hands and see through walls with my supersonic eyes. I have turbo disks on my arms and can knock out evil characters, and I drive a Turbo-mobile. (Hébert & Beardsley, 2001, p. 96)

In this manuscript, Turbo Man's adventure concluded with Jermaine's heroic character capturing a kidnapper and returning peace and tranquility to his community.

The young author who created Turbo Man also had developed a solid sense of ethics by fifth grade. He described a school incident in which a jar of pennies collected by students for a fund-raising project was stolen from a classroom. Jermaine found this very upsetting, and he could not understand how young people could steal from one another. As he shared this with me, he shook his head and expressed concern for his community. The young man who was upset by the school crime dreamed of becoming a lawyer in the future; however, he pointed out that his legal career might have to serve as his second profession, as he planned to first spend several years working as a Hollywood film producer.

Discussion and Implications

The findings from this case study of Jermaine shed light on a number of important issues that are critical to the education of young gifted Black males and provide specific implications for educators and counselors. This study accentuated the need to identify the gifts and talents of Black males early in their school experience. Jermaine was recognized for his creativity at an early age, and he eventually gained continual recognition for his abilities within his community. For Jermaine, being recognized for his creative talents as a young child was critical to his eventual success in school. The early recognition of talent appeared to make a difference in shaping his emerging self-identity as a young scholar, creative writer, and athlete. This finding highlights the need for schools to identify gifted children early in their school experiences to ensure that talent is not wasted. The sooner Black males are identified as gifted, the sooner interventions and programming for talent development can occur.

The intellectual precocity displayed by Jermaine was celebrated by adults beyond his immediate family, and this support appeared significant in fostering his positive view of self. The emotional support Jermaine received from his uncles as well as from Sister Sophia, Coach Cooper, and Teresa and her family also played an influential role in shaping his view of self. This finding reminds educators of how communities make a critical difference in how the gifts, talents, and achievements of children are recognized and supported.

Once Jermaine was able to overcome the negative perceptions adults held regarding his family, the school community eventually came to understand him and appreciate his intellectual ability and creativity. This finding highlights how communities must not only recognize gifted behaviors in their children but also work together collaboratively to encourage them and support them in developing their talents. We are reminded, *it takes a village.*

Jermaine's story also illustrates that when working in economically impoverished environments, the support systems needed to provide positive experiences for gifted Black males may include mentoring relationships. Educators and community leaders must recognize the value of mentors in supporting Black males. The guidance of supportive adults beyond families is essential to the academic success of gifted Black males and assists in reinforcing their motivation to achieve. Significant teachers and mentors have the power to influence lives in so many positive ways. A mentor may be recruited to work with a gifted Black male or one may naturally emerge in a gifted young man's life when he becomes involved in extracurricular activities, as shown in Jermaine's connection to Coach Cooper. The findings of this study serve to remind school administrators of the value of incorporating mentoring programs as early as the elementary school years.

Jermaine's experiences as a child growing up in a rural, economically impoverished community indicates that it takes more than intellectual ability to be successful in school. Psychological characteristics such as self-confidence, motivation, self-efficacy, and resilience in the face of adversity play an important role in influencing the achievement of students. If educators are to work with gifted Black males from high-poverty environments they must certainly address their students' intellectual needs; however, they also must pay equal attention to their psychosocial needs. It is important that educators and counselors work with Black males in building confidence in their abilities. They may need to acquire coping skills to combat discrimination and peer rejection. Moreover, they may also require resiliency to persist when setbacks occur in their lives. Jermaine's experience in making the transition from the little boy who was "too bad to handle" to a respected scholar, creative writer, and athlete reminds educators that affective issues in the lives of gifted Black males must be addressed, and psychosocial skills needed for success must be developed. Jermaine found his psychosocial support systems on his own; however, that scenario should not continue. Schools must be empowered to provide students with the psychosocial support they need to succeed at the highest levels of their abilities.

This study calls attention to a significant issue in this country. The horrific conditions I found in the impoverished community of Pine Grove were nothing short of educational genocide. No White school district anywhere in this country is faced with such poor conditions. Jermaine's story reminds us that we must once more return to Selma and pay close attention to the message delivered by Martin Luther King Jr. We cannot continue to turn our backs on African American children in public schools. It is high time for a national policy that addresses racial prejudice in all forms. There are too many children like Jermaine who are depending upon us to bring about this change. In sharing his life story and aspirations for the future, Jermaine has shared his voice for children living in poverty throughout this country. We must listen and respond.

Notes

1. This chapter is a condensed version of Hébert and Beardsley (2001).

2. With the exception of Teresa and her husband, James, for this study the names of the people and the places in Alabama were changed (e.g., to Pine Grove and Milledge County) to protect the identity of the participants.

3. For an in-depth discussion of research methods and procedures employed in this study readers are encouraged to refer to Hébert and Beardsley (2001).

References

Hébert, T. P., & Beardsley, T. M. (2001). Jermaine: A critical case study of a gifted Black child living in rural poverty. *Gifted Child Quarterly, 45*(2), 85–103.

Strasser, T. (1994). *HELP! I'm trapped in my gym teacher's body*. New York, NY: Scholastic.

Voting Rights Act, 42 U.S.C. §§ 1973 to 1973aa-6 (1965).

6

THE SCHOLAR IDENTITY MODEL

Black Male Success in the K–12 Context

Gilman Whiting

The occlusions in the pipeline from kindergarten to college to employ-ment and to becoming productive and contributing members of the nation for far too many Black, Brown, and low-income students has for years now preoccupied academic and lay scholars alike. The issues at the crux of the pipeline seepages—public education, discrimination and access, student achievement, and effective teaching—have been discussed, debated, and presented as a clarion call to the nation (Alexander & West, 2012; Ford, 2010; Harry & Klinger, 2005; Harry, Klinger, Cramer, & Sturges, 2007; Kozol, 1992, 2006, 2012; Ogbu, 1978; Pager, 2009; Whiting, 2009a, 2009b, 2010; Woodson, 1933/2013).

To situate the reader, I begin with a few truisms about teachers and teach-ing to establish what Wiggings and McTighe (2005) call "enduring under-standings" (p. 25): Teaching is a time-honored profession, American society has moved away from truly honoring its teachers, a teacher can be one of the most influential people in a child's life, it takes a visionary believer/teacher to make lasting change. And there is no predetermined genetic requirement for one to create or be a part of that long-term change.

People, unlike mathematical or scientific problems, are not so easily understood or solved. No two humans are genetically identical. Even monozy-gotic twins who develop from one zygote have infrequent genetic differences because of mutations occurring during development. And although research shows that the DNA of any two humans differs by about 0.1%, no one has been able to successfully map the difference that 0.1% means—if it means anything at all of significance (Bruder et al., 2008; "Genographic Project," 2005; Singer, 2012).

I have been asked over the years, mostly by White American women teachers, "Can I be effective in this work that you (read African American/Black man) do?" It is important to note that I have never had any doubt about the sincerity of the interlocutor. The question is at first blush innocuous enough. However, the question also reveals doubts about identity, ability, and possibly empathy. In effect, I am not like them: male and of a different race, culture, and class. The straightforward answer to most of these teachers is, "Yes, you can." Not only is it possible for that teacher to be effective, but it also is impossible to effect positive change if one cannot envision it. And the statistics tell us that without such teachers, systemic and long-term change is not possible.

Statistical data from the National Center for Education Information (NCEI) and the National Center for Education Statistics (NCES) reveal important demographics about teachers and the implications those demographics hold potentially for the aforementioned hypotheses regarding systematic change. A NCES survey of full-time and part-time public school teachers in 2007–08 indicated that some 76% were female, and a slightly lower percentage of private school teachers were female (74%). Additionally, among males and females, 83% of public school teachers were White, 7% were Black, 7% were Hispanic, 1% were Asian; 1% were of two or more races; and less than 1% were Pacific Islander or American Indian/Alaska Native (NCES, 2007–2008).

The NCEI, which has been studying teachers since 1979, conducted five national surveys of teachers. The latest, *Profiles of Teachers in the U.S. 2011* (Feistritzer, 2011) provides very useful data from the teacher's perspectives, showing that nearly 85% (a higher number than the NCES 2008 data) of the teaching force is female. As with the NCES data, European American (White) females are disproportionately represented on the nation's teaching landscape. Even with the rapidly shifting national demographic data on race and ethnicity, the expected numerical impact on the pool of teachers based on trends in college graduation will be minimal for decades to come (Katz & Rodin, 2010).

It is, therefore, incumbent upon all teachers to believe they can be as effective in this work that I, an African American (Black) male educator, do. There are no hidden secrets, no special handshakes, passwords, or street credibility needed. What is needed is a belief in the untapped potential of all who enter our classrooms. A visionary teacher, regardless of gender, race, socioeconomic status, religion, education, or sexual orientation, can have a net positive effect on the educational outlook and attainment of the youths who are entrusted to us.

When, Where, and How I Enter

The work on the scholar identity model (SIM) began in earnest at the moment that I could reflect existentially on my youth and life experiences as they related to real-life issues of self-efficacy, motivation, academic self-confidence, race, poverty, manhood, and so much more. It was at that moment that I better understood what I, and so many millions of others, had been up against.

Although intuitively I had been aware of the academic disengagement of many of my peers, as well as my own at various points in time, it wasn't until 1996 when I began teaching at a small predominantly Black university (BU) in the midwestern part of the United States that the intellectual groundings of the theories that would eventually become the SIM emerged. This BU served primarily those who lived in the nearby communities. Many administrators and teachers could have opted for employment at better-known local institutions (and several made the attempt), but BU was like a family. It was nurturing and somewhat holistic, a mom-and-pop kind of place. Students with extenuating circumstances also found BU more accepting of them. The most salient of these circumstances centered around race, motivation, and preparedness.

While working at this BU for four years, I was asked to be a motivational speaker for a local fatherhood program (FP) that had a simple mission: to assist young fathers with pathways to parenting skills, including being in the child's life; paying child support; having a relationship with their child or children; possibly resolving relationship issues with the mother or mothers of their children; employment preparation, attainment, and sustenance; and educational continuation and completion. After just two visits, I became a volunteer mentor and teacher at this program for young (16 to 26 years old) Black and Brown low-income fathers and fathers-to-be. Working with these two populations helped to crystallize for me the varied and complex issues surrounding Black and Brown men and boys' academic underperformance and achievement. The opportunity for me to work, teach, volunteer, mentor, and conduct research at BU (four years) and FP (six years) provided the foundations for the SIM framework.

Troubling Observations

Within weeks of arriving at each location (BU and FP), I observed through classroom interactions, interviews (informal and formal), and small- and large-group activities that many of the young men had very low beliefs in their own ability to complete tasks. Many failed to time manage or saw the need to be oriented toward the future or long-range goals. Too many were convinced that the lack of opportunities as well as the few missed opportunities that had been presented was just the way it is, and there was very little they could do personally to change their life's outcomes. They also held misplaced notions about gender, race, culture, and masculinity. To a lesser extent, even those at the BU, generally older and more focused students who were returning to college, had strong doubts in their academic abilities often traceable to their elementary and secondary educational experiences and teachers' expectations.

Now That I Know, What Can I Do?

The theory related to the SIM was first published in my doctoral dissertation, *Young Black American Fathers in a Fatherhood Program: A Phenomenological Study* (Whiting, 2004). The SIM as an individual model was published in the summer of 2006 in *Gifted Child Today* as "Enhancing Culturally Diverse Males' Scholar Identity: Suggestions for Educators of Gifted Students" (Whiting, 2006a). A variation appeared later that same year in the *Journal of Secondary Gifted Education* titled "From At Risk to At Promise: Developing Scholar Identities Among Black Males" (Whiting, 2006b). Whiting (2006a) outlined nine constructs that are conceptually combined to illustrate a psychosocial model of achievement. The model was initially designed more specifically to provide educators working with Black and Brown males with a road map for fostering scholar identities. The model demanded that they themselves, the educators, families, communities, and eventually the mass media, view the students through a different, more capable lens; hence, they would expect different efforts from the student and assist in instilling the idea of being a scholar, often by becoming better, more understanding teachers.

The SIM was never designed to fix a problem. The premise of the SIM is not to fix broken, less capable, less intelligent, or less desirous students, but to motivate, educate, and, most important, relate to capable, intelligent students. But in order to relate to a student, a genuine concern and belief in the unseen potential or talent must be developed and honed by the teacher, coach, guardian, or mentor.

Moving the model from theory to practice, in the summer of 2006 the Scholar Identity Institute (SII) was cocreated at Vanderbilt University with Professor Donna Y. Ford. For the next four years, the SII provided intensive engagement for nearly 100 young Black males. The SII was designed to expose the young men (mostly eighth and ninth graders) to the constructs of the SIM. For two weeks during the summer the young men were exposed time and again to Albert Bandura's theories of self-efficacy (1977);

E. A. Locke's theory on goal setting (1968); bell hooks's (2004) discussions of masculinity, sexuality, and popular culture; and other scholarly writings on various topical subjects from Donna Ford, Tarek Grantham, William Cross, William Julius Wilson, Thabiti Lewis, and me.

The young men were provided with a curriculum on psychosocial behavior, aiding them in assessing their personal roles and responsibility as well as ways to cope with the sometimes structurally racist and sexist beliefs present in their everyday lives. The curriculum was extensive and refined over the years with the goal of being accessible, engaging, personal, relevant, and fun. In 2009, after four summers directing intensive programming, four pillars or supports were added to the nine SIM constructs. Additionally, in 2009, I wrote two follow-up articles: *Gifted Black Males: Understanding and Decreasing Barriers to Achievement and Identity* and *The Scholar Identity Institute: Guiding Darnel and Other Black males*. What follows is a brief description of each of the nine constructs and the four pillars of the SIM.

The Conceptual Model

The SIM (see Figure 6.1) is often depicted in pyramid form, signifying strength, wisdom, and beauty. The selection of the pyramid structure was quite deliberate, for it is also one of the most iconic symbols of genius and wonder in the modern world. The pyramid is composed of the nine constructs. Because of space limitations, I provide brief descriptions of the first two constructs and abbreviated descriptions of the remaining seven. The constructs are inextricably linked and all have individual as well as collective importance.

Figure 6.1 Scholar Identity Model

Self-Efficacy

According to Bandura (1994),

> self-efficacy is defined as people's beliefs about their capabilities to pro-
> duce designated levels of performance that exercise influence over events
> that affect their lives. Self-efficacy beliefs determine how people feel, think,
> motivate themselves and behave. Such beliefs produce these diverse effects
> through four major processes. They include cognitive, motivational, affec-
> tive and selection processes. (p. 71)

Self-efficacy (SE) is the foundational construct for the SIM that all the other constructs are built on and ascend from. SE is the belief in one's self to accomplish a given task with the full knowledge and comprehension of the requirements for completion. In the development of the SIM and the popula-tions worked with, SE is central to academic achievement/attainment (Zimmer-man, Bandura, & Martinez-Pons, 1992). The SIM is also concerned with the intersections of race, gender, culture, and socioeconomic status with SE.

Working with young men at BU, FP, and in the more formal SII, we found an increased level of academic SE across the board. These young men demonstrated an increased self-confidence, self-control, and resiliency. They began to believe they could succeed at problem solving when fully com-prehending a task (e.g., when using the scale of SE, it was noted that when faced with a task of cognitive ability, the students did not feel what Steele and Aronson [1995] refers to as a *stereotype threat*). As the summer's SII pro-gressed, the participants' increased levels of SE became stronger. In words and deeds, they were more than whistling Vivaldi (Steele, 2011), they pushed back against negative stereotypes about Black males. Time and again, they exceeded the requirements and sought out new ways to challenge themselves. Initially, many of the young men would wing it when they did not know an answer; many would also blame extenuating circumstances for their mis-steps. Issues relating to masculinity and stereotype threat initially interfered with asking for assistance. However, after one summer's work, when faced with an unfamiliar or difficult obstacle, they asked for assistance. Once the young men understood the importance of their SE, they were ready for future orientation.

Future Orientation

The construct future orientation is concerned with the relationship between conscious goals, intentions, and task performance. According to E. A. Locke (1968), (a) hard goals produce a higher level of performance (output) than easy goals, (b) specific hard goals produce higher level of output than a goal of do your best, and (c) behavioral intentions regulate choice behavior. The theory also views goals and intentions as mediators of the effects of incentives on task performance and that an individual's conscious ideas regulate his or her actions.

Much of the goal setting is identified with the task at hand. For example, if one interrogates a student entering college, the student's focus or field of vision into the future is usually one semester and often one class or the next exam at a time, whereas, fifth and sixth graders could only envision that week and usually just the day or what the afternoon held. Based on the age of the individual, realistic goal setting will vary; goal setting is a learned and practiced skill, as students mature they are able to plan further into the future. When working with junior high (11–14 years old) and high school students (15–18 years old) who are from low-income and minority groups, knowledge of and plans for setting goals for postsecondary educational studies or careers cannot be emphasized enough. And with those in college, conversations about postgraduate work and employment preparation should begin in the first year. The thought process is a trained process; the more frequently one envisions goals, the more preparation goes into making them a reality.

Motivation theories indicate that people who have aspirations tend to stay focused and prepare for success (Deci & Ryan, 1985, 2002; Dweck & Elliott, 1988; Graham, 1991, 1994). They think about the present and the future, particularly regarding how one's current behaviors and decisions influence future achievements. Diverse males with future targets are not overly concerned about immediate gratification and short-term passing interests and ephemeral goals. These students set realistic goals; likewise, they recognize the importance of a high grade point average, excellent school attendance, and participation in challenging courses as helpmates to reaching their dreams. They also not only have a plan, but a plan B and a plan C. Because very few of these young 18- to 21-year-olds know fully what they want or are actually capable of achieving, having productive alternative scenarios are encouraged.

Willing to Make Sacrifices

To accomplish one's set academic goals, choices have to be made concerning time, effort, or resources. Sociologist Robert K. Merton (1948) coined the familiar phrase *self-fulfilling prophecy*, which is the process whereby a person or group that has a strongly held value, belief, or an expectation, true or false, affects the outcome of a situation. Many adults have learned through experiences of trials and tribulations that sacrifices are necessary for reaching short-term, medium, and long-term goals.

Black males who possess or are working toward a scholar identity also understand that sacrifice may be necessary to attain various goals. They believe and understand and are more likely to relinquish some aspects of a social life (e.g., particular friends, parties, too many social organizations, popularity, etc.) and other distractions (e.g., Internet surfing and social networking sites), gaming (from Bored.com to Zynga and Xbox), and television (including hours of watching sports) to reach those desired goals. They will plan or limit social time, allocating the bulk of their time and efforts toward becoming more productive scholars.

Internal Locus of Control

A student receives (in his or her estimation) a poor grade on an exam. Many of us have been there; what we attribute that grade to makes all the difference in future endeavors. Was it bad luck? Fate? Were we incapable, or did we not muster enough effort? (Weiner, 1980). Knowing which of these categories (luck, fate, ability, and effort) the student chooses to associate with or attribute to the examination results are at the core of internal locus of control. Black males who have a strong internal locus of control are optimistic, even when faced with poor results; these males believe they can do well because they (a) believe they can, (b) planned for the difficult (time consuming) work, (c) made the time to study and prepare for the examination, and (d) when not sure, they are willing to ask for help. Thus, when they receive a less than expected result, they don't blame the test, where they were seated, or a teacher with malevolent intentions. These males take responsibility and live with the results. And most important, they challenge themselves to do better next time.

Self-Awareness

The teacher says, "Young man, please pull your pants up." The young man complies, but thinks, "This is the style and everyone thinks I look/ am cool." As soon as he is out of the teacher's view, and until called on the infraction again, he continues his *sagging* (wearing pants below the waist). Self-awareness is an honest appraisal and understanding of one's perceived and real strengths and limitations. It is not only how you see yourself but also how you are viewed by others and how you contribute to that view. Self-awareness is bound up with effort, etiquette, sincerity, character, and self-control (G. Pesare, personal communication, April 15, 1991). Black males who have a realistic grasp on those areas in need of work are willing to consider and process new information, ideas, and societal expectations toward their self-improvement (e.g., they seek a tutor in classes where they are not doing well, they study longer and more often, and they realize that certain attire triggers negative assumptions). And finally, they take immediate and sustained actions to make appropriate transitions based on their situation.

While the current youth culture of sagging comes from a troubled and negative place (American prisons), it has become part of a contemporary vogue similar to women smoking in the Roaring Twenties, the greaser style of the 1950s, or the long hair of hippies in the 1960s. And as with other periods in time, these various fads are seen as troubling to the status quo. In this era, though, and particularly for Black males, the stakes appear much higher: criminalization, incarceration, and even murder (e.g., Trayvon Martin). Therefore, as a part of self-awareness, young Black and Brown men must be able to code switch as they make the transition into adulthood.

Achievement Greater Than Affiliation

The need for achievement and the need for affiliation are found in varying degrees in all students. Neither is inherently wrong. The need-for-achievement student is *achievement motivated* and therefore seeks attainment of realistic but challenging goals, and academic advancement. The student has a strong need for feedback as it relates to achievement and progress, and a need for a sense of accomplishment. The need-for-affiliation student is *affiliation motivated* and has a need for friendly relationships and seeks interaction with other people. The affiliation driver produces motivation and the need to be liked and held in popular regard (McClelland, 1978).

When the goal of academic success is foremost, but the student assigns the need for affiliation greater importance and yet still expects to receive high academic marks, discontinuity arises. Harvard economist Roland Fryer (2006) found that Black and Brown students often opt for more friends and forego higher grade point averages. A student with a strong scholar identity knows this and makes the sacrifice of having friends who are not motivated toward similar academic goals. For these diverse males, the need for achievement is stronger than the need for affiliation; thus, the number of friends they have or their popularity does not determine their identity.

While they may be social and desire meaningful friendships, they are not troubled about being popular for the sake of popularity. Black and Hispanic males with a strong need for achievement understand that high academic achievement will take them far in life. Conflicts about a student turning his back on his community, culture, or race in pursuit of academic goals may exist. The scholar identity student possesses an unassuming confidence, preferably drawn from having family and friends who respect and support him and do not impede his progress.

Academic Self-Confidence

A teacher wields unimaginable power. A child's academic self-confidence is developed through a series of successful encounters. Unfortunately, seemingly inconsequential microaggressions (Cross & Vandiver, 2001; Sue, Capodilupo, & Holder, 2008) set the standard for how students view themselves. Teachers' expectations drive student achievement; therefore, developing a strong sense of academic self-confidence in young Black males must be understood as an imperative—pushing without coddling.

Black males who believe they are strong students feel comfortable and confident in academic settings, learning, and playing with ideas. Most important, they do not feel inferior in school, and they do not feel the need to negate, deny, or minimize their academic abilities and skills. These males have a strong work ethic—they spend time doing schoolwork, they study, and they require little prodding from parents and teachers. An often underused cog in the teacher tool kit is the role of the teacher as a facilitator, a guide, and a confident person who will allow himself or herself to see and not be threatened by an outgoing young student with verve. (*Verve* is the propensity for energetic, intense, highly stylized body language and is an essential component of a learning style of expression for African American children [Boykin, 1994].)

This does not mean allowing a student to be the class clown or disruptive to the goals of the agenda but merely understanding and having the savvy to use the behavior as a teachable moment, even if the student is doing the teaching. I often use the concept of Academic Aikido in my workshops. Here I am referring to the ability to understand the underlying battles taking place in all classrooms every day, with students pushing against authority merely as a stage of development. For most males (as with females), the onset of puberty marks a point where students, even when faced with the fact that they are wrong, once they commit to leaning into an idea, thought, or position, they are unable or unwilling to back down. It is at this point when the adult drawn into this battle of wills must appear to concede ground, turn (only momentarily), and give way in the direction the student is pushing. It is then and only then that the student can relax enough to hear the adult. While listening and learning from the student, we begin to turn them in the direction we wanted to go all along. The turn may be subtle, or it may be a hairpin turn, but we must be willing to hear and see it when they cannot. Ultimately, students with a high academic self-concept understand that in order to be successful, effort is just as important as, or more important than, ability. In essence, a student does not care what we (the adults) know until they know we (the adults) care. The application of Academic Aikido provides the adult with the opportunity to display care and redirect the student's focus.

Racial Identity and Pride

Even before the election of America's first African American president, keyboards across the nation could be heard tapping away about the so-called Obama effect, writers across the nation seemed to be signaling the arrival of a new postracial society. It was as if the 2008 election of President Barack Obama marked the end of race and racism. That notion has been beaten back (Bonilla-Silva, 2006; Hughey & Jost, 2011; Kaplan, 2011; Metzler, 2008; Sharpley-Whiting, 2009; Touré & Dyson, 2012; Wise, 2010). In too many ways, society has and continues to remind Black and Brown boys and men of their race and what that race means. The average Black teen acts in line with (and sometimes against) stereotypical racialized scenarios daily. In any case, self-esteem and self-concept, racial identity, and pride still affect students' achievement and motivation (Cross & Vandiver, 2001). Teachers and others in positions of authority in teaching and learning capacities must receive continued professional development regarding the persistent significance of race, identity, and racism.

For Black males, possessing race and a scholar identity has high salience; they are comfortable being Black boys or men. They seek greater self-understanding as a racial being but are also aware of the importance of adapting to their environment and being bi- or multicultural (Cross & Vandiver, 2001). Just as important, they do not equate achievement with acting White or selling out (Ferguson, 2001; Ford, 2010; Fordham, 1988; Fryer, 2006; Whiting, 2006b). These young men refuse to be constrained by social injustices based on gender, socioeconomic status, and race or ethnicity.

Masculinity

Masculinity is often a difficult concept to pin down. Broadly, masculinity is recognized as possessing the qualities or characteristics of manliness or of being a man. There are nonetheless myriad ways of being a man and expressing manliness, even though as a culture we tend to accept hegemonic masculinity—tough, hard, domineering, and dominating—as normative. Contemporary representations of and ideas about American Black masculinity tend to lean toward the negative—hypersexual, thug, gangster, violent, abusive, less intelligent athlete, and absent father. Out of whole cloth and against the grain of mainstream culture, Black men, women, and boys have attempted to craft an oppositional narrative of Black masculinity that at times conforms with hegemonic American masculinity, confirms the worst stereotypes of American Black Masculinity, or upends the former narratives.

The role of the SIM in schools is crucial to combatting retrogressive notions about Black masculinity. Studies like Kozol's *Savage*

Inequalities: Children in America's Schools (1992), *The Shame of the Nation: The Restoration of Apartheid Schooling in America* (2006), and *Fire in the Ashes: Twenty-Five Years Among the Poorest Children in America* (2012) reveal how schooling, teachers, administrators, and peer pressure can exacerbate negative self-concepts and destroy academic self-confidence. Using ethnographic accounts, Ann Arnett Ferguson's (2001) *Bad Boys: Public Schools in the Making of Black Masculinity* also presents the structural rituals that lead to the hardening of young Black boys during their school years that often contribute to feelings of uselessness and desperation.

But here I counter that Black males with a scholar identity do not equate hard work, the pursuit of high academic ranking, intelligence, and studiousness with being unmanly. Moreover, they do not equate success with selling out or acting White. Rather, being a scholar is taught and celebrated as an integral part of a self-possessed masculinity. Such students do not feel the need to belittle and resist learning opportunities; in fact, students with a scholar identity feel empowered as young *men* in that they are able to access knowledge that will add to their future goals and expectations.

Four Pillars: Home, School, Community, Mentoring

The nine constructs of my SIM must not only be understood as something that happens in one classroom on a Saturday morning or at a two-week summer camp. The SIM must be woven into the fabric of the young scholar's life. The mere comprehension and knowledge of any construct is insufficient for full integration of information. For the constructs to become an integral part of daily life choices, the scholar's ability to apply and analyze what is learned as well as synthesize, evaluate, and ultimately create from that information is at the heart of transferring the theory (Bloom, 1984). Therefore, it is necessary that the four pillars support and encourage the scholar outside the model.

Home is the first place students should receive positive messages about being a scholar. Students from single-parent and two-parent families need to have family training on SIM.

School is where children between 5 or 6 years old (often earlier) spend a significant portion of their day. If successful, this process goes on for at least 13 years. Therefore, the formative years are crucial; what is learned must be sustained and continue across the grades, especially from elementary into middle school, between middle school and high school, and again between high school and college. Educators need continued professional development. While working with teachers across the country, I have noticed that more than three quarters of those surveyed had not read an entire book relating to professional development since graduating from their last college class. Many have read brief articles (less than 10 pages), and if funds are available, they have attended half-day or full-day seminars once a year. This type of ad hoc professional development falls woefully short of what should be provided for one of our nation's most valuable resources. The SIM is more than professional development; it shifts into personal development. It empowers teachers, and it can be the answer to knowing how to establish and maintain that special learning relationship with all students.

Community is inclusive of home and school, but SIM defines *communities* as those spaces between and around the home and the formal school settings. They are the nerve centers that may occupy a significant portion of a student's life, particularly those students who have working or uninformed or uninvolved, or for other reasons, absentee guardians. Community leaders (local youth centers, YMCAs, gyms, sport teams as well as community police) should all be exposed to a much pithier version of the SIM; they should be made aware of the constructs, their definitions, and the basics on how to assist in the affirming qualities of the model.

I can remember my first thoughts when I heard former National Basketball Association Most Valuable Player Charles Barkley state, "I am not a role model." "How silly!" I mused. "Does he not know that a person who is considered a role model seldom if ever chooses to become someone's role model?" I have yet to meet a student who did not have a role model outside the home. In my life I've had three or four, all male, none of them my father. My first was someone I'd never meet: Julius "Dr. J." Erving. He never knew it, but I wanted to be as famous as he was. Dr. J never asked for my attention, but to me it didn't matter. He was a symbol of a strong, well-liked, and all-powerful Black male. With my academic pursuits, my high school track coach filled the void. He was someone I could talk to, watch, and attempt to emulate. Indeed, he recently sent me a picture of himself and a group of students visiting the White House. He is still a role model; he too never asked to take up that mantle. He told me that I had *potential* before I knew what the word meant, and that has made a difference ever since.

The role model/mentor is critical in the life of young boys. A successful mentor is able to guide, push, and support the young Black male, which is central to success. A mentor's wise and good counsel can last a lifetime.

From Here to Where?

The SIM and the SII were not developed to live on the pages of journals or books. As with all research, they were conceived as a response to a very real human need. There are numerous next steps, projects in the works, that relate to the model.

In 2012 the Heinz Endowments awarded $1.5 million to two school districts for training and implementation of the SIM. Although the two school districts are in the same city, the schools have differing needs. One is a public school district developed during the late 1970s and early 1980s, now more than 30 years old. The other is a charter school district less than 10 years old, which has the feeling of a new car. As different as the two districts are, they have several things in common: They both have students who need and can benefit from the SIM, they have teachers and administrators who truly care about children, and they now have the financial support to implement the work. The trick is the transfer of knowledge for self-sustainability as well as the ability to believe that an intrinsic paradigm shift is possible.

Also in 2012, my SIM went international. For two months I worked with hundreds of educators across India, from New Delhi to the Assam Valley to Gujarat. Teachers there are now faced with what America had been forced to confront in 1954. India has joined 135 other countries from the United Nations in the Right to Educate Act of 2010.[1] And as with _Brown v. Board of Education_ (1954), there is bottlenecking and confusion about how to implement equal schooling for all its citizens. India is the world's largest democracy, but access to schooling is not equal. The SIM is poised to assist administrators and teachers with a modified way of thinking, and the model was modified to address their needs. For example, after brainstorming with several groups of teachers in different parts of the country, the constructs race pride and masculinity evolved into global awareness and gender equity.

Finally, the model was originally intended to work within the nine-month school calendar with an intensive summer training component. The work with the school districts funded by the Heinz Endowments, will provide the opportunity for that implementation. Continued evaluation, assessment, and validation of the SIM and SII are foremost from the research perspective.

Recommendations for Practice

Michelle Alexander and Cornell West (2012), Devah Pager (2009), and William Julius Wilson (2009) are just a few of the researchers who have provided credible evidence regarding the dismal landscape of opportunities made available to America's Black, Brown, and other low-income males, and increasingly to females, without adequate academic credentials. These citizens will encounter far greater difficulty in locating and securing employment in the nation's workforce. Future employment opportunities are based almost solely on educational attainment; although a young student may be able to name entertainers and athletes who have become successful without completing college. The fact remains that being able to name them attests to their rarified existence. As fortunate and famous or infamous as they are, they are also outliers, anomalies, statistical blips on the radar of life and therefore should not be used as one's life model.

The SIM provides Black males with more holistic, realistic, positive, and motivational ways to think about themselves as well as ways to plan and cope with what life may throw their way.

Things We Can Do Today

As educators, parents, caregivers, coaches, mentors, and administrators, we have a model to assist us in moving the needle in a positive direction. Regardless of race, gender, or pedigree, we adults must first view young Black males through a positive lens. We must ignore the negative stereotypes offered up willy-nilly via mass media. If we can watch *The Three Stooges, Dumb and Dumber,* and any and all sundry White males from politicians to policemen behaving badly and not think stereotypically of the young White males sitting in our classrooms, we must apply that same logic to Black men and boys.

Saying we must change our views is the easy part. Doing the work to overcome and replace those historic and corrupt stereotypes dangling over the heads of unsuspecting children sitting in our classrooms will prove understandably more difficult. So it is necessary that we *read more,* have more open and honest *conversations about race and racism* in America, and *practice social action.* Stepping out of our racial, cultural, and class zones is not easy. Every teacher who ever spent one day in a classroom attempting to assist a struggling student whom the teacher believed he or she could not relate to and did not know why understands that stepping out is just the beginning— jumping in is what is needed. We place all these steps under the umbrella of professional development. All who work with students need to continually enhance their cultural competency. We need to seek out effective mentors for students and learn from those mentors. We need to not only attend to personal and professional development but also encourage administrators to be more proactive in seeking out those who can best assist teachers in that development. After all, what we profess to love about this career—helping others, teaching others—demands it. The SIM is but one small step in the right direction.

Note

1. The Constitution (Eighty-Sixth Amendment) Act, 2002 inserted Article 21-A in the Constitution of India to provide free and compulsory education of all children in the age group of six to fourteen years as a fundamental right in such a manner as the state may, by law, determine. The Right of Children to Free and Compulsory Education (RTE) Act, 2009, which represents the consequential legislation envisaged under Article 21-A, means that every child has a right to full-time elementary education of satisfactory and equitable quality in a formal school that satisfies certain essential norms and standards.

Article 21-A and the RTE Act came into effect on April 1, 2010. The title of the RTE Act incorporates the words "free and compulsory." Free education means that no child, other than a child who has been admitted by his or her parents to a school that is not supported by the appropriate government, shall be liable to pay any kind of fee or charges or expenses that may prevent him or her from pursuing and completing elementary education. Compulsory education casts an obligation on the appropriate government and local authorities to provide and ensure admission, attendance, and completion of elementary education by all children in the 6–14 age group. With this, India has moved forward to a rights-based framework that casts a legal obligation on the central and state governments to implement this fundamental child right as enshrined in Article 21-A of the constitution, in accordance with the provisions of the RTE Act.

References

Alexander, M., & West, C. (2012). *The new Jim Crow: Mass incarceration in the age of colorblindness*. New York, NY: The New Press.

Bandura, A. (1977). Self-efficacy: Toward a unifying theory of behavioral change. *Psychological Review, 84*(2), 191–215.

Bandura, A. (1994). Self-efficacy. In V. S. Ramachaudran (Ed.), *Encyclopedia of human behavior* (pp. 71–81). New York, NY: Academic Press.

Bloom, B. S. (1984). *Taxonomy of educational objectives book 1: Cognitive domain*. New York: Longman.

Bonilla-Silva, E. (2006). *Racism without racists: Color-blind racism and the persistence of racial inequality in America*. Lanham, MD: Rowman & Littlefield.

Boykin, A. W. (1994). Afrocultural expression and its implications for schooling. In E. R. Hollins, J. E. King, & W. C. Hayman (Eds.), *Teaching diverse populations: Formulating a knowledge base* (pp. 243–274). Albany, NY: SUNY Press.

Brown v. Board of Education, 347 U.S. 483 (1954).

Bruder, C. E., Piotrowski, A., Gijsbers, A. A., Andersson, R., Erickson, S., Diaz de Ståhl, T., . . . J. P. Dumanski. (2008). Phenotypically concordant and discordant monozygotic twins display different DNA copy-number-variation profiles. *The American Journal of Human Genetics, 82*(3), 763–771. doi:10.1016/j.ajhg.2007.12.011

Cross, W. E., Jr., & Vandiver, B. J. (2001). Nigrescence theory and measurement: Introducing the cross racial identity scale. In J. Ponterotto, J. M. Casas, L. A. Suzuki, & C. M. Alexander (Eds.), *Handbook of multicultural counseling* (pp. 371–393). Thousand Oaks, CA: Sage

Deci, E. L., & Ryan, R. M. (1985). *Intrinsic motivation and self-determination in human behavior (perspectives in social psychology).* New York, NY: Plenum Press.

Deci, E. L., & Ryan, R. M. (2002). *The handbook of self-determination research.* Rochester, NY: University of Rochester Press.

Dweck, C. S., & Elliott, E. S. (1988). A social-cognitive approach to motivation and personality. *Psychological Review, 95*(2), 256–273. doi:10.1037/0033-295X.95.2.256

Feistritzer, E. C. (2011). *Profile of teachers in the U.S. 2011.* Washingon, DC: National Center for Education Information.

Ferguson, A. A. (2001). *Bad boys: Public schools in the making of Black masculinty.* Ann Arbor: University of Michigan Press.

Ford, D. Y. (2010). *Reversing underachievement among gifted Black students.* Waco, TX: Prufrock Press.

Fordham, S. (1988). Acelessness as a factor in Black students' school success: Pragmatic strategy or pyrrhic victory. *Harvard Educational Review, 58*(1), 54–85.

Fryer, R. G. (2006). "Acting White." *Educationnext, 6*(1), 1. Retrieved from http://educationnext.org/actingwhite/

Genographic project. (2005). Retrieved from https://genographic.nationalgeographic.com/

Graham, S. (1991). A review of attribution theory in achievement contexts. *Educational Psychology Review, 3*(1), 5–39.

Graham, S. (1994). Motivation in African Americans. *Review of Educational Research, 64,* 55–117. doi:10.3102/00346543064001055

Grantham, T. C. (2004). Rocky Jones: Case study of a high-achieving Black male's motivation to participate in gifted classes. *Roeper Review, 26,* 208–215.

Harry, B., & Klinger, J. K. (2005). *Why are so many minority students in special education? Understanding race & disability in schools.* New York, NY: Teachers College Press.

Harry, B., Klinger, J. K., Cramer, E. P., & Sturges, K. M. (2007). *Case studies of minority student placement in special education.* New York, NY: Teachers College Press.

hooks, b. (2004). *We real cool: Black men and masculinity.* New York, NY: Routledge.

Hughey, M., & Jost, J. (2011). *The Obamas and a (post) racial America? Series in political psychology.* New York, NY: Oxford University Press.

Kaplan, R. H. (2011). *The myth of post-racial America: Searching for equality in the age of materialism.* Lanham, MD: R & L Education.

Kozol, J. (1992). *Savage inequalities: Children in America's schools.* New York, NY: Harper Perennial.

Kozol, J. (2006). *The shame of the nation: The restoration of apartheid schooling in America.* New York, NY: Broadway.

Kozol, J. (2012). *Fire in the ashes: Twenty-five years among the poorest children in America.* New York, NY: Crown.

Katz, B., & Rodin, J. (2010). *An impending national transformation.* Retrieved from http://www.brookings.edu/research/opinions/2010/05/09-demographics-katz

Locke, E. (1968). Toward a theory of task motivation and incentives. *Organizational Behavior and Human Performance, 3*(2), 157–189. doi:10.1016/00305073(68)90004-4

McClelland, D. C. (1978). Managing motivation to expand human freedom. *American Psychologist, 33*(3), 201–210. doi:10.1037/0003-066X.33.3.201

Merton, R. K. (1948). The self-fulfilling prophecy. *The Antioch Review, 8*(2), 193–210.

Metzler, J. (2008). *The construction and rearticulation of race in a post-racial America.* Bloomington, IN: AuthorHouse.

National Center for Education Statistics. (2007–2008). *Schools and staffing survey.* http://nces.ed.gov/surveys/sass/tables/sass0708_029_t12n.asp

Ogbu, J. U. (1978). *Minority education and caste: The American system in cross-cultural perspective.* New York, NY: Academic Press.

Pager, D. (2009). *Marked: race, crime, and finding work in an era of mass incarceration.* Chicago, IL: University of Chicago Press.

Sharpley-Whiting, T. D. (Ed). (2009). *The speech: Race and Barack Obama's "a more perfect union."* New York, NY: Bloomsbury.

Singer, E. (2012). A comprehensive map of human genetic diversity. *MIT Technology Review.* Retrieved from http://www.technolgyreview.com/web

Steele, C. (2011). *Whistling Vivaldi: How stereotypes affect us and what we can do.* New York, NY: Norton .

Steele, C., & Aronson, J. (1995). Stereotype threat and the intellectual test performance of African Americans. *Journal of Personality and Social Psychology, 69*(5), 797–811.

Sue, D. W., Capodilupo, C. M., & Holder, A. (2008). Racial microaggressions in the life experience of Black Americans. *Professional Psychology: Research and Practice, 39*(3), 329–336.

Touré, & Dyson, M. E. (2012). *Who's afraid of post-Blackness? What it means to be Black now.* New York, NY: Free Press.

Weiner, B. (1980). A cognitive (attribution)-emotion-action-model of motivated behavior: An analysis of judgements of help-giving. *Journal of Personality and Social Psychology, 39*(2), 186–200.

Whiting, G. W. (2004). Young Black American fathers in a fatherhood program: A phenomenological study (Doctoral dissertation). Available from http://docs.lib.purdue.edu/dissertations/AAI3150849/

Whiting, G. W. (2006a). Enhancing culturally diverse males' scholar identity: Suggestions for educators of gifted students. *Gifted Child Today, 29*(3), 46–50.

Whiting, G. W. (2006b). From at risk to at promise: Developing scholar identities among Black males. *Journal of Secondary Gifted Education, 17*(4), 222–229.

Whiting, G. W. (2009a). The scholar identity institute: Guiding Darnel and other Black males. *Gifted Child Today, 32*(4), 53–56, 63.

Whiting, G. W. (2009b). Gifted Black males: Understanding and decreasing barriers to achievement and identity. *Roeper Review, 31*(4). 224–233.

Whiting G. W. (2010). Overrepresentation of African American males in special education: A clarion call for action and change. In E. M. Gallaher, & V. C. Polite (Eds.), *The state of the African American male* (pp. 19–44). East Lansing: Michigan State University Press.

Wiggings, G., & McTighe, J. (2005). *Understanding by design* (2nd ed.). Alexandria, VA: Association for Supervisor and Curriculum Development.

Wilson, W. J. (1996). *When work disappears: The world of the new urban poor.* New York, NY: Knopf.

Wilson, W. J. (2009). *More than just race: Being Black and poor in the inner city.* New York, NY: Norton.

Wise, T. J. (2010). *Colorblind: The rise of post-racial politics and the retreat from racial equity.* San Francisco, CA: City Lights Books.

Woodson, C. G. (2013). *The mis-education of the Negro.* Trenton, NJ: Africa World Press. (Original work published 1933)

Zimmerman, B., Bandura, A., & Martinez-Pons, M. (1992) Self-motivation for academic attainment: The role of self-efficacy beliefs and personal goal setting. *American Educational Research Journal, 29*(3), 663–676.

PART TWO

POSTSECONDARY FRAMEWORKS AND MODELS

7

ACADEMICALLY GIFTED AFRICAN AMERICAN MALES

Modeling Achievement in the Historically
Black Colleges and Universities and
Predominantly White Institutions Context

Fred A. Bonner II

The engagement of African American males with institutions of higher education has been chronicled in the extant literature from a number of key vantage points. Whether it has been the work of scholars who have attempted to shed light on the experiences of this cohort in predominantly White institutions (PWIs; Allen, 1981, 1986, 1988, 1992; Astin, 1975; Cuyjet & Associates, 2006; Fleming, 1984; Smith, Altbach, & Lomotey, 2002; Smith & Associates, 1997; Watson, Terrell, Wright, & Associates, 2002) or whether the context has been the historically Black college and university (HBCU) setting, the Black male in postsecondary institutions has provided fodder for critical discourse over the last several decades (Roebuck & Murty, 1993). The Black male experience in academe has been broad and it has also been narrowly tailored for more pointed analysis in some fields, in particular fields such as science, technology, engineering, and mathematics (STEM; Bonner, Alfred, Lewis, Nave, & Frizell, 2009; Chubin, May, & Babco, 2005; Hrabowski, Maton, Greene, & Grief, 2002; Maton & Hrabowski, 2004; May & Chubin, 2003) or their negotiation of certain identities (i.e., gifted and high achieving [Bonner, 2001, 2010; Fries-Britt,

1998; Fries-Britt & Turner, 2002; Griffin, 2006; Harper, 2005]; racial [Bonner & Evans, 2004; Cleveland, 2004; Steele, 1997; Steele & Aronson, 1995; Strayhorn & Terrell, 2010]), the plight of these men has served as fodder for serious ongoing dialogue.

Given these multiple and competing choices, there is no *one best* approach to tackle this hydra. Thus, like the age-old maxim that tells us the best way to eat an elephant—one bite at a time—this chapter highlights one key dimension of the research on this population: academic giftedness. This chapter is an attempt to foreground academically gifted postsecondary students using the HBCU and PWI institutional context as a background. The focus on the central question, unique in this research, is: What are the perceptions of an academically gifted African American male undergraduate student attending a PWI, and what are the perceptions of an academically gifted African American male attending an HBCU concerning each student's relationship with the institution in the cultivation of his academic giftedness?

In framing and organizing this chapter, this central question is taken from my book *Academically Gifted African American Male College Students* (Bonner, 2010). Additionally, the model presented in the book is problemized and deconstructed to allow for application to the attendant issues associated with the education pipeline for African American males, especially for those identified as academically gifted. The chapter concludes with practical recommendations for research and practice for those in or associated with HBCUs and PWIs.

Giftedness and the P–16 African American Male

To describe the African American experience with gifted and talented programming in the United States as *dismal* is at best appropriate and at worst woefully understated. In addition to the earlier monumental work by Mary Frasier (1977), which illustrated a need for organizing productive experiences for culturally diverse gifted and talented students, are the continuing and contemporary rumblings of gifted scholars Donna Ford, Tarek Grantham, Deborah Harmon, Malik Henfield, James Moore, Michelle Trotman Scott, and Thomas Hébert, who have consistently underscored deficit modeling and marginalizing practices affecting this group that functions at the intersection of giftedness and African American culture. The question I posed in an article published in the *Journal of Black Studies*, "Why do we continually fail to recognize gifted and talented African American students?" (Bonner, 2000, p. 643), sadly is as valid today as it was more than a decade ago.

Highlighting the P–12 Experience

To initiate the consumption of the metaphorical elephant mentioned earlier, an exploration of the issues for the academically gifted African American male in the P–12 setting is warranted. Rhodes (1992) asserted that a focus on gifted Black children in the aggregate should be jettisoned for a more nuanced review of the individual gifted child. Thus, according to Bonner (2010), a number of issues are in critical need of foregrounding if the problems of underachievement and underidentification are going to be addressed. Namely, "These issues include standardized testing, teacher nomination procedures, learning style preferences, family and peer influences, screening and identification, and gifted underachievement" (Bonner, 2010, p. 10). In this section, I highlight three of the most salient issues—standardized testing, teacher nomination procedures, and family and peer influences—affecting this population (for a more comprehensive discussion of these issues as well as those not treated here, please refer to Bonner, 2010).

Standardized Testing

The late Asa Hilliard (1976) was troubled more than three decades ago by the often orthogonal relationship found to exist between African American student achievement and standardized tests. Hilliard said these assessments ask two fundamental questions: Do you know what I know? What is it that you know? He went on to report that it is the strict reliance on the first question that creates disequilibrium for African American students attempting to gain solid footing in education venues that use these tests as tools in the admission and identification process. His research draws on the arguments concerning the advantages that the acquisition of *cultural* and *social capital* provide in gaining access to coveted academic and intellectual spaces.

A major outcry from communities invested in diffusing the disparate impact of standardized tests on student populations of color is to generate processes that do not solely rely on these measures. A number of scholars (Bonner, 2001, 2010; Ford, 1994, 1995; Grantham, 2004; Hébert, 1997, 2002) have said that providing more comprehensive processes that include standardized testing as one of the assessment tool is a more appropriate approach. According to Bonner (2010):

> The sole reliance on traditional assessment measures such as standardized tests runs the risk of putting African American students at a great disadvantage. Yet, it is important to note that attempting to ameliorate these disadvantages by lowering standards and "cut off" scores or by adding points to the scores received by these students obfuscates the true problem—the

actual standardized test itself. It is important to recognize that standardized tests have some usefulness as assessment instruments, but they should never be used as the sole indicator of a complex and multifaceted concept such as giftedness. (p. 11)

Teacher Nomination Procedures

The status of the American P–12 teaching force has been a hotly debated topic for many years. One of the concerns leveled by those in and outside school settings has been the browning and blackening of student populations and the concomitant whitening of teaching populations (Corbett, 2011; Hyland, 2005; Landsman & Lewis, 2011; Noguera, 2008). What many of these scholars lament is the lack of teachers who represent the cultural and ethnic communities of the students they serve. Said differently, Black and Hispanic youths need to be exposed to Black and Hispanic teachers in class-room and schooling contexts. The lack of teachers of color becomes significantly more pronounced among the ranks of those who serve as instructors for gifted and talented students.

With the gifted and talented student of color, especially the academically gifted African American male student, the teacher is often woefully unfamiliar with the student's cultural background and experiences. According to Bonner (2010), "White, middle-class society often serves as the template upon which teacher nominations of gifted and talented students are based. Students who are essentially 'out of cultural sync' with their teachers often go unidentified, regardless of their intellectual abilities and prowess" (p. 12). Thus, for the academically gifted African American male to find his way into gifted programming, a realignment of his cultural habits has to be morphed into a framework that is more congruent with those exhibited by his teacher.

A few cautionary tales must be provided concerning the negative impact this morphing of cultural identity exacts on these high-achieving African American males. Irvine (1990) said that when students are required whether through explicit or implicit means to deny their cultural background and heritage, the resultant effect is often self-hatred, lowered self-esteem, heightened anxiety, and lower academic achievement. Similarly, Torrance (1973) said that if educators are genuinely interested in identifying gifted students within minority cohorts they must eschew one-size-fits-all templates and embrace characteristics that are valued by these communities.

Family and Peer Influences

Family and peer units have an impact on the academically gifted African American male in important ways. Early in his negotiation of a gifted identity, the African American male learns he must assume multiple identities across multiple contexts, sometimes in very narrow windows of space and time. One moniker used to describe this behavior is *code switching*, which has been touted by some educators as one of the most essential tools an African American male should have at his disposal (Comer, 1988; hooks, 2004; White & Cones, 1999; Whiting, 2006).

Although family and peer networks serve as sources of great support, they can also serve as enclaves that constrain potential. Some of the negative outcomes for African American males associated with these interactions are the perceived need to be *raceless* (Ford, 2011; Hébert, 2002) or that by being smart in some way means that one is *acting White* (Ford, 2011). An even further disheartening outcome is that because of these pressures, the academically gifted African American male attempts to create more distance from his gifted designation and chooses *disidentification* (Bonner, Lewis, Bowman-Perrott, Hill-Jackson, & James, 2009) as a means to pull away from this identity.

Another and perhaps the most debilitating effect of a nonsupportive family and peer unit is the behavioral outcome Whitten (1992) called *survival conflict*, a reaction by the gifted male to his success, feeling that his academic accomplishments will move him away from these individuals who have been important in his life's journey. Bonner (2010) wrote:

> This behavior can essentially manifest itself in one or several responses: guilt, ambivalence, anxiety, and depression. The manifestation of these feelings is frequently subconscious and can be debilitative if they are not addressed and handled appropriately; hence, self-sabotage, procrastination, decreased productivity, and devaluation of one's self-concept, accomplishments, and ambitions can ensue. (p. 15)

Highlighting the Postsecondary Experience

The extant literature on the experiences of African American students in academe has been far reaching in its coverage (Allen, 1988, 1992; Allen, Epps, & Haniff, 1991; Cuyjet & Associates, 2006; D'Augelli & Hershberger, 1993; Palmer & Wood, 2012; Watson et al., 2002). Although most of the focus has been on the African American collegiate population in general, a dismantling of this monolith provides essential constituent group data that often go undetected. I have spent considerable time investigating academically gifted African American males.

Several of my contemporaries focus on this cohort of African American males in the college and university environment (Fries-Britt, 1998; Harper,

2005). Their important work has lent voice to what has ostensibly been a quiescent field. Notwithstanding the critical work these scholars are engaging in, their focus has tended to underscore the population they have referred to as *high achieving*. Although similar from an etymological perspective, terms such as these are somewhat different from an epistemological perspective. Beyond the grade and grade point average foundation that give rise to many of the high achieving approaches, the term *academic giftedness* carries with it the gravitas of gifted theory that envelopes such ancillary appendages as *creativity, task commitment, practicality*, and even *luck* (Renzulli, 1986; Sternberg, 1985, 2007; Tannenbaum, 1979).

As in the preceding section, this overview reflects three of the most salient issues influencing the college-going experience for this group in the HBCU and PWI context: relationships with faculty, peer relationships, and institutional environment (see Bonner, 2010, for a more in-depth review).

Relationships With Faculty

A recapitulated theme across the literature focusing on students of color, particularly African American students, is the importance of establishing solid relationships with individuals capable of assisting these students to navigate the postsecondary terrain. The primary go-to individuals for this role are faculty members. The importance of these relationships should not be understated given the number of challenges these students face during their matriculation experiences. Beyond the rudimentary transition from high school to college, African American students also endure the vicissitudes of integrating into an academic and social milieu that at best seems *tepid* and at worst *chilly* (Bonner & Bailey, 2006; Bonner, Marbley, & Howard Hamilton, 2011; Fleming, 1984; Guiffrida, 2004; Smith & Associates, 1997; Strayhorn & Terrell, 2010).

Faculty members provide much-needed mentoring and role modeling to support the matriculation experiences of these collegians. However, for these relationships to form organically, fertilization and cultivation are necessary for healthy growth. Namely, a study by Fries-Britt and Turner (2002) revealed that 100% of the African American males in their investigation reported feeling that they had to prove themselves academically competent to accomplish this task of gaining faculty member's attention. They expressed attendant feelings and perceptions that they had to essentially reveal to faculty that they possessed the intellectual capital to be successful. In addition, D'Augelli and Hershberger (1993) reported that African American males were more likely to be perceived as possessing poor academic and socialization skills and were less likely to seek out faculty for assistance because of perceived maltreatment.

In looking more narrowly at the experiences of academically gifted African American males, matriculation concerns are even more pronounced. The common refrain, "He's smart, he doesn't need my help" serves as the proverbial death nail in getting the assistance these students need to remain successful. Maton and Hrabowski (2004), reporting on gifted students in STEM fields, found that even those undergraduates with good grades and standardized test scores were experiencing school failure at high levels. Addi... Ford, Webb, and Sandidge (1994) argued that, "the psychological, cu... and social issues confronting gifted college students have received only scant attention. One of the more plausible explanations for this paucity is the myth that gifted college students have no problems" (p. 36).

Peer Relationships

Bonner (2001) said, "Peer groups are important in that they often expose students to viable social circles of similar achievement-oriented peers, thereby reifying these students' aspirations and goals" (p. 21). It is the peer group that serves as sounding board and mirror in the college student development experience. These enclaves also serve a critical role in positively affecting persistence. Carroll (1988) reported that the frequency and the quality of students' interactions with peers and their participation in extracurricular activities are positively associated with persistence (i.e., remaining at the institution). In these groups students are able to test assumptions and sometimes tackle ill-structured problems (King & Kitchner, 1994).

The peer group provides a safe zone for the African American male to simply be himself. White and Cones (1999) said that these groups meet important needs such as offering belonging, feedback, and new learning experiences. These zones become even more critical for these men who are placed in nonminority settings in which every fiber of their being is analyzed and problemized using incongruent and unfamiliar templates. Peers provide sociocultural support, which for many of these students account for more variance in the undergraduate experience than their academic engagements. Thus, Sedlacek (1993) and his exploration of noncognitive variables (e.g. self-concept, realistic self-appraisal, handling system/racism, long-range goals, leadership, strong support person, community, and nontraditional learning) found to have an impact on the undergraduate African American experience are quite applicable in this instance.

For the gifted African American male collegian, the peer group serves to mediate the multiple and intersecting identities these students assume in the higher education setting. Not only are these students navigating their identities as academically gifted in a context that sometimes disparages or is woefully unprepared to facilitate their high achievement, but they are also combating stereotypical notions that they are accessing higher education either through an affirmative action mandate or their athletic prowess.

Institutional Environment

Foundational to student development theory and the field of student affairs is Kurt Lewin's (1936) interactionist paradigm B = f(P, E). The equation, read as behavior is a function of the person times the environment, underscores how behavioral outcomes are determined by the interaction of the individual and the environmental setting. It is essential to note about this heuristic that by altering either the P or the E, the behavioral outcome in some way will be influenced. The argument has been that the impact the environment can exact on behavior has not been fully investigated. And if this argument is extended to certain subpopulations in higher education, the need to explore the resultant effect is even more dire.

In Tinto's (1975) seminal research highlighting student-institution-fit, he concluded that the more a student is integrated into academic and social systems, the more committed the student will be to the institution. Clearly the literature paints a picture of two different educational contexts—the HBCU as being supportive in the development of African American students but with key challenges regarding access to better facilities and resources, and the PWI as creating opportunities for education and career advancement but with an often chilly and inhospitable campus climate. Yet, both types of these institutions must commit to ensuring that the environment is facilitative of academic potential (Berger & Milem, 2000; Bonner, 2010).

Academically gifted African American males require an institutional environment that recognizes and supports their gifted as well as their African American identities. And foundational to this support is their gender identity (Whiting, 2006). Combating isolation in majors (e.g., science, technology, engineering, mathematics) that are not highly popular with their African American peers or by participating in settings (e.g., academic societies, honors colleges, predominantly White Greek organizations) where they might find themselves the only person of color in attendance becomes a unique challenge for this cohort on the PWI campus, and finding environments that pull together like-minded peers or settings that promote intellectual pursuits that fall outside the typical interests of other Black males in the HBCU setting becomes a problem. According to Bonner (2010), "The gifted African American male can find himself locked outside of the African American community, which does not relate to him at an academic level, and the White community, which does not relate to him at a cultural level—a virtual academic purgatory" (p. 30).

The academically gifted Black male engagement framework (AGBME; see Figure 7.1) provides a visual display of the six categories uncovered in a prior empirical research investigation (Bonner, 2010) aimed at responding to the question mentioned earlier in this chapter: What are the perceptions of an academically gifted African American male undergraduate student attending an HBCU, and what are the perceptions of an academically gifted African American male attending a PWI, concerning his relationship with the institution in the cultivation of his academic giftedness? Additionally, I asked a number of subquestions in an attempt to better understand how these individuals experienced giftedness in these two different institutional contexts.

This empirical investigation (Bonner, 2010) involved conducting case studies at Texas A&M University–Commerce (TAMUC) and Grambling State University (GSU). A primary case study participant was identified at each institution—Trey Williams at TAMUC and Stephen James at GSU. Both males were chemistry majors, had attained at least junior class standing, and were identified as gifted using a number of criteria including such measures as grades, faculty nominations, and test scores (Renzulli, 1986).

In addition to these two primary case participants, administrators and faculty as well as friends (other academically gifted African American males) who interacted with the participants were interviewed. Two grounded theories emerged from this investigation:

Theory 1: The research-oriented approach to education maintained by TAMUC supported Trey Williams's academic giftedness in the institutional setting but did not thoroughly support his academic giftedness outside the institutional setting.

Figure 7.1 Academically Gifted Black Male Engagement Framework

Theory 2: The liberal arts approach to education maintained by GSU supported Stephen James's academic giftedness in and outside the institutional setting. (Bonner, 2010)

Highlighting the AGBME Framework

The AGBME Framework (Bonner, 2010) is ensconced in an important point in the *education pipeline* (the links between pre–K and elementary school, middle school and high school, high school and postsecondary). Located in the postsecondary end of the pipeline, this model offers key insight on crucial components found to support the success of academically gifted African American male undergraduates. I am presently engaged in quantitative testing of each constituent category to allow for *genernalizability*. In its current form, this model is based on qualitative methods and lends itself to *transferability*, thus allowing the reader to determine its relative fit in particular educational contexts.

Lessons and Recommendations Across the Categories

Relationships with faculty. These are critical in the HBCU and PWI setting. At the core of these relationships both students derived important mentoring advice and role modeling cues that assisted them in navigating the higher education terrain. In HBCU settings, *faculty relationships should focus on providing room for the academically gifted African American male to embrace his gifted identity*, what Whiting (2006) refers to as the development of a scholar identity. In the PWI settings, *a focus on race and what it means to be African American* in many instances becomes the topic for investigation. The suggestion that focusing on academics in the Black college setting and focusing on race in the White college setting will serve as a panacea is too simple; this population is too complex for such rudimentary solutions. However, these are key starting points in the process of addressing these students needs.

Peer relationships. In the HBCU and PWI setting, while primarily serving the same purpose, these relationships are the outgrowths from somewhat different places of origin; for example, in the HBCU context, peer relationships *served as enclaves in which the academically gifted African American male could reify behaviors that he found produced growth and dissolve those behaviors that were found to inhibit growth*. In the PWI context, peer groups served as more of safe spaces and zones for continued survival. These groups provided a place of refuge from the constant pressures of fitting into foreign and unfamiliar cultural molds. They also served as buffers against a sometimes hostile and inhospitable campus climate. Administrators of institutions should consider ways to ensure that students are engaging in productive peer relationships.

Family influence and support. Essential in the successful matriculation process for these males, and given their status as academically gifted, the family has probably played a key role in their education experiences across their P–12 careers. Also, given the proclivity for students of color, especially African American students, to remain close to the family unit subsequent to high school graduation, it would behoove higher education institutions to find ways to ensure that parents remain connected. A good showing of intentions to keep parents involved during orientation programming must be followed up with consistent communication throughout the undergraduate experience.

Factors influencing college selection (college choice). These factors play a key role in fostering the success of this gifted cohort in both contexts. Understanding what motivated the student to choose the institution is critically important information in persistence and retention interventions. Keeping in the background and eliciting when necessary the student's initial drivers to select the institution via questions as simple as "Why did you choose this institution?" or "What do you find exciting about your major?" are sometimes warranted. Although the rationale for college choice can become muddied, effective faculty and administrators are able to pull students from the morass they sometimes find themselves in during their matriculation experience.

Self-perception. This is one of the most important categories to consider when interacting with academically gifted African American male populations. In this research investigation (Bonner, 2010) and in a grant-funded research study for the National Science Foundation (NSF), an empirical investigation that I completed with a team of researchers, it became clear that many academically gifted African American students did not know how to negotiate their gifted identities, particularly in light of engagements with other African American peers, nonminority peers, and nonminority faculty. An even more basic issue is that many of these high achievers struggled to not only define but also to see themselves as *gifted*. This is yet another complex category that defies solutions of a singular nature; hence, I offer a point of initiation in tackling this issue. While both HBCUs and PWIs must assist these men in dealing with a congeries of self-perception maladies—acting White, disidentification, and stereotype threat, to name a few—they must find ways to create and support campus-based initiatives that explore the development of healthy identities. Also, programs that recognize and celebrate scholarly achievement should be promoted.

Institutional environment. This along with campus climate concerns are at the center of all the identified categories. The institutional environment sets key parameters, whether explicitly or implicitly, around the actions of the key actors in the environmental setting. For the academically gifted African American male participating in this study, the HBCU environment was supportive of his high achievement, and finding spaces on campus that celebrated his scholarly success were not too difficult to find. For the PWI participant, he found the environment in the classroom and laboratory settings supportive of his academic success; however, outside these venues the greater campus environment was found to be unsupportive. Assessments of campus climate and environments can not be divorced from the individuals who are experiencing these contexts. Studies in the aggregate do not provide nuanced assessments of how certain subpopulations are experiencing these settings. The HBCU and PWI need to specifically look at how African American males in general and academically gifted African American males in particular experience the institutional context.

Conclusion

It would be a huge mistake on the part of those invested in addressing the issue of the education pipeline to ignore academically gifted African American male college students. The tendency to focus efforts on those students who present academic deficiencies should not obfuscate the focus on efforts to ensure that the academically talented are being supported. The either/ or proposition must be replaced by a both/and approach in identifying the most effective practices in ensuring the seamless flow of students through the education pipeline. Additionally, the same limited and mutually exclusive discourse that tends to inform the HBCU and PWI debate as it relates to the experiences of African American students too has to be excised to allow for more seamless pipeline conversations. This chapter and the presentation of the AGBME model is but one cog in the wheel of offering empirically derived data to support initiatives aimed at improving the educational experiences of one of our most important higher education communities.

References

Allen, W. R. (1981). Correlates of Black student adjustment, achievement, and aspirations at a predominantly White southern institution. In G. Thomas (Ed.), *Black students in higher education: Conditions and experiences in the 1970s* (pp. 127–141). Westport, CT: Greenwood Press.

Allen, W. R. (1986). *Gender and campus race differences in Black student academic performance, racial attitudes and college satisfaction*. Atlanta, GA: Southern Education Foundation.

Allen, W. R. (1988). Black students in U.S. higher education: Toward improved access, adjustment, and achievement. *Urban Review, 20*(3), 165–188.

Allen, W. R. (1992). The color of success: African-American college student outcomes at predominantly White and historically Black public colleges and universities. *Harvard Educational Review, 62*(1), 26–44.

Allen, W. R., Epps, E. G., & Haniff, N. Z. (Eds.). (1991). *College in Black and White: African American students in predominantly White and in historically Black public universities*. Albany, NY: SUNY Press.

Astin, A. W. (1975). *Preventing students from dropping out*. San Francisco, CA: Jossey-Bass.

Berger, J. B., & Milem, J. F. (2000). Promoting undergraduate self-concept: Differences between historically Black and predominantly White colleges. *Journal of College Student Development, 41*(4), 381–394.

Bonner, F. A., II. (2000). African American giftedness. *Journal of Black Studies, 30*, 643–664.

Bonner, F. A., II. (2001). *Academically gifted African American male college students: A phenomenological study*. Storrs, CT: The National Research Center on the Gifted and Talented, University of Connecticut.

Bonner, F. A., II. (2010). *Academically gifted African American male college students*. Santa Barbara, CA: ABC-CLIO.

Bonner, F. A., II, Alfred, M. V., Lewis, C. W., Nave, F. M., & Frizell, S. S. (2009). Historically Black colleges and universities (HBCUs) and academically gifted Black students in science, technology, engineering and mathematics (STEM): Discovering the alchemy for success. *Journal of Urban Education: Focus on Enrichment, 6*(1), 122–136.

Bonner, F. A., II, & Bailey, K. (2006). Assessing the academic climate for African American men. In M. Cuyjet (Ed.), *African American men in college* (pp. 24–46). San Francisco, CA: Jossey-Bass.

Bonner, F. A., II, & Evans, M. (2004). Can you hear me? Voices and experiences of African American students in higher education. In D. Cleveland (Ed.), *Broken silence: Conversations about race by African American faculty and students on the journey to the professorate* (pp. 3–18). New York, NY: Peter Lang.

Bonner, F., Lewis, C. W., Bowman-Perrott, L., Hill-Jackson, V., & James, M. (2009). Definition, identification, identity, and culture: A unique alchemy impacting the success of gifted African American millennial males in school. *Journal for the Education of the Gifted, 33*(2), 176–202.

Bonner, F. A., II, Marbley, A. F., & Howard Hamilton, M. (Eds.). (2011). *Diverse millennial students in college*. Sterling, VA: Stylus.

Carroll, J. (1988). Freshman retention and attrition factors at a predominantly Black urban community college. *Journal of College Student Development, 29*(1), 52–59.

Cleveland, D. (Ed.). (2004). *Broken silence: Conversations about race by African American faculty and students on the journey to the professorate*. New York, NY: Peter Lang.

Comer, J. (1988). Educating poor minority children. *Scientific American, 259*(5), 42–48.

Corbett, A. (2011). *Can White teachers effectively teach Black students?* Retrieved from http://nbpa.info/2011/01/can-white-teachers-effectively-teach-black-students/

Chubin, D., May, G. S., & Babco, E. L. (2005). Diversifying the engineering workforce. *Journal of Engineering Education, 94*(1), 73–86.

Cuyjet, M. J., & Associates. (2006). *African American men in college.* San Francisco, CA: Jossey-Bass.

D'Augelli, A. R., & Hershberger, S. L. (1993). African American undergraduates on a predominantly White campus: Academic factors, social networks, and campus climate. *Journal of Negro Education, 62*(1), 67–81.

Fleming, J. (1984). *Blacks in college.* San Francisco, CA: Jossey-Bass.

Ford, D. Y. (1994). *The recruitment and retention of African-American students in gifted education programs: Implications and recommendations.* Storrs: University of Connecticut, The National Research Center on the Gifted and Talented.

Ford, D. Y. (1995). Desegregating gifted education: A need unmet. *Journal of Negro Education, 64*(1), 52–62.

Ford, D. Y. (2011). *Reversing underachievement among gifted Black students.* Waco, TX: Prufrock Press.

Ford, D., Grantham, T., Henfield, M., Harmon, D., Scott, M., Porchér, S., & Price, C. (Eds.) (in-press). *Gifted and advanced Black students in school: An anthology of critical works.* Waco, TX: Prufrock Press.

Ford, D. Y., Webb, K. S., & Sandidge, R. F. (1994). When gifted kids grow up. *Gifted Child Today, 17*(3), 34–42.

Fries-Britt, S. (1998). Moving beyond Black achiever isolation: Experiences of gifted Black collegians. *Journal of Higher Education, 69*(5), 556–576.

Fries-Britt, S. L., & Turner, B. (2002). Uneven stories: The experiences of Black collegians at a historically Black and a traditionally White campus. *Review of Higher Education, 25*(3), 315–350.

Grantham, T. (2004). Rocky Jones: Case study of a high-achieving Black male's motivation to participate in gifted classes. *Roeper Review, 26*(4), 208–215.

Griffin, K. A. (2006). Striving for success: A qualitative exploration of competing theories of high-achieving Black college students. *Journal of College Student Development, 47*(4), 384–399.

Guiffrida, D. A. (2003). African American student organizations as agents of social integration. *Journal of College Student Development, 44*(3), 304–320.

Harper, S. R. (2005). Leading the way: Inside the experiences of high-achieving African American male students. *About Campus, 10*(1), 8–15.

Hébert, T. P. (1997). Jamison's story: Talent nurtured in troubled times. *Roeper Review, 19,* 142–148.

Hébert, T. P. (2002). Gifted Black males in a predominantly White university: Portraits of high achievement. *Journal for the Education of the Gifted, 26*(1), 25–64.

Hilliard, A. G., III. (1976). *Alternatives to IQ testing: An approach to the assessment of gifted "minority" children.* Retrieved from ERIC database. (ED147009)

hooks, b. (2004). *We real cool: Black men and masculinity.* New York, NY: Routledge.

Hrabowski, F. A., III, Maton, K. I., Greene, M. L., & Greif, G. L. (2002). *Overcoming the odds: Raising academically successful African-American young women.* New York, NY: Oxford University Press.

Hyland, N. E. (2005). Being a good teacher of Black students? White teachers and unintentional racism. *Curriculum Inquiry, 35*(4), 429–459.

Irvine, J. J. (1990). *Black students and school failure.* New York, NY: Greenwood Press.

King, P. M., & Kitchener, K. S. (1994). *Developing reflective judgment: Understanding and promoting intellectual growth and critical thinking in adolescents and adults.* San Francisco, CA: Jossey-Bass.

Landsman, J., & Lewis, C. (Eds.). (2011). *White teachers/diverse classrooms: Creating inclusive schools, building on students' diversity and providing true educational equity* (2nd ed.). Sterling, VA: Stylus.

Lewin, K. (1936). *Principles of topological psychology.* New York, NY: McGraw-Hill.

Maton, K., & Hrabowski, F. (2004). Increasing the number of African American PhDs in the sciences and engineering: A strengths-based approach. *American Psychologist, 59*(6), 547–556.

May, G. S., & Chubin, D. E. (2003). A retrospective on undergraduate engineering success for underrepresented minority students. *Journal of Engineering Education, 92*(1), 1–13.

Noguera, P. A. (2008). *The trouble with Black boys and other reflections on race, equity and the future of public education.* San Francisco, CA: Wiley.

Palmer, R., & Wood, J. L. (Eds.). (2012). *Black men in college: Implications for HBCUs and beyond.* New York, NY: Routledge.

Renzulli, J. S. (1986). The three-ring conception of giftedness: A developmental model for creative productivity. In R. J. Sternberg & J. E. Davidson (Eds.), *Conceptions of giftedness* (pp. 53–92). New York, NY: Cambridge University Press.

Rhodes, W. C. (1992). Navigating the paradigm change. *Journal of Emotional and Behavioral Problems, 1*(2), 28–34.

Roebuck, J. B., & Murty, K. S. (1993). *Historically Black colleges and universities: Their place in American higher education.* Westport, CT: Praeger.

Sedlacek, W. E. (1993). Employing noncognitive variables in the admission and retention of nontraditional students. In Corland Lee (Ed.), *Achieving diversity: Issues in the recruitment and retention of underrepresented racial/ethnic students in higher education* (pp. 33–39). Alexandria, VA: National Association of College Admission Counselors.

Smith, D., & Associates. (1997). *Diversity works: The emerging picture of how students benefit.* Washington, DC: Association of American Colleges and Universities.

Smith, W. A., Altbach, P. G., & Lomotey, K. (2002). *The racial crisis in American higher education: Continuing challenges for the twenty-first century.* Albany, NY: SUNY Press.

Steele, C. M. (1997). A threat in the air: How stereotypes shape intellectual identity and performance. *American Psychologist, 52*(6), 613–629.

Steele, C. M., & Aronson, J. (1995). Stereotype threat and the intellectual test performance of African Americans. *Journal of Personality and Social Psychology, 69*(5), 797–811.

Sternberg, R. J. (1985). *Beyond IQ: A triarchic theory of human intelligence.* New York, NY: Cambridge University Press.

Sternberg, R. J. (2007). Intelligence and culture. In S. Kitayama & D. Cohen (Eds.), *Handbook of cultural psychology* (pp. 547–568). New York, NY: Guilford Press.

Strayhorn, T. L., & Terrell, M. C. (Eds.). (2010). *The evolving challenges of Black college students: New insights for policy, practice, and research.* Sterling, VA: Stylus.

Tannenbaum, A. (1979). Pre-Sputnik to post-Watergate concern about the gifted. In A. H. Passow (Ed.), *The gifted and the talented* (pp. 5–27). Chicago, IL: National Society for the Study of Education.

Tinto, V. (1975). Dropouts from higher education: A theoretical synthesis of the recent literature. *A Review of Educational Research, 45*(1), 89–125.

Torrance, E. P. (1973). Assessment of disadvantaged minority group children. *School Psychology Digest, 2*(4), 3–10.

Watson, L., Terrell, M., Wright, D., & Associates. (2002). *How minority students experience college: Implications for planning and policy.* Sterling, VA: Stylus.

White, J. L., & Cones, J. H. (1999). *Black man emerging: Facing the past and seizing a future in America.* New York, NY: Routledge.

Whiting, G. W. (2006). From at risk to at promise: Developing scholar identities among Black males. *Journal of Secondary Gifted Education, 17*(4), 222–229.

Whitten, L. (1992). Survival conflict and survival guilt in African-American college students. In M. Lang & C. A. Ford (Eds.), *Strategies for retaining minority students in higher education.* Springfield, IL: Charles C Thomas.

8

GIFTED, BLACK, MALE, AND POOR IN SCIENCE, TECHNOLOGY, ENGINEERING, AND MATHEMATICS

Achieving Despite the Odds

Alonzo M. Flowers

Over the past nine years I have amassed critical work experience in secondary and postsecondary settings as a classroom instructor and as an administrator. Each of these positions has given me the opportunity to advance my ideas not only about the importance of quality teaching but also about what constitutes quality learning for diverse student populations across the P–20 continuum. The emphasis in my research agenda comes primarily from secondary experiences in environments in which Black male students lacked exposure to equitable opportunities to learn. These experiences led me to the realities regarding the frequent disconnection that occurs when students move from the secondary level to the postsecondary level. This disconnection results primarily from inequitable funding of the K–12 system, which creates an unbalanced starting point for Black male students who do not attend schools comparable to those of their more affluent counterparts. Flowers's 2011 study explores perceptions of academically gifted, poor, Black male undergraduate students in engineering disciplines in order to identify factors that contribute to academic and social development.

Through an exhaustive literature review and extensive data collection process, I reaffirm and extend the findings of other researchers (Bonner, 2001a, 2010b; Chubin, 2002; Hrabowski, 2003; Maton & Hrabowski, 2004; National Science Foundation [NSF], 2002; Palmer, Davis, & Hilton, 2009) that Black males have been understudied in the gifted and science, technology, engineering, and mathematics (STEM) literature. S. A. Jackson (2003) predicted that over the next 10 to 20 years workers in science and technology in the United States would be retiring at record rates, and there would not be enough people in the pipeline to replace them. Based on participants' responses in my research, seven categories emerge to identify aspects of the participants' experiences in college: (a) self-perceptions, (b) financial obstacles, (c) engineering as a major, (d) family influence and support, (e) peer relationships, (f) relationships with faculty, and (g) the students' perceptions of the institution. Like many other groups that are marginalized in socioeconomic status, generational status, and race and ethnicity, this cohort has critical obstacles to overcome; however, by investing in an asset approach as opposed to a deficit-based approach regarding their educational experiences, it is possible to identify ways academically gifted poor Black males can contribute to the STEM workforce in meaningful ways.

The historical Black male experience in education is steeped in a context that cannot be disregarded when examining academically gifted, poor Black males. In the United States, the educational experiences of Black males consist of academic disparities, inequality of opportunity, and unjustified treatment based on race and socioeconomic status. According to Lucas (1994), the primary purpose of higher education was originally to produce a learned clergy. Over time, higher education also became a social institution for the elite who had the financial means to attend college. For Black males, educational opportunities were initially nonexistent. Even though some provisions were made historically, there are still numerous limitations in access, funding, and opportunity for academically gifted, poor Black male college students (Davis, 1994). For instance, prior to the 1970s, African American's participation in STEM academic programs and professional communities was virtually nonexistent (Babco, 2001). Black males were not effectively recruited and retained in research-driven institutions of higher education (Moore, 2006). A significant portion of Black students who earned degrees in STEM received them from historically Black colleges and universities (HBCUs; Babco, 2001; Hines, 1997; Hurtado, 1992). The historical development of higher education in the United States has been and continues to be influenced by racial, social, economic, and cultural factors, which have a direct effect on the academic outcomes of academically gifted, poor Black males (Bonner, 2001b; Cross & Burney, 2005). Conceptually, the notions of academic and social integration and connectedness are equally important when exploring issues concerning gifted poor Black male students (Bonner, 2010b; Harper, 2006). The extent of students' racial identity development and levels of self-efficacy influences the level of integration into postsecondary environments (Harper, 2004). The variety of theories used as the framework for this chapter emphasize the interrelatedness of Sternberg's (2003) triarchic theory of intelligence, Tinto's (1993) student integration model, and Whiting's (2006b) scholar identity model as frameworks that have constructed perceptions of academically gifted, poor Black male students attending predominantly White institutions (PWIs) and HBCUs.

Conceptual Framework

Historically, the definitions of *giftedness* and *achievement* were based on a hegemonic construct, failing to recognize social, cultural, or economic indicators (Bonner, 2010b). According to some educators, the problem of identifying minority gifted students is more a problem of how to integrate the information from a set of multiple criteria into the screening and identification process (Baldwin, 1980; Eby, 1983; Frasier, 1989; Renzulli, 1981). Bonner (2000) contended that giftedness is defined, shaped, and adjudged in a societal milieu and is not something merely inside a person's head (p. 656). Sternberg (1985) illustrated multiple means for understanding extraordinary levels of intelligence in his triarchic theory of intelligence. Considering the importance of improving educational opportunities for Black males in STEM disciplines, it is crucial to examine the complexities of Black male's educational experiences. To frame this chapter, it is imperative to examine the definition of *giftedness* and how students' conceptualizations of their abilities affect their academic development and persistence. The purpose of this chapter is to provide a historical and conceptual understanding of the complex educational experiences of Black males. This chapter illustrates the linkages among poverty, culture, academic giftedness, and two distinct institutional types (i.e., HBCUs and PWIs) in relation to the Black male college experience. The theories that frame this study (see Figure 8.1) are derived from research on giftedness (Sternberg, 1985), research on student integration (Tinto, 1993), and research on student's self-assessment (Whiting, 2006b).

Sternberg's Triarchic Theory of Intelligence

Sternberg's (1985) triarchic theory of intelligence outlines intelligence based on one's internal world, one's experience with tasks or situations, and one's external world. Sternberg used the triarchic theory to explain exceptional

Figure 8.1 Conceptual Framework

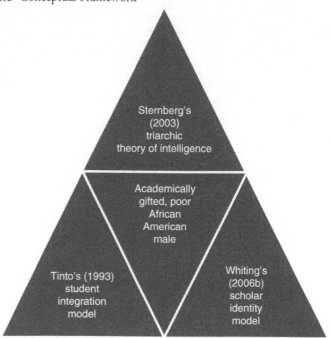

intelligence, such as giftedness and levels of retardation in children. The triarchic theory is a general theory of human intelligence that focuses on analogies and syllogistic reasoning. For instance, in a study that involved adults and children solving simple analogies, Sternberg found that the youngest children solved problems differently from older children. Sternberg theorized that this happened because the younger children had not yet developed the ability to discern higher-order relationships. Applying this theory, defining *giftedness* becomes an individualized and holistic process that requires examination of multiple congruous factors that affect the development of academic abilities.

Tinto's Student Integration Model

Research by Tinto (1993) contributes to the theoretical framework of this study. According to Tinto, Black students face unique challenges in academic development and social integration into PWIs. Tinto's model suggests that students' personal background characteristics, their educational and occupational goals, their commitment to their goals and to the institution, and the degree of academic and social involvement and investment in the institution interact to predict whether the students will leave the institution before completing a degree program. Tinto's model comprehensively accounts for the interaction between an individual's characteristics and the institutional conditions that affect integration. Thus, Tinto's theory explores personal as well as environmental components that affect students' integration into college environments.

Whiting's Scholar Identity Model

Gifted Black males find that their identity development, particularly their racial identity development, influences their achievement, motivation, and attitudes toward school (Grantham & Ford, 2003). Whiting's (2006b) scholar identity model examines how gifted Black males construct their self-perception, their self-concept, and their racial identity in relation to their perceptions of themselves as students. Their identity is further defined by interaction between the school environment and several internal characteristics, such as self-efficacy, self-awareness, and masculinity. Establishment of a positive identity for the Black male student is significant in that it serves as the foundation for the student to develop some sense of agency and in turn determine where he fits in the academy (Bonner & Bailey, 2006, p. 28). Establishing a coherent sense of one's self is an essential part of the collegiate experience. For academically gifted, poor Black males, the college experience is a multifaceted process that requires a psychological evaluation of the multiple forces that affect their academic success in higher education.

Usage of Framework

Sternberg's (2003), Tinto's (1993), and Whiting's (2006a) theories serve as a frame to understanding the participant's experiences in Flowers's (2011) study of academically gifted engineering students and their conceptualization of their colleague experiences. Figure 8.2 shows the intersection of the three theories that make up the conceptual framework.

The components of the conceptual framework led to a holistic understanding of achievement identity. Specifically, the models enabled an understanding of giftedness, college academic and social integration, and the participants' self-perceptions of being gifted. Based on the participant's conceptualization of their experiences, the conceptual framework illustrates the interconnectedness between participants' experiences and these three theories. Study participants' perceived notions of their ability, willingness to socially and academically integrate, and framing of their giftedness all occurred simultaneously to create an *achievement identity* (Flowers, 2011).

Figure 8.2 Achievement Identity Triarchic Theory of Intelligence

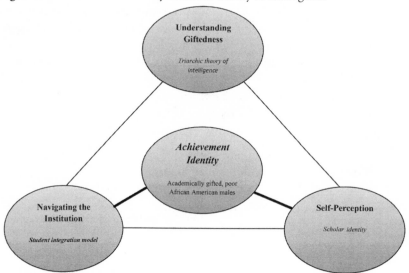

Triarchic theory of intelligence. Sternberg (2003) characterized intelligence as the cognitive ability to learn from experience, to rationalize, to remember important information, and to manage successfully the demands of daily living. Sternberg suggested that the notion of giftedness is constructed from an individualized and holistic ideology that emphasizes the interactions among multiple factors in the development of academic abilities. In other words, giftedness is multidimensional as social, academic, and environmental factors influence and broaden the traditional definition of *giftedness*. Sternberg said that various forms of intelligence, such as *analytical, creative,* and *practical,* can be attributed to innate characteristics associated with student learning.

Sternberg (2003) noted that analytical intelligence is based on the joint operations of metacomponents and performance components as well as knowledge acquisition. Study participants claimed that while they were always cognizant of their academic abilities, their opportunity to acquire knowledge was sometimes limited. Consequently, they had to be proactive in their pursuit of knowledge acquisition. For instance, one of the ways the participants acquired knowledge in engineering was to enroll in STEM bridge programs or attend STEM charter academies.

Sternberg (2003) also acknowledged the importance of creative intelligence, which he stated involves insights. He held that people who embodied creative intelligence could synthesize information and solve life problems. He asserted that this creative intelligence allows people to adjust creatively in new situations and generate new ideas. Study participants indicated that since a young age they had felt creative. One participant related that in primary school he disassembled and reassembled a computer in an entirely new way. All the participants mentioned that majoring in engineering requires a high level of creativity. For example, three participants made the comment that engineering requires you to think outside the box. When asked for clarification, each claimed that engineers must consider what will be necessary for the future rather than simply what will be necessary today.

Sternberg (2003) also discussed practical intelligence, which he claimed involves the ability to manage everyday tasks, to live and balance the demands of the external world successfully. Study participants described how the monetary demands of college often prompted them to negotiate elements of their academic process. For instance, the cost of textbooks was a recurring theme. Students noted that to be successful without the textbook they had to hustle, meaning they had to negotiate their available resources by determining which textbooks to purchase, borrow from classmates, or borrow from the library. Participants also had to find ancillary support in lieu of the resources they could not afford to purchase. Regardless of their socioeconomic situation, participants persisted beyond the sophomore benchmark that most engineering students do not meet.

Sternberg's (2003) theory suggests that the integration of analytical, creative, and practical intelligence was evident in the participants of this study. While several of the participants acknowledged giftedness as a positive characteristic, self-identifying as gifted was rare. Rather than perceiving themselves as gifted, the participants recognized themselves as *high achieving*, a term Sternberg used to refer to the ability to apply knowledge. Participants' notions of their intelligence were based on their ability to achieve academically and to use knowledge to persist in educational pursuits. Their perceptions about their academic abilities (i.e., giftedness) were influenced by academic and social factors.

Social and academic integration. According to Tinto (1993), Black students face unique challenges in their academic and social integration at institutions of higher education. Tinto's model suggests that students' personal background characteristics, as well as educational and occupational goals, are strong predictors of academic success. Tinto asserted that individual characteristics and institutional context both affect the student's ability to persist. In this study, the participants' ability to integrate academically and socially into their college environments was a significant component of their academic success. Findings indicated that social and academic integration, campus climate, and financial aid were major contributors to the academic and social development of the participants.

The way students integrate socially into the university has been noted as a compounding process (Tinto, 1993). Social integration is a cumulative process that continues throughout the student's college experience. For most students, particularly Black males, peer relations and faculty mentors are important factors in student integration, academically and socially (Cabrera, Colbeck, & Terenzini, 2001; Love, 1995; Pascarella & Terenzini, 1991). Peer relationships and faculty mentors were important factors in the experiences of the participants. Study participants discussed how peers had influenced their college experience; their interactions with peers were sometimes positive and sometimes negative. For instance, some participants noted that their peers had inspired them to pursue engineering as a major. One participant credited his roommate's influence on his decision to explore civil engineering as a possible major. With regard to negative peer interaction, several participants reported that peers sometimes disapproved of their giftedness. Some reported being called names such as nerd, school boy, and library-head because of their commitment to education. Others reported that peers referred to them as White boy, judging their drive to be academically successful as wanting to be White. Participants indicated they did not care about being teased but noted frustration about being called White. In several studies, Ford (1992, 1996, 2005) asserted that gifted Black males were more likely than their gifted female counterparts to report negative pressures from peers when they performed well academically. One participant declared that because you are a Black male who is achieving academically does not mean you want to be White; it just means you want to achieve something in your life.

Participants who attended University PWI had to seek faculty mentorship through their involvement in an engineering organization. They declared that because faculty interaction outside the classroom was minimal, they sought mentors through other avenues (e.g., honors programs, organizations). Study participants at University HBCU reported that finding a faculty mentor was not a problem, as the nature of the engineering department was built on the concept of student support. Study participants at University HBCU noted that a lack of student success was a result of the individual and not the environment. On the contrary, participants at University PWI claimed that individual competition was embedded within every aspect of the institutional context. Student success is based on the students' ability to remain competitive in unbalanced circumstances, many of which are out of students' control.

Scholar identity model. Establishing a coherent sense of one's self is an essential part of the collegiate experience for academically gifted, poor Black males. Whiting's (2006a) scholar identity model suggested that Black males' identities are constructed by interaction between the school environment and several internal characteristics, such as self-efficacy and willingness to make sacrifices. *Self-efficacy* refers to one's belief about one's ability to perform a specific task. According to Bandura (1997), *efficacy* is a generative capability in which cognitive, social, emotional, and behavioral subskills must be organized and effectively orchestrated to serve innumerable purposes (pp. 36–37). In other words, by organizing and executing a necessary course of action, students begin to self-regulate their learning by setting goals as a means to not only increase their ability to perform a task but also their persistence in the task. Leading scholars on gifted Black students (Bonner, 2001b, 2010a; Ford, 1996; Grantham, 2004; Hilliard, 2003) have maintained that a strong sense of self is an essential characteristic of academically gifted Black males. Whiting (2006a) asserted that when self-efficacy is positive for Black males, they tend to share similar characteristics: (a) high resilience, (b) high self-confidence, (c) high self-control, (d) a strong sense of self-responsibility, and (e) a clear understanding of the tasks they face and the belief they can accomplish all the subtasks associated with their goal.

All the study participants stressed that they believed in their ability to achieve (Flowers, 2011). As a result, they were able to perform successfully in their majors. However, each participant asserted that academic success was dependent on the willingness to make sacrifices. For instance, Isaiah said that his need to achieve was greater than the need to participate in unimportant social experiences such as parties. He claimed that other students considered him an outsider but that their perceptions were irrelevant. His academic goals took precedence over nonacademic events. Whiting (2006a) indicated that Black males who have a scholar identity understand the necessity for self-sacrifice to reach academic goals. The participants stressed that the time commitment to homework, study, and in-class assignments seemed to be more daunting in their major than in other college majors, but they declared they were willing to sacrifice now to achieve gains in the future.

Recommendations for Research

The findings of this study provide insight into the experiences of academically gifted, poor Black male students majoring in engineering disciplines. While this study provided insight into the academic and social perceptions of the participants, research that extends to various other aspects of their experiences is necessary. First, researchers should reframe traditional notions of giftedness to reflect inclusiveness of multiple perspectives (e.g., analytical, creative, and practical intelligence). Second, research should focus on multiple statuses (e.g., race, masculinity, socioeconomic, workforce transition) that academically gifted, poor Black males encounter as they navigate their engineering undergraduate degrees. A holistic understanding of this demographic is warranted if researchers and universities intend to meet the needs of academically gifted, poor Black males in engineering disciplines. Third, future studies should explore issues of academics and masculinity, the influences of mentoring, and effects of long-term goal setting by Black male students in engineering disciplines. Fourth, researchers need to examine the factors that motivate Black males to study engineering disciplines. Finally, more research publications that contribute to the dialogue about African American male engineers and their transition into the engineering workplace are needed. The findings in this study serve as a basis for future inquiry into areas of student and academic development of academically gifted Black males pursuing undergraduate engineering degrees. More important, this study created a frame for understanding issues of poverty and student academic achievement.

Recommendations for Practice

The findings of this study indicate that the support received by the participants (peers, faculty, family, and financial sources) significantly contributed to their academic achievement. Based on the findings, four recommendations for practice are presented.

Implement family involvement in the college transitional process via community-based practices. Study participants noted that family influence and support was a critical component in their collegiate experiences. Guiffrida (2003) asserted that minority students' families play an important role in the development of their educational and social identities as college students. Study participants described family support as essential; however, opportunities for family involvement on campus were minimal. Many of the participants reported that the more time they spent in college, the more they felt disconnected from their family. In most cases, their experiences were rooted in the fact that their families had limited knowledge about the participants' daily experiences as college students. Although every participant claimed he always felt academically supported by his family, that support was not necessarily indicative of the family's understanding of the college process. Thus, it is vital to establish family-friendly transitional programs for academically gifted, poor Black male students, specifically in STEM disciplines. Department-based programs should be designed to support family inclusion, especially for economically disadvantaged families. Administrators at institutions of higher education must realize that initiatives focusing on family involvement should be systemic. With regard to HBCUs, Kimbrough and Harper (2006) recommended,

> Given that most HBCUs are nestled in the heart of Black neighborhoods or in close geographic proximity to large concentrations of African Americans, they are in a unique position to reinforce college-going messages to young boys and teenage males. After-school, summer, and special outreach programs should be created to nurture pools of prospective Black male college-goers. (p. 205)

Consequently, all programs should move beyond just recruiting students at the high school level and should focus on community-based initiatives. It is essential that community-based family involvement programs engage not only the nuclear family but also various community stakeholders (e.g., community social organizations, local businesses, and churches). Community-based programs should be initiated to create connections between the student, the community, and the institution.

Establish P–20 initiatives to provide academic, social, and financial support to academically gifted, poor, Black males as an institution-based initiative supported by all stakeholders. The aim of the P–20 initiatives would be to target, as early as preschool, Black male students from low-income backgrounds. The intent of the program would be to expose Black students to engineering majors and related career opportunities. The recommended P–20 initiatives would focus on financial aid, recruitment and admissions, academic services, student services, and curriculum and instruction. The initiative would be designed as a collaborative effort by all stakeholders (students, parents, school, community, and the university). Traditional P–20 programs have distinct programming characteristics that differ by school and state (Yonezawa, Jones, & Mehan, 2002). State and federal stakeholders should genuinely encourage and enable academic support programs for low-income Black males. Effective P–20 programs are marked by the following characteristics: (a) high standards for program students and faculty, (b) personalized attention for students, (c) interaction with role models, (d) peer support, (e) college/community-based program schools, (f) financial aid and scholarship assistance, and (g) focus on problem-based curricula (Flowers, 2011). These administrative and instructional practices could serve as preparatory tools for Black male students in their navigation of the educational pipeline, specifically in engineering disciplines.

HBCUs and PWIs should incorporate P–20 programs to capitalize on the long-term development and success of students, particularly low-income

Black males. For institutions of higher education, the goal of providing students increased academic opportunities must include all students, regardless of socioeconomic status or race. The purpose of P–20 programs is to promote collaboration among secondary schools, their communities, and institutions of higher education. Ultimately, P–20 programs can create dual opportunities for collaborative conversations between universities and area primary and secondary schools. While myriad issues affect the experiences of academically gifted, poor Black males in college, a P–20 initiative could provide critical academic support and college preparatory skills.

Conclusion

The enrollment and persistence of Black males in STEM programs remains one of the most urgent issues in higher education. For the United States to remain globally competitive and move forward technologically, there must be a continuous reproduction of gifted and talented citizens with new and fresh ideas. As the demands for technology innovation increase, and the demographic trends in the workplace change, it is vital that Black male college students have the resources to gain skills to participate in the technologically advanced marketplace (Jackson & Moore, 2006, 2008). The findings of Flowers' study suggest that financial hardships that participants encountered did not inhibit their ability to be successful. All indicated that financial issues were the most significant challenge in their academic experience. Nevertheless, analysis of data indicated that participants who maintained high self-efficacy and a willingness to make sacrifices did not let financial issues derail their academic goals. This finding indicates that feeling efficacious increased participants' confidence to be successful academically. While much still remains to be learned about the experiences of academically gifted, poor Black males in higher education, particularly with regard to success in STEM programs, one essential fact was learned from this study: Despite all the odds, a positive sense of self was one of the primary contributors to the participants' achievement identity.

References

Babco, E. (2001). *Under-represented minorities in engineering: A progress report.* Washington, DC: Commission on Professionals in Science and Technology.

Baldwin, A. (1980, April). *The Baldwin identification matrix, its development and use in programs for the gifted child.* Paper presented at the annual meeting of the Council for Exceptional Children, Philadelphia, PA.

Bandura, A. (1997). *Self-efficacy: The exercise of control.* New York, NY: Freeman.

Bonner, F. A., II. (2000). African American giftedness: Our nation's deferred dream. *Journal of Black Studies, 30*(5), 643–663.

Bonner, F. A., II. (2001a). *Gifted African American male college students: A phenomenological study* (Research Monograph No. RM01148). Storrs: University of Connecticut, National Research Center on the Gifted and Talented.

Bonner, F. A., II. (2001b). Making room for the study of gifted African American males. *Black Issues in Higher Education, 18*(6), 80.

Bonner, F. A., II. (2010a). *Academically gifted African American males in college.* Santa Barbara, CA: ABC-Clio.

Bonner, F. A., II. (2010b). *Gifted African American male college students.* Santa Barbara, CA: Praeger.

Bonner, F. A., II, & Bailey, K. W. (2006). Enhancing the academic climate for African American college men. In M. J. Cuyjet (Ed.), *African American men in college* (pp. 24–46). San Francisco, CA: Jossey-Bass.

Cabrera, A. F., Colbeck, C. L., & Terenzini, P. T. (2001). Developing performance indicators for assessing classroom teaching practices and student learning. *Research in Higher Education, 42*(3), 327–352.

Chubin, D. (2002). Who is doing science—and who will? In S. J. Lita, S. D. Nelson, & A. H. Teich (Eds.), *AAAS science and technology policy yearbook 2002* (pp. 345–354). Washington, DC: American Association for the Advancement of Science.

Cross, T. L., & Burney, V. H. (2005). High ability, rural, and poor: Lessons from Project Aspire and implications for school counselors. *Journal of Secondary Gifted Education, 16*(4), 148–156.

Davis, J. E. (1994). College in Black and White: Campus environment and academic achievement of African American males. *Journal of Negro Education, 63*(4), 620–633.

Eby, J. W. (1983). Gifted behavior: A non-elitist approach. *Educational Leadership, 41*(8), 30–36.

Flowers, A. M. (2011). *Academically gifted, poor African American male undergraduates in engineering disciplines: Perceptions of factors contributing to success in a predominantly White institution (PWI) and historically Black college and university (HBCU) context* (Unpublished doctoral dissertation). Texas A&M University, College Station, TX.

Frasier, M. M. (1989). Poor and minority students can be gifted, too! *Educational Leadership, 50*(7), 16–18.

Ford, D. Y. (1992). Determinants of underachievement as perceived by gifted, above-average, and average Black students. *Roeper Review, 14*(3), 130–136.

Ford, D. Y. (1996). *Reversing underachievement among gifted Black students: Promising practices and programs.* New York, NY: Teachers College Press.

Ford, D. Y. (2005). Welcoming all students to room 202: Creating culturally responsive classrooms. *Gifted Child Today, 28*(4), 28–30.

Grantham, T. C. (2004). Multicultural mentoring to increase Black male representation in gifted programs. *Gifted Child Quarterly, 48*(3), 232–245.

Grantham, T. C., & Ford, D. Y. (2003). Beyond self-concept and self-esteem for African American students: Improving racial identity improves achievement. *The High School Journal, 87*(1), 18–29.

Guiffrida, D. A. (2003). African American student organizations as agents of social integration. *Journal of College Student Development, 44*(3), 304–320.

Harper, S. R. (2004). The measure of a man: Conceptualizations of masculinity among high-achieving African American male college students. *Berkeley Journal of Sociology, 48*(1), 89–107.

Harper, S. R. (2006). Peer support for African American male college achievement: Beyond internalized racism and the burden of "acting White." *Journal of Men's Studies, 14*(3), 337–358.

Hilliard, A. G. (2003). *Young, gifted, and Black: Promoting high achievement among African American students.* Boston, MA: Beacon Press.

Hines, S. M. (1997). *Factors influencing persistence among African-American upper-classmen in natural science and science-related majors.* Retrieved from ERIC database. (ED406898)

Hrabowski, F. (2003). Raising minority achievement in science and math. *Educational Leadership, 60*(4), 44-48.

Hurtado, S. (1992). The campus racial climate: Contexts of conflict. *Journal of Higher Education, 63*(5), 539–569.

Jackson, J. F. L., & Moore, J. L., III. (2006). African American males in education: Endangered or ignored? *Teachers College Record, 108*(2), 201–205.

Jackson, J. F. L., & Moore J. L., III. (2008). The African American male crisis in education: A popular media infatuation or needed public policy response? *American Behavioral Scientist, 51*(7), 847–853.

Jackson, S. A. (2003). *Envisioning a 21st-century science and engineering workforce for the United States: Tasks for university, industry, and government.* Washington, DC: National Academy Press.

Kimbrough, W. M., & Harper, S. R. (2006). African American men at historically Black colleges and universities: Different environments, similar challenges. In M. J. Cuyjet (Ed.), *African American men in college* (pp. 189–209). San Francisco, CA: Jossey-Bass.

Love, P. (1995). Exploring the impact of student affairs professionals on student outcomes. *Journal of College Student Development, 36*(2), 162–170.

Lucas, C. (1994). *American higher education: A history.* New York, NY: St. Martin's Press.

Maton, K. I., & Hrabowski, F. A., III. (2004). Increasing the number of African American PhDs in the sciences and engineering: A strengths-based approach. *American Psychologist, 59*(6), 547–556.

Moore, J. L., III. (2006). A qualitative investigation of African American males' career trajectory in engineering: Implications for teachers, school counselors, and parents. *Teachers College Record, 108*(2), 246–266.

National Science Foundation. (2002). *Women, minorities, and persons with disabilities in science and engineering* (NSF 03-312). Arlington, VA: Author.

Palmer, R. T., Davis, R. J., & Hilton, A. A. (2009). Exploring challenges that threaten to impede the academic success of academically under-prepared African American male collegians at an HBCU. *Journal of College Student Development, 50*(4), 429–445.

Pascarella, E., & Terenzini, P. (1991). *How college affects students.* San Francisco, CA: Jossey-Bass.

Renzulli, J. S. (1981). The revolving door model: A new way of identifying the gifted. *Phi Delta Kappan, 62*(9), 648–649.

Sternberg, R. J. (1985). *Beyond IQ: A triarchic theory of human intelligence.* Cambridge, UK: Cambridge University Press.

Sternberg, R. J. (2003). Giftedness according to the theory of successful intelligence. In N. Colangelo & G. Davis (Eds.), *Handbook of gifted education* (pp. 88–99). Boston, MA: Allyn & Bacon.

Tinto, V. (1993). *Leaving college: Rethinking the causes and cures of student attrition* (2nd ed.). Chicago, IL: University of Chicago Press.

Whiting, G. W. (2006a). From at risk to at promise: Developing scholar identities among Black males. *Journal of Secondary Gifted Education, 17*(4), 222–229.

Whiting, G. W. (2006b). Promoting a scholar identity among African American males: Implications for gifted education. *Gifted Education Press Quarterly, 20*(3), 2–6.

Yonezawa, S., Jones, M., & Mehan, H. (2002). Partners for preparation. In W. G. Tierney & L. S. Hagedorn (Eds.), *Increasing access to college: Extending possibilities for all students* (pp. 145–168). Albany, NY: SUNY Press.

9

THEORIZING MANHOOD

Black Male Identity Constructions
in the Education Pipeline

T. Elon Dancy II

Experiences among Black men in college are the subject of countless books, articles, and reports (Allen, 1988; Bonner, 2010; Brown,
Dancy, & Davis, 2013; Cuyjet, 2006; Dancy, 2012; Dancy & Brown,
2007, 2012; Davis, 1994; Harper, 2009, 2012; Palmer & Wood, 2012;
Strayhorn, 2008, 2010). Disparate trends of enrollment, retention, and
graduation in comparison to Black women are critical in much of this work
(Brown & Hurst, 2004; Brown, Dancy, & Davis, 2013; Harper, 2006). For
instance, reports on the high school to college transition find differential
factors between Black men and women. In 1976, 35% of Black high school
graduates who enrolled in college were men compared with 32% of women
(Brown & Hurst, 2004). And while the number of Black men awarded the
bachelor's degree increased by 52% from 1977 to 2000, the number of Black
women awarded the bachelor's degree increased by 112% in the same period
(Brown & Hurst, 2004). In addition, the ways that discrimination, bias, and
stereotyping play out in Black male education also seem to motivate research
foci on identity and inequity on campus (Brown, Dancy, & Davis, 2007;
Dancy, 2010a, 2012).

Black boys and men are enigmatic in educational spaces. Many admire
yet despise them across schooling and collegiate contexts (Davis, 1994, 2001).
Furthermore, pedestrian praise of Black heroics in peer and athletic circles
across educational institutions suggests a false campus centering that beyond

the surface reflects oppressive interests (Brown & Davis, 2000; Dancy, 2012; Ferguson, 2000). Black males are also labeled as hypersexual and dangerous and then punished disparately in society and education (Ferguson, 2000). Since the 1990s, when the *New York Times* urgently described Black males as a group in crisis, Black males have occupied a place in the public psyche (Dancy, 2012). Unfortunately, Black male collegiate experiences are eclipsed as media pundits scurry to sensationalize the experiences of Black men in ghettos or prisons.

College participation trends are also complicated in light of a study that found Black male self-ratings of their abilities increasing over time (Allen, Griffin, Jayakumar, Kimura-Walsh, & Wolf, 2007). These trends, all of which implicate race, gender, and various identities, demand additional research and diversified methodologies. Sadly, Black manhood—what it means to be a man—goes largely understudied in education in general and postsecondary education in particular. Even more, the latest studies in the field lag behind decades of sociological, anthropological, and cultural studies that maintain the importance of understanding the relevance of manhood construction in the social, developmental, and educational outcomes of Black males. Over 10 years ago, James Earl Davis (2000) argued, "What it means to be a Black male is so marginalized and suppressed in [educational institutions] and at home, that the manhood of Black men is developed with great difficulty" (p. 64). Disrupting this context across the educational pipeline motivates my scholarship.

In this chapter I review studies of Black boyhood and identity construction in schools. Next, I synthesize the landscape of Black manhood and masculinities research in college. Then in the following section, I revisit the background of my study and then offer a model of manhood to inform thinking and practice about the role of these matters in educational settings. The chapter ends with implications for research and practice and a conclusion.

Black Boyhood Construction in Schools

The behavioral experiences of Black boys are salient for understanding school (mis)comprehension of masculine identities. Previous studies argued that young boys construct masculine identities and ideologies through overcoming obstacles and subsequently earning a sense of autonomy and mastery (Chodorow, 1978; Wainrib, 1992). However, scholars hypothesize the understudied pathways of Black boys as eclectic representations of a combination of Afrocentric, Eurocentric, and alternative standards (Dancy, 2012; Harris, 1995). While Black boy constructions are less clear, many stereotypical ways of knowing this group abound.

Scholars found that common stereotypes including popular youth and classroom terror lead to a range of behaviors, strategies, and constructions within and beyond schooling spaces that influence how Black boys make meaning of themselves over time (Billson, 1996; Davis, 2000; Ferguson, 2000, 2007; Majors & Billson, 1992; Sewell, 1997). Black men who have attended school in American educational systems tell graphic stories that bear out this argument (Cose, 2003; Wright, 1945/2005). Their autobiographical sketches reveal the impact of disparate schooling and collegiate experiences on the construction of early manhood. For example, *Black Boy* by Richard Wright provides an autobiographical description of an early Black boy's experience in school. This account has been the subject of scholarship interrogating the policing of Black male bodies in education. For instance, hooks (2004b) writes, "a reader and a thinker, Wright was constantly interrogated by classmates and teachers who wanted him to remain silent. They wanted to know 'why do you ask so many questions?'" (p. 35).

In *The Envy of the World: On Being a Black Man in America*, Cose (2003) writes that poor Black children during Richard Wright's time were classified as unable to learn. In fact, Wright (1945/2005) argues that learning to read and write in his early childhood angered White American communities that wanted him to remain uneducated. The narratives of Black feminist scholars recall sobering contemporary stories of Black men similar to those of the 1920s (hooks, 2004b). Cose reflects:

> That elementary school experience made it difficult for me to take school seriously. I was never a bad student, but I simply didn't see it as a venue where much learning would take place or where my mind would be stretched. And the more schooling I received, the more my assessment was confirmed. . . . [I learned to be] so mistrustful of school, so alienated from its methods, and so convinced that I was too smart to be there, that I was in no mood to give it my heart. (as cited in hooks, 2004b, p. 35)

In *Makes Me Wanna Holler*, McCall describes the racial harassment he encountered as an 11-year-old alone in a predominantly White school:

> I was the only [Black] in most of my classes. When I walked into one room and sat down, the students near me would get up and move away. . . . It wasn't much better dealing with White teachers. They avoided eye contact with me as much as possible. . . . It was too much for an eleven-year-old to challenge, and I didn't try. Instead, I tried to become invisible. I kept to myself, remained quiet during class discussions, and never asked questions in or after class. I kept my eyes glued to my desk or looked straight ahead to avoid drawing attention to myself. I staggered, numb and withdrawn, through each school day. (as cited in hooks, 2004b, p. 37)

Some studies note the ways the Wright (1945/2005) and Cose (2003) narratives demonstrate why Black boys find it necessary to trouble schools and influence other Black boys to act similarly (Harris, 1995; Kunjufu, 1986). Subsequently, the school peer group becomes a precarious incubator for orthodox Black boyhood. In fact, some schooling experiences are so transformative in the lives of Black boys that they can even reverse homegrown values (hooks, 2004a; Steinberg, Dornbusch, & Brown, 1992). Years ago, scholars contended that Black boys learn to behave in accordance with a culture in which *coolness* is most respected and attained by breaking rules or receiving poor grades in school (Kunjufu, 1986). Outcomes usually include social rewards, such as security in peer groups, achievement, belonging, status, and self-validation (Harris, 1995; Taylor, 1989). Furthermore, peers *adultify* Black boys, shaping perceptions as manly as early as in the third grade following success in athletics, fighting, risk taking, or playing the dozens well (Kunjufu, 1986). *Playing the dozens* is defined as a competitive ritual characterized by an exchange of verbal insults related to the participants or members of the participants' families (Harris, 1995). Conversely, Black males who perform well academically and exhibit different instincts are potentially labeled by same-race peers as selling out and acting White (Fordham & Ogbu, 1986). The likelihood of peer group acceptance or rejection, however, is not the only force that shapes masculine identity (Kunjufu, 1986; Steinberg et al., 1992).

In fact, Noguera (2003) adds that there is also an institutional dynamic at play. He writes, "[Black] males may engage in behaviors that contribute to their underachievement and marginality, but are more likely to be channeled into marginal roles and to be discouraged from challenging themselves by adults who are supposed to help them" (p. 452). Ferguson (2000) makes a similar argument, asserting that Black males display aggressive behavior because they are labeled as unsalvageable at the beginning of their educational experiences. In *Bad Boys: Public Schools in the Making of Black Masculinity*, Ferguson studies how institutional norms and procedures in the field of education are used to maintain a racial order, and how images and racial myths frame how individuals perceive themselves and others in a racial hierarchy.

Ferguson (2000) found evidence that the school environment contributes to the marginalization of Black boys. Specifically, labels such as *troublemakers* imposed by authorities (teachers, principals, staff) predispose Black boys to socially unaccepted and deviant life outcomes. Additionally, Ferguson found that Black boys in the study become less eager to persist in their fourth grade year and learn to model themselves after future professional athletes or Black men in urban neighborhoods at the same time. Unfortunately, this plan is shaped for them by contexts that have labeled them as unsalvageable.

Garibaldi (1992) argues that teachers play a seminal role in reversing unsalvageable perceptions as well as harmful academic and social behaviors of Black boys. However, he further contends that teachers are susceptible to internalizing and projecting negative stereotypes and myths to unfairly describe Black boys as a "monolithic group with little hope of survival and success" (p. 8). Garibaldi ultimately maintains that teacher locus may resist positive self-concepts and personal expectations among Black boys leading to disassociation with the learning experience. Similarly, hooks (2004b) recalls how Black boys were unfairly stereotyped despite excelling in schools:

> White teachers were not eager to teach Black boys and White parents were not eager to have Black boys sitting next to their sons and daughters. Suddenly, smart Black boys were invisible. When a "special" Black boy was allowed to be in the gifted classes it was only after he had proven himself to be appropriately subordinate. Always, he was the one smart boy who managed to excel, learned to be obedient, to keep his mouth shut. Smart Black boys who wanted to be heard, then and now, often find themselves cast out, deemed troublemakers, and placed in slow classes or in special classes that are mere containment cells for those deemed delinquent. Individual poor and working-class boys who excel academically in the public school system without surrendering their spirit and integrity usually make it because they have an advocate, a parent, parental caregiver, or teacher who intervenes when the biased educational system threatens them with destruction. (pp. 38–39)

Ferguson (2000) notes three key behaviors that emerge from the biased educational system hooks (2004b) mentions. These behaviors, Ferguson argues, provide evidence that Black boys, to a large degree, perceive manhood as a power struggle. The first behavior, heterosexual power (understood as male heterosexual), refers to the physical, biological, and representational differences to perform acts (i.e., physical touching) that define Black boys as perpetrators and Black girls as victims. Personal violations of heterosexual power include transgressive behaviors (i.e., same-sex curiosity and attraction). When Black boys want to show supreme contempt for another boy they call him a girl or liken his behavior to a girl's behavior (Ferguson, 2000). In general, transgressing rigidly heterosexual masculine codes likely results in victimization and alienation from Black boy cultures at school (Davis, 2000).

A second behavior involves usage of confrontational voice or classroom performances that engage and disrupt the normal direction of the flow of power. While Black boys use power to disrupt school standards and well-scripted roles in classrooms (i.e., constant noise, rapping, laughing, crumpling paper), schools negatively sanction these behaviors (Ferguson, 2007).

Furthermore, Black boy peer groups perceive these behaviors as lively, fun, exciting, and cool in an otherwise bland context (Davis, 1999). However, when Black males use confrontational voices in schools, the goal is likely to make a name for themselves (Ferguson, 2007). Harper (1996) adds that how Black boys use their voice becomes an identifying marker for masculinity and that "a too-evident facility in White idiom can quickly identify one as a White-identified Uncle Tom who must also be weak, effeminate, and probably a fag" (p. 11).

Black males potentially use the third behavior, fighting, as a mechanism to demonstrate mistrust of authority figures in school because of sociohistorical and present power relations in their communities (Ferguson, 2007). Ferguson's work further contends that fighting is usually either an exploratory site to construct media-endorsed manhood, a social practice of entertainment, or an attempt to scare others to avoid future confrontations. Black boys who show competence in fighting, participating in sports, teasing, and reporting actual or contrived sexual conquests are bestowed with greater privileges than those perceived as less adequate in these areas. Corbin and Pruitt (1999) write that Black boys turn to sexual promiscuity, machismo, risk taking, and aggressive social skills to compensate for feelings of insecurity in a Eurocentric world. Such insecurity likely manifests itself in changes in posture, clothing, dialect and language, walking style, and demeanor (Harris, 1995). Majors and Billson (1992) further characterize this behavior as a coping mechanism labeled *cool pose*, which they define as:

> the presentation of self that many [Black boys and] men use to establish their male identity. Cool pose is a ritualized form of masculinity that entails behaviors, scripts, physical posturing, expression management, and carefully crafted performances that deliver a single, critical message: pride, strength and control. (p. 4)

Majors and Billson (1992) argue that prior to college, Black boys learn early to project a facade of emotionlessness, fearlessness, and aloofness to counter the poor self-image and confidence expected from people of their race. Majors and Billson also suggest that the cool pose becomes pathological in a sense, or self-sustaining, because of its continued use as a coping mechanism. To view Black boys (and men) in only this light, however, is problematic. Scholars and activists write that the endorsement of a behaviorally restrictive or unidimensional conception of manhood, (i.e., tough guy, player of women) is viewed as dysfunctional in a cultural frame of racism and economic oppression (Hunter & Davis, 1992). Unfortunately, families either intentionally or unintentionally reinforce notions of unidimensional boyhood.

Black boys may also consider academic engagement less masculine because of how it is valued in families. In fact, hooks (2004b) argues that "soul-murdering" (p. 40) in families detrimentally affects the self-esteem of Black boys and potentially shames their authentic selves:

> In some [Black] families where reading is encouraged in girl children, a boy who likes to read is perceived as suspect, as on the road to being a "sissy." Certainly as long as [Black] people buy into the notion of patriarchal manhood, which says that real men are all body and no mind, [Black boys] who are cerebral, who want to read, and who love books will risk being ridiculed as not manly. (p. 40)

Hooks reflects on experiences in her home in which her brother was constantly humiliated by her father for "not measuring up to the standards of patriarchal maleness" (p. 89). Her suggestion that Black boys are valued and indulged for being male but also shamed for not conforming to acceptable "patriarchal boyhood" (p. 89) charges educational systems with failing to impart or inspire learning in Black boys. Both conditions infect the masculine identities of Black boys with powerlessness and hopelessness (hooks, 2004b).

Because of these early socialization experiences, researchers claim that Black men quickly understand the social rewards associated with exhibiting masculine behaviors and the derogatory name calling and peer disapproval associated with feminine behaviors (Davis, 2001; Ferguson, 2007). Discipline and retention trends support this assertion. For instance, Black boys have the highest suspension and dropout rates at elementary and high school levels. Widely, the academic performance of Black boys is lower than that of their White and Asian counterparts in urban and nonurban settings (Hrabowski, Maton, & Grief, 1998). These experiences subsequently inform Black men's collegiate perceptions. In fact, a number of well-rehearsed gender roles negatively correlate with Blacks men's collegiate perceptions by the time Black men reach traditional college age (Fleming, 1984; Polite & Davis, 1999).

Studies of Black Males and College Masculinities

For decades, gender-sensitive inquiry into the study of males in college, particularly Black males, has been slow to emerge. In general, studies of college men, manhood, and masculinities are emerging yet scarce across higher education and student development literature (Dancy, 2010b, 2011a, 2011b; Davis, 1999, 2002; Laker & Davis, 2011). Overall, current trends in research on Black men focus on two areas: how constructions of masculinity influence college gains and the group or fraternity dynamic influencing college manhood and masculinity.

Studying the nexus among masculinities and college gains, Czopp, Lasane, Sweigard, Bradshaw, and Hammer (1998) compared Black men enrolled in historically Black colleges and universities (HBCUs) to White men enrolled in predominantly White institutions (PWIs). The aim was to understand how these constructions affect the academic and social gains of men enrolled in four-year colleges. In both contexts, the authors found that men with pronounced masculine attributes who present themselves as unconcerned about academic performance on a test were evaluated by college students to be more socially attractive and more masculine than men who were concerned about test performance. In a related study, participants identified that men college students are more likely than women college students to present themselves with a disorganized academic self-presentation (Lasane, Sweigard, Czopp, Howard, & Burns, 2000). In addition, the study found that college students perceived an academically organized, studious student as less masculine and less socially attractive than a disorganized, less conscientious student. Additional studies consider the impact of different racial populations on the gender role development of Black men.

Davis (2013) studied the link between gender roles and collegiate engagement for Black men in an HBCU in the South and a PWI in the Midwest. Regression analyses indicated that gender role orientations (competitiveness and hypermasculinity) significantly predicted academic engagement behaviors. Black men at HBCUs scored higher than their peers at historically White colleges on subscales that measured hypermasculinity and antisocial behaviors/competitiveness, while there were no differences between groups on the mastery competitiveness subscale. Thus, specific aspects of masculinity were related to level of academic engagement.

Following qualitative study, Tatum and Charlton (2008) found four factors to be teachers of masculinity among college men: male authority figures, sports and competition, media and society, and influence of male peers. Tatum and Charlton's findings, notwithstanding the small sample size, emphasize how this phenomenon may not be easily measured quantitatively, as the delicacy and nuances of this topic require flexibility in gleaning the data. In another study, conceptualizations of masculinity included (a) dating and pursuing romantic or sexual relationships with women, (b) athletic activity (organized sports, individual exercise/bodybuilding), and (c) competition (Harper, 2007). When paired with Davis (1995), complexities among college men's masculinities and college achievement, retention and persistence are more apparent.

The pathological perception that Black men in groups evoke fear, suspicion, and concern has provided a backdrop for investigations of masculinity primarily in Black Greek-letter fraternities (Jones, 2004; McClure, 2006). In these groups, elusive gender normative scripts demand masculine behaviors that are reflections of those ideals (Kimmel & Messner, 2007). Like Black men's groups throughout American history, groups of Black college men (i.e., fraternities, friendship groups) are found to enact a more amalgamated definition of *manhood* in which African ideals of community largely blend with Eurocentric notions about capitalism and American patriarchy (McClure, 2006).

Men's groups are additionally found to endorse hegemonic masculinity or behaviors and actions that reflect patriarchal ideals and may reflect the following types of thinking in college: (a) homophobia, the fear or hatred of nonheterosexual men; (b) devaluing femininity; (c) increasing masculine bravado; and (d) claiming masculine space in spaces deemed feminine or feminized (Anderson, 2007). Men are potentially encouraged by men's groups to treat women as sexual objects to confirm heterosexuality, but this also prevents true intimacy with women (Capraro, 2007). Therefore, a hegemonic masculine script likely offers little room for Black men's vulnerabilities, grievances, and emotions in contexts (i.e., men's groups, teams, and fraternities) purporting to accommodate them.

In *Black Haze: Violence, Sacrifice, and Manhood in Black Greek-Letter Fraternities*, Jones (2004) suggests that Black men enact ritualized aggression on each other to shape and define masculine identity among aspiring fraternity members. Fraternity rituals, which are largely traced to the sacrificial rituals of ancient times, are found to establish prevalence and relevance for individual and collective Black male identity (Jones, 2004). Additionally, Jones suggests that Black men in fraternities experience pressures to shape a four-dimensional masculinity that is "cool," "hard," "down," and "real" (Jones, 2004, p. 108). These descriptors endorse ideas that Black men who are in control and unemotional are authentic Black men. The social locations of these ideals are not far removed from historical constructions of Black men as beasts, bucks, and Sambos (Dancy, 2012). Presently, pathologies constructed around Black men create little difference in how society regards *unacceptable* groups of Black men (e.g., gangs) and *acceptable* groups of Black men (e.g., Black collegiate Greek-letter fraternities). In both groups, linguistic and physical violence represent a subconscious need in Black men to shape a definition of manhood that bonds men (Jones, 2004). While these issues are important, the knowledge that Black males potentially enter college with an oppositional identity also has implications for colleges that seek to engage and retain them.

Background of the Study

The Brother Code: Manhood and Masculinity Among Black Men in College (Dancy, 2012), details a larger qualitative study that investigated Black manhood in college and the institutional role in shaping these constructions. Grounded theory, phenomenological, and case study approaches complemented micro- and macrolevels of data analysis. More specifically, grounded theory guided participant selection and initial coding of data, while phenomenological and case study methods guided categorical and contextual analyses.

The men selected for this study attended 12 four-year colleges situated across the 19 southern and border states of America. Arguably, these states continued to operate dual systems of higher education despite Title VI of the Civil Rights Act of 1964 barring legalized segregation (Brown, 1999). The 12 institutional sites for this study were selected according to their Carnegie (2010) classification. Using the latest classifications, doctorate-granting institutions, master's institutions, and baccalaureate institutions were selected. These institutions were disaggregated according to their historical and predominant student population (HBCUs and PWIs) and institutional funding (public, private). This matrix resulted in four colleges per Carnegie classification. Given this site selection design, tribal colleges and special-focus institutions were ineligible.

Twenty-four men enrolled in four-year colleges and universities were selected to participate in the study. Respondents were Black, traditional college-age (18–24), and upperclassmen (sophomores, juniors, and seniors). The participants were majoring across a breadth of disciplines, maintained at least a 2.5 grade point average (GPA) and were involved, or engaged, students in college. This study's understanding of engagement is from Chickering and Gamson's (1987) seven principles (e.g., student-faculty contact, cooperation among students) of student activities that reflect good institutional practice. Therefore, activities reflecting good institutional practice may include using an institution's human resources, curricular and extracurricular programs or organizations, and other opportunities for learning and development.

Data were gathered in face-to-face interviews; the average interview lasted over two hours. Interviews were reviewed for accuracy and then compared with my journals. In general, the interview instrument prompts and protocols were modified as appropriate to inform research questions. Specifically, the interview instrument to gather this data partially included questions from Terenzini and colleagues' (1992) transitions to college interview instrument that assessed participant precollege, in-class, and out-of-class experiences in college. Questions from this instrument included, What is it like for you as a Black man getting used to life as a student at (institution)?

and Are Black men valued here? If no, who is valued? In what ways? If yes, in what ways? Other questions included, What identities have been significant for you as you grew up? and Tell me what went into your decisions to go to college? Additional questions were informed by theory and research on Black male behavior and identity development in schools and colleges.

Grounded theory guided participant selection and initial coding of data. A rigorous coding technique described by Charmaz (2006) was used to keep codes close to data and provide responses on how and why participant experiences were as they described. In addition, phenomenological methods were used to add rigor to the analysis of the interviews. After an initial coding, statements were compared with the research questions to discover horizons, or perspectives on identity development in college (Moustakas, 1994). Last, case study methodologies were elected to draw contextual understandings (HBCUs and PWIs); I drew heavily on the process of *correspondence* (Stake, 1995), which Stake defines as the search for patterns or consistency that emerge when data are aggregated.

Patterns were grouped across respondents' collegiate classification (i.e., Carnegie classification; collegiate funding type, public versus private; and collegiate context, for example, HBCU versus historically White) to display themes that are consistent across these categories. After conducting analysis on each interview, textural-structural descriptions of spiritual identity constructions and collegiate experiences were compiled for each participant. Textural-structural descriptions, which entail the whats and hows of experiences (Moustakas, 1994), captured the themes of each participant's interview and were e-mailed to participants to serve as vehicles for member checking.

Manhood and Masculinity: Identity, Behavior, and the In Between

As other scholars, I have found manhood a multidimensional concept referring to the self-expectations, relationships and responsibilities to family, and worldviews or existential philosophies that men accept or acknowledge (Dancy, 2010b, 2011a, 2011b; Hunter & Davis 1992). Unsurprisingly, manhood development is informed by intersecting raced, gendered, classed, sexual-oriented, religious, and other realities. Manhood is identity based, a state of being, unlike masculinity, which is behavior based, or a state of doing. Masculinity refers to the observable enactments, affectations, and performances men use to honor or dishonor their manhood. Dislodging these two concepts forces us to see how the two are linked but are not the same, just as identity and behavior are linked but not the same. Separating these concepts requires researchers to study not only expressions or behaviors but the constructed meanings that inform, undergird, or are potentially concealed by these behaviors (see Figure

9.1). Hunter and Davis (1992) also note this difference in the observation that Black men understand manhood in multiple arenas and contexts within and beyond traditional notions of masculinity and the male role.

Masculinity and femininity are not separate personality traits assigned to either men or women. Rather, perceptions of men and women as masculine or feminine reflect cultural stereotypes as opposed to psychological realities (Bem, 1987; Constantinople, 1973). Therefore, bodies can exhibit both masculine and feminine behaviors. Unfortunately, the curious dislocation of gender and femininity in men's studies' push for the study of masculinities potentially confuses the masculinity-femininity dialectic.

The body is a vessel for which there is a "materialization of possibilities" (Butler, 1990b, p. 272), and often the ways the possibilities emerge are through the body performance—masculinity (Alexander, 2006; Butler, 1990a, 1990b, 1995; Courtenay, 2000; Kimmel, 2002). Furthermore, performance is the presentation of the body itself in its stylized repetition of acts that are socially validated and discursively established (Butler, 1990b). The ways that Black male bodies move in fulfilling goals and desires in social contexts are replete with complex negotiations of the real and the authentic. In *Performing Black Masculinity*, Alexander (2006) argues:

> The Black male body is [controversial]. It is a site of public and private contestation. . . . The diversity that exists within the character of the Black man is not acknowledged, hence he is relegated to a stereotypically pathologized position, in which any variation of performance might be constructed as inauthentic or not being real, passing for something that he is not. (p. 74)

Inhabiting masculinity as a space of performance also brings to mind the previously mentioned cool pose idea (Majors & Billson, 1992). Notwithstanding, adherence to the code makes cultural borders between groups

Figure 9.1 Conceptual Framework for Manhood and Masculinity

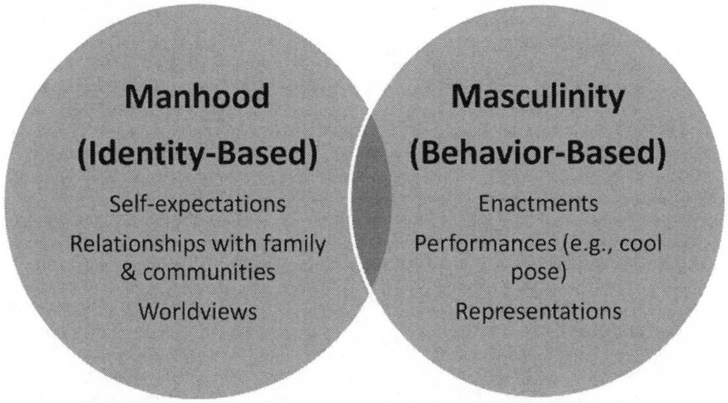

**Manhood
(Identity-Based)**

Self-expectations

Relationships with family & communities

Worldviews

**Masculinity
(Behavior-Based)**

Enactments

Performances (e.g., cool pose)

Representations

more discernible, separates us from them, and enables individuals to connect or identify with others in similar positions (Rhoads, 1994).

The model is robust across my analyses of Black masculine experiences. One compelling example is the way mothers and fathers differentially affect manhood and masculinity in their sons. While the hegemonic strongholds of manhood development, or the brother code, would not allow the men to credit their mothers with teaching manhood, mothers or women guardians clearly were responsible for shaping the major themes of manhood reported in this chapter. Notwithstanding, the men insisted fathers taught them how to be men when directly asked but struggled to locate the lessons. Beyond this question, mothers were clearly identified as teachers of the themes of manhood emergent in the study. In contrast, fathers or men guardians were linked to teaching masculinity, or the demonstrations, enactments, and performances of men (Dancy, 2012).

Implications and Conclusion

This model requires common thought and consideration among all educational personnel—in schools, colleges, and other settings—who care about the educational experiences of Black males. Related to masculine identity, many strategies capture the attention of school administrators, local communities, and parents as possible solutions to the problems associated with Black males in public schools. First, mentoring programs that assign professional Black men as role models for young boys, typically in elementary and middle schools, have been established in many school districts, urban and suburban. Second, teachers play a critical role in reversing Black boys' academic and social behaviors that conflict with educational achievement. Teachers are leaders of the classroom experience, and the messages teachers consciously or subconsciously give to Black males will manifest themselves in Black male's perceptions of schools and American society. Counselors must also refrain from stereotypical thinking about the intellectual capacity and aptitude of Black males. Additionally, there are a number of implications for postsecondary educational settings.

This research joins with previous research that encourages institutions to mine the sources for improving institutional context and climate (Altbach, Lomotey, & Rivers, 2002; antonio, 2004; Bowman & Smith, 2002; Brown & Freeman, 2004; Cabrera, Nora, Terenzini, Pascarella, & Hagedorn, 1999; Dancy, 2010a; Hurtado, Milem, Clayton-Pedersen, & Allen, 1998). Postsecondary institutional efforts to deconstruct oppressive environments are salient for Black male retention and the elimination of stereotypes. My studies (Dancy, 2011a, 2011b, 2012) clearly discover suspicions that college faculty, other college personnel, and students reference stereotypes as ways of knowing Black men. Stereotypes attempting to authentically locate Black male identities have no place in college and only fuel divisiveness among students (Dancy, 2012). Stereotypes include, but are not limited to, former gang member, soft, hard, hypersexual, sexually endowed, nerd, sell-out, dangerous, pimp, athlete, player, stupid, lazy, criminal, or thug. All Black men deserve an equal opportunity, as does any student group, to feel entitled to institutional resources deemed good institutional practice. The delivery of these resources should not reflect a colonized institutional axiology of intolerance, closedness, and presumptuousness.

As is the case in the K–12 settings, mentoring is salient for Black men in college; it builds Black male worldviews, particularly through communal notions of giving back (Dancy, 2012). In addition, the strongest mentoring relationships must provide spaces for disclosure, vulnerability, and coping. Culturally relevant mentoring models, such as those in the work of Brown, Davis, and McClendon (1999), provide three options in mentoring and advising relationships toward eliminating unintended assumptions. The first option, academic midwifery, involves college personnel assisting students in producing new ideas and intellectual insights. The second option, role molding, involves college personnel taking an active role in shaping intellectual and professional aspirations. The third option, *frientoring*, infuses a friendly relationship into the faculty, administrative, and staff posture with students (Brown et al., 1999). In addition, colleges must challenge the notion that it takes a man to mentor a man. While the embodied experience matters more or less, women demonstrate compelling ability to shape Black men's understandings of themselves as men (Dancy, 2012).

The critical finding about women, particularly Black men's mothers, also implicates collegiate practice on what these institutions expect from male mentors. Indeed, mothering matters. *Mothering* is defined as treating a person with kindness and affection, trying to protect him or her from anything dangerous or difficult, and nurturing (Brown & Davis, 2000). Mothers, grandmothers, and even college personnel who "mother" largely influence Black manhood development in college (Dancy, 2012). Thus, male mentors may learn from women's and feminist approaches in mentoring. Underwood (2000), who is a Black man, describes his epiphany about how mothering has no gender and is also a call to action for men:

> Looking back over the past ten years, I have learned that motherhood is not necessarily determined by gender. . . . In Black families, roles are often flexible, with a support system to help adjust, meet, and cope with life demands. . . . The Black male has multiple cultural roles to play. . . . Primary care-giving, mentoring, modeling, nurturing, and assessing were probably the most important responsibilities for me as a mother (p. 47).

Finally, what works for students' educational best is in many ways incompatible with what works for many Black males. It may be a burden for education workers to add to and constantly rethink how they deliver education to Black males. However, the implications in this chapter are likely relevant across student groups. A turbulent history of exclusion, a changing national populace, and the federal policy landscape demand change and accountability.

References

Alexander, B. K. (2006). *Performing Black masculinity: Race, culture, and non-heterosexual identity.* Lanham, MD: AltaMira.

Allen, W. R. (1988). The education of Black students on White college campuses: What quality the experiences? In M. Nettles (Ed.), *Toward Black undergraduate student equality in American higher education* (pp. 57–86). Albany, NY: SUNY Press.

Allen, W. R., Griffin, K. A., Jayakumar, U. M., Kimura-Walsh, E. F., & Wolf, D. S. (2007, April). *Ebony and the ivory tower: Trends in the socioeconomic status, achievement, and self-concept of Black male freshmen between 1971 and 2004.* Paper presented at a meeting of the American Education Research Association, Chicago, IL.

Altbach, P. G., Lomotey, K., & Rivers, S. (2002). Race in higher education: The continuing crisis. In W. A. Smith, P. G. Altbach, & K. Lomotey (Eds.), *The racial crisis in American higher education* (pp. 23–42). Albany, NY: SUNY Press.

Anderson, E. (2007). Orthodox and inclusive masculinity: Competing masculinities among heterosexual men in a feminized terrain. In M. Kimmel & M. Messner (Eds.), *Men's lives* (7th ed., pp. 208–220). Boston, MA: Allyn & Bacon.

antonio, a. (2004). When does race matter in college friendships? Exploring men's diverse and homogeneous friendship groups. *The Review of Higher Education, 27*(4), 553–575.

Bem, S. L. (1987). Masculinity and femininity exist only in the mind of the perceiver. In J. M. Reinisch, L. A. Rosenblum, & S. A. Sanders (Eds.), *Masculinity/femininity: Basic perspectives* (pp. 304–311). New York, NY: Oxford University Press.

Billson, J. M. (1996). *Pathways to manhood: Young Black males struggle for identity.* New Brunswick, NJ: Transaction.

Bonner, F. (2010). *Academically gifted African American male college students.* Santa Barbara, CA: Praeger.

Bowman, P., & Smith, W. A. (2002). Racial ideology in the campus community: Emerging cross-ethnic differences and challenges. In W. A. Smith, P. G. Altbach, & K. Lomotey (Eds.), *The racial crisis in American higher education: Continuing challenges for the twenty-first century* (pp. 103–120). New York, NY: SUNY Press.

Brown, M. C. (1999). *The quest to define collegiate desegregation: Black Colleges, Title VI compliance, and post-Adams litigation.* Westport, CT: Bergin & Garvey.

Brown, M. C., Dancy, T. E., & Davis, J. E. (2007). Drowning beneath a rising tide: The common plight of public schools, disadvantaged students, and African American males. In S. P. Robinson & M. C. Brown (Eds.), *The children Hurricane*

Katrina left behind: Schooling contexts, professional preparation, and community politics (pp. 54–72). New York, NY: Peter Lang.

Brown, M. C., Dancy, T. E., & Davis, J. E. (2013). *Educating African American males: Contexts for consideration, possibilities for practice.* New York, NY: Peter Lang.

Brown, M. C., & Davis, J. E. (2000). *Black sons to mothers: Compliments, critiques, and challenges for cultural workers in education.* New York, NY: Peter Lang.

Brown, M. C., Davis, G. L., & McClendon, S. A. (1999). Mentoring graduate students of color: Myths, models, and modes. *Peabody Journal of Education, 74*(2), 105–118.

Brown, M. C., & Freeman, K. (2004). *Black colleges: New policies and perspectives for practice.* Westport, CT: Praeger.

Brown, M. C., & Hurst, T. (2004). *Educational attainment of African American males post-Brown v. Board of Education.* Washington, DC: Frederick D. Patterson Institute of the United Negro College Fund.

Butler, J. (1990a). *Gender trouble: Feminism and the subversion of identity.* New York: Routledge.

Butler, J. (1990b). Performative acts and gender constitution: An essay in phenomenology and feminist theory. In S. E. Case (Ed.), *Performing feminisms: Feminist critical theory and theatre* (pp. 270–282). Baltimore, MD: Johns Hopkins University.

Butler, J. (1995). Contingent foundations. In S. Benhabib, J. Butler, D. Cornell, & N. Fraser (Eds.), *Feminist contentions* (pp. 35–57). New York, NY: Routledge.

Cabrera, A. F., Nora, A., Terenzini, P. T., Pascarella, E., & Hagedorn, L. S. (1999). Campus racial climate and the adjustment of students to college. *Journal of Higher Education, 70*(2), 134–160.

Capraro, R. L. (2007). Why college men drink: Alcohol, adventure, and the paradox of masculinity. In M. Kimmel & M. Messner (Eds.), *Men's lives* (7th ed., pp. 182–195). Boston, MA: Allyn & Bacon.

Carnegie Foundation for the Advancement of Teaching. (2010). *Classification descriptions.* Retrieved from http://classifications.carnegiefoundation.org/descriptions/

Charmaz, K. (2006). *Constructing grounded theory: A practical guide through qualitative analysis.* Thousand Oaks, CA: Sage.

Chickering, A. W., & Gamson, Z. F. (1987). Seven principles for good practice in undergraduate education. *AAHE Bulletin, 39*(7), 3–7.

Chodorow, N. (1978). *The reproduction of mothering.* Berkeley: University of California.

Constantinople, A. (1973). Masculinity-femininity: An exception to a famous dictum. *Psychological Bulletin, 80*(5), 389–407.

Corbin, S. K., & Pruitt, R. L. (1999). Who am I? The development of the African American male identity. In V. Polite & J. E. Davis (Eds.), *African American males in school and society: Practices and policies for effective education* (pp. 68–81). New York, NY: Teachers College Press.

Cose, E. (2003). *The envy of the world: On being a Black man in America.* New York, NY: Simon & Schuster.

Courtenay, W. H. (2000). Constructions of masculinity and their influence on men's well-being: A theory of gender of health. *Social Science and Medicine, 50*(10), 1385–1401.

Cuyjet, M. (2006). *African American men in college.* San Francisco, CA: Jossey-Bass.

Czopp, A. M., Lasane, T. P., Sweigard, P. N., Bradshaw, S. D., & Hammer, E. D. (1998). Masculine styles of self-presentation in the classroom: Perceptions of Joe Cool. *Journal of Social Behavior and Personality, 13*(2), 281–294.

Dancy, T. E. (2010a). *Managing diversity: (Re)visioning equity on college campuses.* New York, NY: Peter Lang.

Dancy, T. E. (2010b). Manhood and masculinities in college: Connecting theory and research to practice. In T. E. Dancy (Ed.), *Managing diversity: (Re)Visioning equity on college campuses* (pp. 159–180). New York, NY: Peter Lang.

Dancy, T. E. (2011a). African American males, manhood, and college life: Learning from the intersections. *College Student Affairs Journal, 29*(1), 17–32.

Dancy, T. E. (2011b). Colleges in the making of manhood and masculinity: Gendered perspectives on African American males. *Gender and Education, 23*(4), 477–495.

Dancy, T. E. (2012). *The brother code: Manhood and masculinity among African American males in college.* Charlotte, NC: Information Age.

Dancy, T. E., & Brown, M. C. (2007). Unintended consequences: African American male educational attainment and collegiate perceptions after Brown v. Board of Education. *American Behavioral Scientist, 51*(7), 984–1003.

Dancy, T. E., & Brown, M. C. (2012). *African American males and education: Researching the convergence of race and identity.* Charlotte, NC: Information Age.

Davis, J. E. (1994). College in Black and White: The academic experiences of African American males. *Journal of Negro Education, 63*(4), 620–633.

Davis, J. E. (1995, April). *Campus climate, gender, and achievement of African American college males.* Paper presented at the annual meeting of the Association for the Study of Higher Education, Orlando, FL.

Davis, J. E. (1999). What does gender have to do with the experience of African American College men? In V. Polite & J. E. Davis (Eds.), *African American males in school and society: Policies and practices for effective education* (pp. 134–148). New York, NY: Teachers College Press.

Davis, J. E. (2000). Mothering for manhood: The (re)production of a Black son's gendered self. In M. C. Brown & J. E. Davis (Eds.), *Black sons to mothers: Compliments, critiques, and challenges for cultural workers in education* (pp. 51–70). New York, NY: Peter Lang.

Davis, J. E. (2001). Black boys in school: Negotiating masculinities and race. In R. Majors (Ed.), *Educating our Black children: New directions and radical approaches* (pp. 169–182). New York, NY: RoutledgeFalmer.

Davis, J. E. (2013). Negotiating masculinity in college: African American males and academic engagement. In M.C. Brown II, T.E. Dancy, and J. E. Davis, (Eds.), *Educating African American males: Contexts for consideration, possibilities for practice,* (53–66). New York: Peter Lang.

Davis, T. L. (2002). Voices of gender role conflict: The social construction of college men's identity. *Journal of College Student Development, 43*(4), 508–521.

Ferguson, A. A. (2000). *Bad boys: Public schools in the making of Black male masculinity*. Ann Arbor: University of Michigan Press.

Ferguson, A. A. (2007). Making a name for yourself: Transgressive acts and gender performance. In M. Kimmel & M. Messner (Eds.), *Men's lives* (7th ed., pp. 154–166). Boston: Allyn & Bacon.

Fleming, J. (1984). *Blacks in college*. San Francisco, CA: Jossey-Bass.

Fordham, S., & Ogbu, J. U. (1986). Black students' school success: Coping with the "burden of acting White." *The Urban Review, 18*(3), 179–205.

Garibaldi, A. (1992). Educating and motivating African American males to succeed. *Journal of Negro Education, 61*(1), 4–11.

Harper, P. B. (1996). *Are we not men? Masculine anxiety and the problem of African-American identity*. New York, NY: Oxford University Press.

Harper, S. (2006). Peer support for African American male college achievement: Beyond internalized racism and the burden of "acting White." *Journal of Men's Studies, 14*(3), 337–358.

Harper, S. R. (2007). The measure of a man: Conceptualizations of masculinity among high-achieving African American male college students. In M. Kimmel & M. Messner (Eds.), *Men's lives* (7th ed., pp. 89–107). Boston, MA: Allyn & Bacon.

Harper, S. (2009). Niggers no more: A critical race counternarrative on Black male student achievement at predominantly White colleges and universities. *International Journal of Qualitative Studies in Education, 22*(6),697–712.

Harper, S. (2012). *Black male student success in higher education: A report from the National Black Male College Achievement Study*. Philadelphia: University of Pennsylvania, Center for the Study of Race and Equity in Education.

Harris, F. (1995). Psychosocial development and Black male masculinity: Implications for counseling economically disadvantaged African American male adolescents. *Journal of Counseling Development, 73*, 279–287.

hooks, b. (2004a). *The will to change: Men, masculinity, and love*. New York, NY: Atria Books.

hooks, b. (2004b). *We real cool: Black men and masculinity*. New York, NY: Routledge.

Hrabowski, F. A., III., Maton, K. L., & Grief, G. L. (1998). *Beating the odds: Raising academically successful African American males*. New York, NY: Oxford University Press.

Hunter, A., & Davis, J. E. (1992). Constructing gender: An exploration of Afro-American men's conceptualization of manhood. *Gender and Society, 6*(3), 464–479.

Hurtado, S., Milem, J. F., Clayton-Pedersen, A. R., & Allen, W. R. (1998). Enhancing campus climates for racial/ethnic diversity: Educational policy and practice. *Review of Higher Education, 21*(3), 279–302.

Jones, R. L. (2004). *Black haze: Violence, sacrifice, and manhood in Black Greek-letter fraternities*. Albany, NY: SUNY Press.

Kimmel, M. (2002). Global masculinities: Restoration and resistance. In B. Pease & K. Pringle (Eds.), *A man's world? Changing men's practices in a globalized world* (Vol. 4, pp. 21–38). London, UK: Zed Books.

Kimmel, M., & Messner, M. (Eds.). (2007). *Men's lives* (7th ed.). Boston, MA: Pearson.

Kunjufu, J. (1986). *Countering the conspiracy to destroy Black boys*. Chicago, IL: Afro American Publishing.

Laker, J. A., & Davis, T. (2011). *Masculinities in higher education: Theoretical and practical considerations.* New York, NY: Routledge.

Lasane, T., Sweigard, P., Czopp, A., Howard, W., & Burns, M. (2000). The effects of student academic presentation on gender and sociability. *North American Journal of Psychology, 1*(2), 229–242.

Majors, R., & Billson, J. M. (1992). *Cool pose: The dilemmas of Black manhood in America.* New York, NY: Lexington Books.

McClure, S. (2006). Voluntary association membership: Black Greek men on a predominantly White campus. *Journal of Higher Education, 77*(6), 1036–1057.

Moustakas, C. (1994). *Phenomenological research methods.* Thousand Oaks, CA: Sage.

Noguera, P. A. (2003). The trouble with Black boys: The role and influence of environmental and cultural factors on the academic performance of African American males. *Urban Education, 38*(4), 431–459.

Palmer, R. T., & Wood, L. (2012). *Black men in college: Implications for HBCUs and beyond.* New York, NY: Routledge.

Polite, V. & Davis, J. E. (1999). *African American males in school and society: Practices and policies for effective education.* New York, NY: Teachers College Press.

Rhoads, R. A. (1994). *Coming out in college: The struggle for a non-heterosexual identity.* Westport, CT: Bergin & Garvey.

Sewell, T. (1997, April). *Teacher attitude: Who's afraid of the big Black boys?* Paper presented at the annual meeting of the American Educational Research Association, Chicago, IL.

Stake, R. E. (1995). *The art of case study research.* Thousand Oaks, CA: Sage.

Steinberg, L., Dornbusch, S. M., & Brown, B. B. (1992). Ethnic differences in adolescent achievement: An ecological perspective. *American Psychologist, 45*(8), 347–355.

Strayhorn, T. (2008). The role of supportive relationships in facilitating African American males' success in college. *NASPA Journal, 45*(1), 26–48.

Strayhorn, T. (2010). When race and gender collide: Social and cultural capital's influence on the academic achievement of African American and Latino males. *Review of Higher Education, 33*(3), 307–332.

Tatum, J. L., & R. Charlton. (2008). A phenomenological study of how selected college men construct and define masculinity. *Higher Education in Review, 5,* 99–126.

Taylor, R. (1989). Black youth, role models, and the social construction of identity. In R. Jones (Ed.), *Black adolescents* (pp. 155–174). Berkley, CA: Cobb & Henry.

Terenzini, P. T., Allison, K. W., Millar, S. B., Rendon, L. I., Upcraft, M. L., Gregg, P., et al. (1992). *The Transition to College Project: Final report.* University Park, PA: Pennsylvania State University, National Center on Postsecondary Teaching, Learning, and Assessment.

Underwood, E. (2000). From son to mother?: Intellectualizing the personal. In M. C. Brown & J. E. Davis (Eds.), *Black sons to mothers* (pp. 35–50). New York, NY: Peter Lang.

Wainrib, B. R. (1992). *Gender issues across the lifecycle.* New York, NY: Springer.

Wright, R. (2005). *Black boy.* New York, NY: HarperCollins. (Original work published 1945)

10

EXPLORATORY STUDY OF THE FACTORS AFFECTING THE ACADEMIC AND CAREER DEVELOPMENT OF AFRICAN AMERICAN MALES IN SCIENCE, TECHNOLOGY, ENGINEERING, AND MATHEMATICS

James L. Moore III, Lamont A. Flowers, and Lawrence O. Flowers

The importance of increasing the representation of African American males in the science, technology, engineering, and mathematics (STEM) workforce is well established in the scholarly literature (Beede et al., 2011; Flowers, Moore, Flowers, & Clarke, 2011; Moore, 2006; Williamson, 2010). Despite the fact that national estimates suggest that STEM jobs will proliferate throughout the next decade (Beede et al., 2011; Langdon, McKittrick, Beede, Khan, & Doms, 2011), African American males are still underrepresented among college students and recent graduates in the STEM fields. In 2010, African American males represented about 6%

This study was supported by two grants from the National Science Foundation (HRD-0929148 and HRD-1332555).

of males earning degrees in science and engineering (National Science Foundation, 2013). According to data from the National Science Foundation, the number of bachelor's degrees awarded to African American males in science and engineering fields increased from 12,018 to 15,852 between the years 2001 and 2010 (National Science Foundation, 2013). While the number of African American male graduates in STEM has increased since 2001, this percentage remains disproportionately low compared with the percentage of males from other racial groups for the same period.

In a recent article, Esters and Toldson (2013) indicated that African American males are underrepresented in STEM degree programs compared with their representation in the United States. Additionally, Reid (2013) found that African American males in STEM disciplines had lower grade point averages than African American males majoring in non-STEM disciplines. To explain these trends in STEM education, prior research has sought to identify critical factors that influenced the recruitment, retention, graduation, and career development outcomes of African American males (Flowers et al., 2011; Moore, 2006). For example, to increase the likelihood that African American males graduate with STEM degrees, Williamson (2010) suggested that higher education administrators and student affairs professionals should attempt to enhance African American male students' social experiences on campus. Harper (2010) identified factors that positively influence African American males' success in STEM at postsecondary institutions, such as participation in minority student organizations. Toldson and Esters (2012) found that more than half of the African American males in their multi-institutional study reported that they were prepared to enter a career following graduation. Though this finding is noteworthy, many of the African American males who participated in their study were not as confident in their future job prospects following graduation.

Previous studies have investigated the challenges faced by African American male college students in STEM disciplines and have explored various topics, such as economic issues, institutional barriers, academic readiness, limited career development opportunities, and negative stereotypes (Hrabowski, Maton, & Grief, 1998; Moore, 2006; Owens, Lacey, Rawls, & Holbert-Quince, 2010; Palmer & Maramba, 2011). Researchers also suggest that having African American male role models in academic settings enables African American male students to interact with individuals who understand the difficulties of pursuing a STEM degree as well as how to navigate academic and social challenges on campus (Gasman, 2011; Moore, Flowers, Guion, Zhang, & Staten, 2004). Moreover, African American male STEM college faculty may be able to provide African

American male STEM students with strategies on how to succeed in higher education while mitigating potential obstacles pertaining to race and gender (Gasman, 2011; Griffin, Pérez, Holmes, & Mayo, 2010). In light of previous research that suggests we need to examine issues that impact African American males in STEM disciplines (Lundy-Wagner, 2013), we conducted a qualitative study. The purpose of the study was to investigate the academic and career development experiences of African American male college students in STEM disciplines and to explore the impact of individual- and institutional-level factors on African American males' persistence in STEM degree programs.

Methods

To develop the methodology, we reviewed several studies regarding the impact of race on educational outcomes (Pascarella & Terenzini, 2005). Collectively, this area of research suggests that students' perceptions of their academic experiences informs their social experiences and affects their educational outcomes. Moreover, a salient theme embedded throughout the scholarly literature highlights the importance of strong academic and social support networks (Adelman, 2006; Coleman, 1988; Crosnoe, 2004; Moore, 2006; Reid & Moore, 2008). Consistent with this assertion, White and Glick (2000) described the relationship between students' social capital and their educational outcomes. Additionally, González, Stoner, and Jovel (2003) found that academic enrichment experiences, such as participation in honors classes, gifted and talented programs, and advanced placement courses, positively influenced students' social capital. Stated differently, increased social capital, obtained from school programs and personnel, enhanced educational opportunities for those students who had access to challenging academic opportunities, exposure to information that stimulates career interests in STEM fields, and supportive educational environments, are strong predictors of student outcomes in STEM.

To investigate the primary issues in this study, we interviewed 30 African American male STEM students from a historically Black college and university. Using the grounded theory approach (Glaser & Straus, 1967; Lincoln & Guba, 1985), which enables researchers to collect and analyze data simultaneously to develop theoretical and thematic explanations, the aim of this qualitative study was to explore African American male students' perceptions of their academic and career development experiences. Consistent with prior research assessing college students (Pascarella & Terenzini, 2005), we also examined students' precollege experiences, perceptions of institutional characteristics, and social experiences. Qualitative research strategies advanced by Jorgensen (1989) were utilized to analyze our data. During the research process, we relied heavily on the transcripts for analyzing the interview data and the data from the completed biographical questionnaires. Additionally, the qualitative study used constant comparative approaches (Glaser & Strauss, 1967; Lincoln & Guba, 1985; Miles & Huberman, 1984; Strauss & Corbin, 1990). Individual interviews ranged from 45 minutes to 1 hour.

As a way of enhancing the overall quality of the data obtained, we also employed traditional qualitative research techniques to increase the reliability and validity of the research process (Miles & Huberman, 1984; Strauss & Corbin, 1990). For example, to enhance dependability in our research, we spent sufficient time with the study's participants to check for discrepancies in responses, verified the accuracy of participants' responses with existing literature, and explored each participant's experience meticulously (Lincoln & Guba, 1985; Rubin & Rubin, 1995). After closely reviewing and analyzing the data, the following themes emerged: (a) family influence and encouragement, (b) K–12 academic experiences, (c) educational interests and career aspirations, (d) academic experiences in college, and (e) relationships with peers, teachers, and college faculty. In the next section, we explain each theme. Quotations from select participants were included where appropriate to capture the essence of the other participants' views and support the particular theme. The exploratory framework, as shown in Figure 10.1, provides an analytical lens for better understanding the factors affecting the academic and career development of African American males pursuing STEM degrees. Additionally, the framework sheds light on the important elements that we need to integrate into the strategies designed to increase the representation and success of African American males pursuing STEM degrees.

Results

Family Influence and Encouragement

The research literature suggests that families play a major role in African American male students' academic and career decisions (Herndon & Moore, 2002; Moore, 2006). For African American male college students, families provide different types and levels of assistance to students. Guidance, support, and encouragement are some of the kinds of assistance provided by families (Moore, 2006). Such assistance and involvement have been shown

Figure 10.1 Academic and Career Development Framework for African American Males in STEM

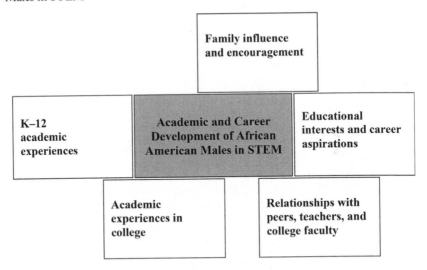

to positively influence African American males as they relate to these students' academic and career development outcomes (Flowers et al., 2011; Moore, 2006). Researchers have also found that students perform better in STEM, when their parents are engaged in their education (Moore, 2006). For this study, many of the African American males described the significant role their family played in their academic and career development. During one interview, an African American male student stated, "In 2008, I had a son born, and my whole thing is if I don't take care of him who else will. What got me to where I am has a lot to do with [the] expectations [of] my family [which] was set for me very early on." Another participant noted the importance of encouragement and support:

> I've got a little brother, and I know, when I was in high school, [that] I really didn't have nobody to actually [help me with planning and preparing for STEM]. He told me now he's going to be a doctor, but I didn't have nobody who actually [asked me] why or make sure this what you want to do. . . . I know my mother believes in me and wants me to be successful. I talk to her all the time, so I know I have support. Basically, I can't let her down.

K–12 Academic Experiences

Clewell, Anderson, and Thorpe (1992) wrote, "The greatest influence on the size and quality of the science and engineering work force is the precollege experience" (p. 15). When asked about their precollege experiences, African American males highlighted the importance of teachers and particular academic experiences as being influential in their decisions to choose to pursue a STEM degree. Pertaining to the importance of precollege experiences, one participant stated, "I was fortunate enough to grow up in one of the [top] four counties in Virginia, known for education around the U.S. It [my school] is very technological driven." In several interviews, African American males illustrated critical incidents and individuals who affected their schooling experiences prior to college. For example, a student noted: "I was fortunate to go to a good high school. It was based on your [academic] talent and ambitious goals."

For many years, researchers have examined the interrelationships between students' academic perceptions, experiences, and interactions with others in school settings to understand the critical set of real and perceived factors that influence academic motivation (Schunk, 1996; Strauss & Corbin, 1990; Vanderstoep, Pintrich, & Fagerlin, 1996). Because academic motivation tends to affect academic achievement, this area of research has been fundamental to our understanding of African American males' cognitive and psychosocial development in STEM disciplines. Viewed collectively, this body of research has attempted to explain how students negotiate their academic pursuits, interests, expectations, and obligations in light of the social context (Nota, Soresi, & Zimmerman, 2004). This social context includes a myriad of factors, such as an individual's self-perceptions of his or her own abilities and skills, an individual's self-perceptions of his or her abilities in relation to others, and an individual's experiences and interactions with family, peers, and school environments (Bandura, 1995; Bandura, Barbaranelli, Caprara, & Pastorelli, 1996; Schunk, 1996; Schunk & Zimmerman, 1994; Zimmerman, 1989).

Educational Interests and Career Aspirations

Consistent with the STEM literature, we discovered that educational interests and career aspirations affect a student's decision to major in a STEM field. Further, this finding suggests that career interests may directly influence the career decision-making process of African American male students (Flowers et al., 2011; Hrabowski et al., 1998; Moore, 2006). Aligned with this finding, Naizer (1993) found that intellectual curiosity also contributes to students' interests in STEM. For this study, African American males discussed the extent to which their academic interests and interactions with teachers influenced their decisions to pursue a STEM career. Related to this theme, a participant noted, "I was in a chemistry course and being in that course and interacting with my [chemistry] teacher made me fall in love with chemistry. So from there, I wanted to be a chemical engineer." Elaborating on this concept, another participant said:

> All of the [high school] courses I took were honors, and as far as preparing me for STEM, early on I didn't know that I wanted to go into STEM. When I took them [STEM] classes, I realized what I was interested in and what I had a talent for and primarily it was math. . . . I felt like it was not only a challenge, but it gave me an opportunity to think outside the box but also think systematically and rationally.

Academic Experiences in College

According to the research literature, a number of factors influence African American male STEM students' academic and career outcomes (Moore, 2006; Moore et al., 2004). For example, it is widely accepted that high-quality learning experiences in rigorous academic programs result in better educational outcomes for African American male students (Moore, 2006). The more students have access to rigorous courses or programs, the more they tend to achieve academically (Reid & Moore, 2008). Combined with strong academic support services, taking advanced courses has shown to positively affect students' educational aspirations (Flowers, Milner, & Moore, 2003). To summarize this theme, one student contended, "More classes are getting harder, which is excellent because it's going to prepare us for when we get out [in the STEM workplace] or, in my case, graduate school or professional school, but I enjoy the classes here and I enjoy my environment here." In a previous study, Moore (2006) found that advanced learning initiatives that emphasize STEM can also increase African American male students' aptitudes for and interests in these career pathways. In this study, many of the African American males expressed how precollege and college-level opportunities influenced their decision to major in STEM. Reinforcing this particular viewpoint, a participant described a critical incident:

> My behavior changed in cell biology. . . . That's when I became a man. But, biochem was my first bad grade I got a C so I flipped out. . . . It made me think about changing my major. I got really upset because it didn't come easy to me. . . . I had to really do some soul searching but it changed my attitude on life.

Relationships With Peers, Teachers, and College Faculty

Creating a learning environment in which students are active participants in their education produces high levels of academic efficacy and educational aspirations (Reid & Moore, 2008). Thus, students are often more engaged in their academic work and motivated to achieve at higher levels when there is a strong sense of belonging to the learning environment (Akey, 2006). Supporting this claim, a participant remarked, "The things that I have learned from them [other students] they have also learned from me.... We all learn from each other about handling our business..., that is mainly we got through just working with each other." Students tend to be more successful in learning environments, when they receive clear and consistent expectations (Akey, 2006). Consistent with this viewpoint, Moore (2006) found that "quality school experiences and interactions with school personnel" (p. 255) positively influence African American male students' academic and career outcomes in STEM. In this study, we found similar results. In this regard, an African American male student remarked about the student-faculty interactions that he has with one of his professors by stating, "Every time I talk to him he makes me want to do better and study harder. He is a good mentor." Many of the students in our study also indicated that their college professors played a role in confirming or reaffirming their decision to persist in a STEM discipline and excel academically. Moreover, data from our study suggested that student-faculty interactions ranged from receiving advice and encouragement to having the opportunity to conduct research with faculty. Consistent with this theme, one African American male student stated:

> There are certain faculty that I knew who really knew what I wanted to do and that [were] behind me 100%. But, [there are] still some faculty who I just really don't feel like they are.... That's the way it feels [but] maybe it could just be me.... I just feel like I can't approach them.... I pretty much stick to certain faculty that I know who are behind me 100%.

Conclusions

The United States loses African American males annually at each segment of the educational pipeline—elementary, secondary, and postsecondary (Jackson & Moore, 2006). To address this issue, informed by a qualitative study of African American males, we developed a potentially useful framework to consider. It illustrates important experiences and interactions that may enhance the study of career development in STEM. The framework is also based on the belief that, throughout students' K–12 educational experiences, they are forming, developing, and changing their attitudes and beliefs about themselves, others, and school (Clewell et al., 1992). Moreover, during this time, students participate in a variety of educational experiences and activities (Lent, 2005). As a result, they may develop preferences, orientations, and behaviors that affect their academic and social development in educational institutions.

Research highlights the importance of family in the education process for African American students (Herndon & Hirt, 2004; Moore, 2006). Furthermore, families who have confidence in their children's ability to excel in STEM tend to have a positive attitude regarding their children's academic attitudes and outcomes (Clewell et al., 1992). Regardless of race, past correlational studies have revealed positive relationships with parental encouragement, parental expectations, and students' interest in STEM careers (Parsons, Adler, & Kaczala, 1982). This line of research has even suggested that educators are influential in shaping students' interests and motivation to pursue a STEM career (Moore, 2006). With this in mind, Clewell et al. (1992) asserted:

> Students who indicate a strong liking for and/or do well in these subjects frequently point to a teacher as an important influential factor. Similarly, students who express negative attitudes and opt out of future mathematics and science course work often attribute their thinking and decisions to a bad experience with a teacher. (p. 80)

Implications for Practice

In many sectors of society, new STEM jobs may significantly improve the American economy by creating novel technologies and innovative industries (Langdon et al., 2011). As a result—in light of national employment statistics that indicate that African Americans comprise only 6% of the STEM workforce (Beede et al., 2011)—we still need to increase the level of academic preparedness of all of our citizens as well as expand diversity efforts. For example, academic stakeholders should consider designing and implementing undergraduate STEM career development programs for African American males that focus on improving their job interview skills, career planning skills, and career management skills to adequately prepare them to enter the STEM workforce. As a result, the present study's qualitative findings suggest that African American males pursuing STEM degrees may need to increase the amount and quality of student-faculty interactions that focus on out-of-class research and laboratory experiences. Our data also suggest that STEM college faculty and the learning experiences they design for students play important roles in the educational process. Thus, it is important for teachers and college faculty to develop pedagogical strategies that enhance African American male STEM students' educational and career aspirations.

It is also important that preK—12 teachers and STEM college faculty understand how their behaviors and attitudes may affect students' motivation to learn in educational settings (Flowers et al., 2003). As justification for this particular recommendation, research suggests that positive student-faculty interactions contribute significantly to African American males' persistence in education, particularly in STEM (Moore et al., 2004). Therefore, preK—12 teachers and college faculty should set high academic and social expectations for African American males. If African American males' interactions with STEM college faculty are inadequate or ineffective, they tend to become reliant on their informal networks (e.g., peers) for guidance and support (Moore et al., 2004), which in this context may have little value for students when they are not able to obtain the needed encouragement, skill development, and support from STEM college faculty.

Implications for Research

This chapter reflects the findings of individual interviews with African American males. Although we present the study's results in an abbreviated manner, we believe these exploratory findings provide great insight that may lead to the development of strategies designed to better understand and support the academic and career development of African American males in STEM disciplines. While exploratory in nature, the findings from this study may serve to encourage university administrators, student affairs professionals, educational researchers, and STEM college faculty to advance the study of student development among African American males in STEM disciplines.

Our qualitative results suggest that, for high-ability African American male students, we may need to begin to question the relationship between academic self-efficacy and career self-efficacy. Moreover, our qualitative findings indicate that we should enable African American male STEM students to participate in programs and learning experiences that will aid in the development of their career aspirations. With respect to the underlying theoretical relationships (Bandura, 1995; Betz, 2007), our qualitative data also suggest that we may need to identify strategies to enhance the career self-efficacy of African American male STEM students. Future research should also attempt to identify factors that influence African American males' career development outcomes. Additionally, future research should also examine the factors that influence African American males' career interests and orientations. In contrast to previous recommendations for research, future studies should test the effectiveness of policies and practices designed to enhance African American male STEM students' educational, affective, and employment outcomes. This line of research may inform higher education administrators, student affairs professionals, and college faculty who are in need of studies that measure the effects of particular educational strategies, curriculum approaches, and educational policies on the recruitment, retention, and career development outcomes of African American males in STEM disciplines.

References

Adelman, C. (2006). *The toolbox revisited: Paths to degree completion from high school through college.* Washington, DC: U.S. Department of Education.

Akey, T. M. (2006). *School context, student attitudes and behavior, and academic achievement: An exploratory analysis.* New York, NY: MDRC.

Bandura, A. (Ed.). (1995). *Self-efficacy in changing societies.* New York: Cambridge University Press.

Bandura, A., Barbaranelli, C., Caprara, G. V., & Pastorelli, C. (1996). Multifaceted impact of self-efficacy beliefs on academic functioning. *Child Development, 67*(3), 1206–1222.

Beede, D., Julian, T., Khan, B., Lehrman, R., McKittrick, G., Langdon, D., et al. (2011). *Education supports racial and ethnic equality in STEM* (ESA Issue Brief No. 05-11). Washington, DC: U.S. Department of Commerce.

Betz, N. E. (2007). Career self-efficacy: Exemplary recent research and emerging directions. *Journal of Career Assessment, 15,* 403–422.

Clewell, B. C., Anderson, B. T., & Thorpe, M. E. (1992). *Breaking the barriers: Helping female and minority students succeed in mathematics and science.* San Francisco, CA: Jossey-Bass.

Coleman, J. S. (1988). Social capital in the creation of human capital. *American Journal of Sociology, 94,* 95–121.

Crosnoe, R. (2004). Social capital and the interplay of families and schools. *Journal of Marriage and Family, 66*(2), 267–280.

Esters, L. L., & Toldson, I. A. (2013). Supporting minority male education in science, technology, engineering, and mathematics (STEM) disciplines. *Texas Education Review, 1,* 209–219.

Flowers, L. A., Milner, H. R., & Moore, J. L., III. (2003). Effects of locus control on African American high school seniors' educational aspirations: Implications for preservice and inservice high school teachers and counselors. *The High School Journal, 87*(1), 39–50.

Flowers, L. A., Moore, J. L., III, Flowers, L. O., & Clarke, M. J. (2011). The relationship between academic self-concept and career self-efficacy among African-American males in STEM disciplines at two historically Black colleges and universities: An exploratory study. In H. T. Frierson & W. F. Tate

(Eds.), *Beyond stock stories and folktales: African Americans' paths to STEM fields* (pp. 73–83). Bingley, UK: Emerald Group Publishing Limited.

Gasman, M. (2011). Black men in the STEM fields at historically Black colleges and universities. In H. T. Frierson & W. F. Tate (Eds.), *Beyond stock stories and folktales: African Americans' paths to STEM fields* (pp. 115–127). Bingley, UK: Emerald Group Publishing Limited.

Glaser, B. G., & Strauss, A. L., (1967). *The discovery of grounded theory: Strategies for qualitative research.* Chicago, IL: Aldine.

González, K. P., Stoner, C., & Jovel, J. E. (2003). Examining the role of social capital in access to college for Latinas: Toward a college opportunity framework. *Journal of Hispanic Higher Education, 2*(2), 146–170.

Griffin, K. A., Pérez, D., II, Holmes, A. P. E., & Mayo, C. E. P. (2010). Investing in the future: The importance of faculty mentoring in the development of students of color in STEM. In S. R. Harper & C. B. Newman (Eds.), Students of color in STEM (*New Directions for Institutional Research, No. 148*, pp. 95–103). San Francisco: Jossey Bass.

Harper, S. R. (2010). An anti-deficit achievement framework for research on students of color in STEM. In S. R. Harper & C. B. Newman (Eds.), *Students of color in STEM. (New Directions for Institutional Research, No. 148*, pp. 95–103). San Francisco: Jossey Bass.

Herndon, M. K., & Hirt, J. B. (2004). Black students and their families: What leads to success in college. *Journal of Black Studies, 34*(4), 489–513.

Herndon, M. K., & Moore, J. L., III. (2002). African American factors for student success: Implications for families and counselors. *The Family Journal: Counseling and Therapy for Couples and Families, 10*(3), 322–327.

Hrabowski, F. A., III, Maton, K. I., & Greif, G. L. (1998). *Beating the odds: Raising academically successful African American males.* New York, NY: Oxford University Press.

Jackson, J. F. L., & Moore, J. L., III. (2006). African American males in education: Endangered or ignored? *Teachers College Record, 108*(2), 201–205.

Jorgensen, D. (1989). *Participant observation: A methodology for human studies.* Newbury Park, CA: Sage.

Langdon, D., McKittrick, G., Beede, D., Khan, B., & Doms, M. (2011). *STEM: Good jobs now and for the future* (ESA Issue Brief No. 03-11). Washington, DC: U.S. Department of Commerce.

Lent, R. W. (2005). A social cognitive view of career development and counseling. In S. D. Brown & R. W. Lent (Eds.), *Career development and counseling: Putting theory and research to work* (pp. 101–127). Hoboken, NJ: Wiley.

Lincoln, Y. S., & Guba, E. G. (1985). *Naturalistic inquiry.* Beverly Hills, CA: Sage.

Lundy-Wagner, V. C. (2013). Is it really a man's world? Black men in science, technology, engineering and mathematics at historically black colleges and universities. *The Journal of Negro Education, 82*, 157–168.

Miles, M. B., & Huberman, A. M. (1984). *Qualitative data analysis: A sourcebook of new methods.* Beverly Hills, CA: Sage.

Moore, J. L., III. (2006). A qualitative investigation of African American males' career trajectory in engineering: Implications for teachers, school counselors, and parents. *Teachers College Record, 108*(2), 246–266.

Moore, J. L., III, Flowers, L. A., Guion, L. A., Zhang, Y., & Staten, D. L. (2004). Improving the experiences of non-persistent African American males in engineering programs: Implications for success. *National Association of Student Affairs Professionals Journal, 7*(1), 105–120.

National Science Foundation. (2013). *Women, minorities, and persons with disabilities in science and engineering: 2013* (Special Report NSF 13-304). Arlington, VA: Author.

Naizer, G. L. (1993). Science and engineering professors: Why did they choose science as a career? *School Science and Mathematics, 93*(6), 321–324.

Nota, L., Soresi, S., & Zimmerman, B. J. (2004). Self-regulation and academic achievement and resilience: A longitudinal study. *International Journal of Educational Research, 41*(3), 198–215.

Owens, D., Lacey, K., Rawls, G., & Holbert-Quince, J. (2010). First-generation African American male college students: Implications for career counselors. *The Career Development Quarterly, 58*(4), 291–300.

Palmer, R. T., & Maramba, D. C. (2011). African American male achievement: Using a tenet of critical theory to explain the African American male achievement disparity. *Education and Urban Society, 43*(4), 431–450.

Parsons, J. E., Adler, T. F., & Kaczala, C. M. (1982). Socialization of achievement attitudes and beliefs: Parental influences. *Child Development, 53*(2), 310–321.

Pascarella, E. T., & Terenzini, P. T. (2005). *How college affects students: A third decade of research* (2nd ed.). San Francisco, CA: Jossey-Bass.

Reid, K. W. (2013). Understanding the relationships among racial identity, self-efficacy, institutional integration and academic achievement of Black males attending research universities. *The Journal of Negro Education, 82*, 75–93.

Reid, M. J., & Moore, J. L., III. (2008). College readiness and academic preparation for postsecondary education: Oral histories of first-generation urban college students. *Urban Education, 43*(2), 240–261.

Rubin, H. J., & Rubin, I. S. (1995). *Qualitative interviewing: The art of hearing data.* Thousand Oaks, CA: Sage.

Schunk, D. H. (1996). *Learning theories: An educational perspective* (2nd ed.). Englewood Cliffs, NJ: Prentice Hall.

Schunk, D. H., & Zimmerman, B. J. (1994). *Self-regulation of learning and performance: Issues and educational applications.* Hillsdale, NJ: Lawrence Erlbaum Associates.

Strauss, A., & Corbin, J. (1990). *Basics of qualitative research: Grounded theory procedures and techniques.* Newbury Park, CA: Sage.

Toldson, I. A., & Esters, L. L. (2012). *The quest for excellence: Supporting the academic success of minority males in science, technology, engineering, and mathematics (STEM) disciplines.* Washington, DC: Association of Public and Land-grant Universities.

Vanderstoep, S. W., Pintrich, P. R., & Fagerlin, A. (1996). Disciplinary differences in self-regulated learning in college students. *Contemporary Educational Psychology, 21*(4), 345–362.

Williamson, S. Y. (2010). Within-group ethnic differences of Black male STEM majors and factors affecting their persistence in college. *Journal of Global and International Studies, 1*(2), 45–73.

White, M. J., & Glick, J. E. (2000). Generation status, social capital, and the routes out of high school. *Sociological Forum, 15*(4), 671–691.

Zimmerman, B. J. (1989). A social cognitive view of self-regulated academic learning. *Journal of Educational Psychology, 81*(3), 329–339.

II

THE FIVE DOMAINS

A Conceptual Model of Black Male Success in the
Community College

J. Luke Wood and Frank Harris III

The community college serves as the primary pathway for Black (and other minority) male students into postsecondary education. In fact, 70.5% of Black men who enter public higher education do so through the community college (National Center for Education Statistics [NCES], 2009). However, the paths that lead students into a community college can differ greatly. Of the Black males enrolled in a community college, 54.4% entered directly after high school; this includes students who earned high school diplomas (85.7%), those who passed a general education development test or other equivalency test (8.6%), those who did not complete high school or earn a certificate (2.3%), and a range of other paths (e.g., high school certificate, home schooling, attending high school abroad; NCES, 2012b).

In addition to those students who have entered a community college directly after high school, a large proportion, 45.6%, enter after having delayed their enrollment into higher education. Among these students, males waited an average of 6.2 years before enrolling in community college (NCES, 2012c), which helps to explain why the average age for Black males in the community college is 27.7 years old (Wood & Essien-Wood, 2012). Black males who delay their enrollment in a community college often enter the workforce (48.8%), serve in the armed forces (13.8%), or in some cases experience more negative outcomes (e.g., incarceration, unemployment; NCES,

2006).[1] Upon entering a community college, students are provided a myriad of potential academic opportunities. Some students set out to earn certificates (10.1%), gain job skills (2.4%), or take courses for personal interest (9.3%), while 78.2% set out to earn associate's degrees (NCES, 2012d).

Of those with the goal of earning an associate's degree, 64.6% desire to earn a traditional associate's degree in arts or science, while 35.4% are pursuing an occupational/applied associate's degree (NCES, 2012e). It should be noted that none of these pathways are completely exclusive. Many of the students who are pursuing associate's degrees and certificates also have the goal of transferring to a four-year institution. In fact, 43.2% of Black males indicate their intent to transfer from a community college to a four-year college or university. With the aforementioned data in mind, the numerous pathways into and through community colleges situate these institutions as essential components of the educational pipeline for Black men. For many Black males, community colleges often serve as the only viable option for them to earn a postsecondary degree (Bush, 2004; Bush & Bush, 2004, 2005, 2010). In light of this, the purpose of this chapter is to propose a conceptual model of Black male student success in community colleges. In doing so we begin with a discussion of research and practice efforts that have been enacted over the past decade to address concerns about the success of Black male students in community colleges. Implications for research and practice that are informed by the proposed model are also presented in this chapter.

Change on the Horizon

Despite the fact that most Black males who participate in postsecondary education are enrolled in community colleges, the literature on this population has just begun to burgeon.[2] In a review of literature on African American males in the community college between 1971 and 2009, Wood and Hilton (2012a) found that prior to 1999, only one peer-reviewed article had been published on this population. However, between 2000 and 2009, eight peer-reviewed articles and four book chapters were written on these men. Ten more peer-reviewed articles and two book chapters have been published since 2010 on Black men in community colleges (Wood & Harris, 2012). These works represent an exponential growth in scholarship that has emerged in tandem with enhanced national interest, discourse, and efforts to facilitate the success of men of color in community colleges. Similarly, over the past decade, minority male initiatives have emerged at community colleges to facilitate persistence, achievement, attainment, and transfer among men of color. A wide variety of approaches are employed in these initiatives to bolster student success for men of color, including tutoring, support groups, conferences, courses, lecture series, and task forces (Nevarez & Wood, 2010).

While the preponderance of male minority initiatives in community colleges illustrates a climate of shifting concern, the efficacy of these efforts is challenged by several factors, one of which is an overreliance on four-year college and university research to inform program models for two-year college men (Wood, 2011a). Two studies illustrate the salience of this point. Flowers (2006) used data from the NCES's (n.d.) Beginning Postsecondary Students Longitudinal Study, which collects data on students during and after postsecondary education, to better understand nuances in academic and social integration between Black men at two- and four-year institutions. His research found significant differences in academic and social integration by institutional type. Specifically, he found that Black men in two-year colleges were less likely than their four-year counterparts to be academically and socially integrated into their college settings. These findings suggest that practitioners and researchers should be cautious in assuming uniformity in the Black male experience across institutional contexts.

Using a similar approach, Wood (2013) examined background differences between Black males in public two- and four-year colleges. His findings suggested numerous differences between these two groups. Specifically, he noted that Black men at two-year institutions were significantly more likely to be older, independent, married, to have dependents, and to have delayed their enrollment in higher education than those enrolled at four-year institutions. Further, Black males at two-year colleges have fewer years of high school preparation in foreign languages, mathematics, and science than Black males enrolled at four-year institutions. Wood concluded that while Black men at two- and four-year institutions share racial or ethnic heritages and gendered experiences, differences between the groups necessitate different programming, structures, policies, and practices.

Given these findings, practitioners interested in supporting the success of Black (and other minority) male students in community colleges must construct program models that address the unique educational challenges they experience. Taking the aforementioned trends and challenges into account, the next section presents a conceptual model of Black male student success in the community college. The model was informed by empirical and theoretical insights on Black male students in community colleges and is presented to serve as a conceptual guide for researchers and practitioners interested in investigating and addressing factors affecting the success of these students.

A Conceptual Model of Black Male Success in the Community Colleges

To develop a conceptual model for Black male success, we reviewed published peer-reviewed articles, book chapters, and reports on Black men in community colleges. This literature has focused primarily on several areas: analyses and evaluations of programs serving Black males (e.g., Bush, Bush, & Wilcoxson, 2009; Leach, 2001; Ray, Carly, & Brown, 2009), correlates and determinants of Black male persistence in community college (Flowers, 2006; Glenn, 2003–2004; Freeman & Huggans, 2009; Hagedorn, Maxwell, & Hampton, 2001–2002; Mason, 1998), and factors associated with academic achievement and success (e.g., Bush & Bush, 2010; Perrakis, 2008; Wood & Essien-Wood, 2012; Wood & Hilton, 2012b, 2012c; Wood, Hilton & Lewis, 2011; Wood & Turner, 2010). The latter two areas provided insight into the factors affecting the success, broadly defined, of these men. While limited to literature on persistence and achievement, the research that informed the development of this model may also have applicability for other student outcomes (e.g., transfer, attainment), since persistence research is often used as a starting point for investigating other academic outcomes (e.g., Dougherty & Kienzl, 2006; Nora & Rendón, 1990; Wood, Nevarez, & Hilton, 2011).

The literature on Black males in community colleges describes correlates and determinants of their success in five variable domains: social, noncognitive, academic, environmental, and institutional. Collectively, these domains are hereafter referred to as the five domains. These variable constructs are influenced by three sets of precollege considerations, including goals, background, and societal norms. Interactions between precollege considerations and the five variable constructs affect the success (e.g., persistence, achievement, attainment, transfer) of Black males in the community college. To provide a fuller understanding of these relationships, the primary components and variables of the model are discussed in the following section.

Precollege Considerations

The three primary precollege considerations are goals, background, and societal norms. While these constructs affect student success in college, their primary importance (in light of the model) is to provide a context for understanding the experiences of Black men prior to entering the community college. These constructs are generally interrelated. Societal norms refer to normative messages about Black men in society specific to their racial or ethnic and gender identity and are usually stereotypical in nature. Often, they depict Black boys or men as indolent, brutish, immoral, and unintelligent. These messages are rooted in historical racism (direct and indirect), perpetuated through social interactions, and reified through media and other societal institutions (e.g., schools, families, sports, churches; Harris, Palmer, & Struve, 2011). As a result, school teachers (who are often White and female) have marred perceptions of Black boys, thereby treating them negatively and communicating with them in ways that suggest schooling is not for them. Thus, as a result of these negative messages about school, many young men redirect their efforts toward success in other arenas, particularly those that society has validated as realistic and "acceptable" pathways for Black males, such as entertainment and sports (Majors & Billson, 1992).

As students progress through the educational pipeline, they establish, clarify, and reassess their goals in three primary areas: career, personal, and educational. Career goals include students' professional aspirations. Prior research has shown that having strong career aspirations, as opposed to mixed or unclear aspirations, is a strong propellant for academic success (Wood, 2010). Personal goals refer to students' aspiration for their own lives (e.g., having a family, civic involvement, living in the local community). While stereotypical perceptions of Black men would suggest otherwise, research by Wood, Hilton, and Hicks (in press) illustrate several primary personal goals for Black men in community colleges, which include creating a better future for themselves and their families, a responsibility to others (with a focus on being a role model to family and friends), and debunking stereotypical perceptions of Black men. Their research indicates that these personal goals serve as motivational factors for Black men to succeed in college. Educational goals refer to the highest degree a student plans to earn (e.g., associate's, bachelor's, doctorate). Educational goals have been shown to be strong predictors of persistence for Black men, with greater aspirations being predictors of enhanced outcomes (Freeman & Huggans, 2009; Hagedorn et al., 2001–2002; Mason, 1998; Wood & Williams, 2013).

Several studies have identified background variables that are predictive of Black male success in the community college. Generally, younger Black male students are more likely to persist than older students (Hagedorn et al., 2001–2002; Perrakis, 2008). Moreover, Strayhorn (2012) has also linked age to greater levels of satisfaction with students' academic experience. We postulate that findings regarding age are significant predictors of success because younger students have more recent experiences in educational settings and fewer life commitments (e.g., familial obligations). Prior academic performance in high school is another piece in the student success puzzle. Greater achievement in high school (e.g., grade point average, higher-level math course work) is predictive of Black males' success in community colleges

(Hagedorn et al., 2001–2002; Perrakis, 2008). In addition, spirituality has been found to be a positive contributor to Black male success in community colleges. Specifically, Wood and Hilton (2012c) found that spirituality and a belief in God aided Black male achievement by serving as an inspiration for excellence, providing a more focused purpose in life, enabling students to overcome societal barriers, reducing relational distractions, and allowing Black men to feel a sense of support when involved in isolating environments.

The Five Domains

Five primary domains that have been the focus of scholarly investigations of Black men in community colleges are influenced by precollege considerations (described previously) and are perceived to have an effect on academic success (directly) and on other domains (see Figure 11.1). These domains (indirectly) influence academic outcomes. Interrelationships between the domains are complex; most of them (e.g., social, environmental, institutional) have an effect on noncognitive and academic factors, which are believed to have a bidirectional relationship.

Figure 11.1 The Five Domains: A Conceptual Model of Black Male Success in Community Colleges

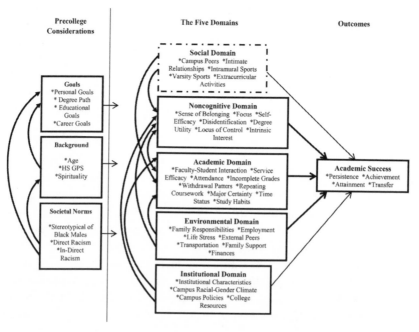

Findings on the effect of social domain variables on Black male success are tenuous. Several studies have assumed that greater involvement in the social landscape of college leads to enhanced success. For instance, Strayhorn (2012) identified social integration as a predictor of Black males' satisfaction in the community college. He suggested that satisfaction leads to retention; therefore, social integration has an effect (direct or indirect) on student success. Seemingly, this connection is sensible. However, some evidence suggests that social integration as a whole is not predictive of student success but rather has a negative (albeit small) effect on persistence (Wood, 2012a). For example, one common measure of social integration is students' establishment of relationships with other collegians. As noted by Bush and Bush (2010), peer group dependence can be a barrier to Black male success: "Peer interaction with African American men is perceived as something that African American male students had to overcome to be successful as opposed to a tool for success" (p. 55). One rationale for this finding is that Black men are often marginalized and alienated in campus environments. Thus, peer interactions with other men, whom *the campus* has failed to incorporate, successfully results in an out group whose members never feel like they are connected to or that they matter in the campus setting. Further, Wood and Williams (2013) examined predictors of Black male persistence using data from the Beginning Postsecondary Students Longitudinal Study (NCES, n.d.). His findings indicated that while participation in intramural sports had a positive effect on persistence, engagement in extracurricular activities had a negative effect. All told, these findings seem to illustrate that the effect of social involvement may be nuanced, with some measures of social integration detracting from student success and others contributing to it.

The noncognitive domain focuses on variables that are an affective response to social environments; as such, these variables are psychosocial in nature. Perrakis (2008) lends some light to the impact of psychosocial variables on Black male success. She found that for Black and White males a sense of belonging in their campus environment was predictive of their success in college. Given the difficult relationships between Black male students and their faculty, this finding is understandable. In his model of urban Black male persistence in the community college, Mason (1998) theorized that several psychosocial outcomes were predictive of success: satisfaction with their collegiate experience, feelings of helplessness and hopeless in their noncollege lives (external locus), their level of stress as it relates to their academic endeavors, and the degree to which they believe their academic pursuits are worthwhile (referred to as *degree utility*). With respect to degree utility, Wood (2011b) also discussed the importance of it, noting that "many Black males may experience a utility-conflict, meaning that their perceptions of the benefits of school conflict with their experiences, perceptions, and immediate needs" (p. 24). These studies illustrate the importance of fostering campus climates that create a sense of belonging and an internal locus of control, and inculcate degree utility for Black males in community colleges.

With regard to variables in the academic domain, positive academic habits such as attending class regularly (Mason, 1998), spending time studying, particularly in groups (Freeman & Huggans, 2009; Riley, 2007), and using academic services (Glenn, 2003–2004; Mason, 1998) are predictors of Black male success. For example, Glenn's examination of Texas community colleges with high graduation rates for Black males indicated that they performed better at institutions with freshman-only advising and mandatory orientation (for credit). Wood and Hilton (2012b) noted that awareness of campus support services is essential, as many Black males have little exposure to the support networks that are available to assist them in college. Being committed to one's academic goals has also been linked to student success (Freeman & Huggans, 2009), as early identification of an academic major (Hagedorn et al., 2001–2002) and major certainty (Mason, 1998) are integral predictors of Black male persistence. Research has also shown the importance of time status. Black males who are enrolled full-time are significantly more likely to persist than part-timers (Freeman & Huggans, 2009; Hagedorn et al., 2001–2002). For example, Wood (2012b) noted that Black males who attend community college full-time have 78.8% greater odds of persisting than part-timer enrollees. This is a particularly important consideration, given that nearly 60% of Black males are enrolled in community colleges part-time (Wood & Essien-Wood, 2012).

Researchers have also given attention to the importance of academic integration on Black male persistence (Flowers, 2006; Freeman & Huggans, 2009; Strayhorn, 2012). For example, Flowers found that Black males in community colleges were significantly less likely to be academically integrated (as measured by participation in study groups, talking with faculty outside class, and meeting with academic advisers) than their four-year counterparts. This is an important consideration, as Wood (2012a) has shown that academic integration is an integral predictor of Black male persistence in the community college. A key measure of academic integration is often students' degree of interactions with faculty. Several studies have focused on faculty-student interaction during class. For instance, Bush and Bush (2010) noted that Black males often have limited interactions with faculty, largely because of the students' perceived lack of affirmation and support. As a result, Wood and Turner (2010) outlined several simple steps that faculty can take to support Black males in class, including being friendly and caring, proactively monitoring their performance, listening to their concerns, and providing encouragement and affirmation.

Variables in the environmental domain also seem to have an effect on Black male persistence. These variables occur in students' lives outside college and serve to pull them away from their academic pursuits. Lack of finances, minimal outside encouragement, and familial responsibilities are all negative predictors of Black male persistence (Freeman & Huggans, 2009; Mason, 1998). For instance, Wood (2012b) noted that Black males were 5.5 times more likely than other male community college students to leave in their first year because of family responsibilities. He also found that these men were more likely to leave, citing personal reasons. Moreover, in Wood and Williams's (2013) model of Black male persistence, he noted that environmental variables accounted for more variance in persistence than did background, academic, and social variables combined. While finding that working part-time had a positive effect on persistence, he noted that stressful life events and supporting others (e.g., children, parents) had a strong negative effect on persistence.

Generally, the literature on Black males in community college overlooks the effect of institutional domain variables (e.g., campus climate, policies) on student success. Some evidence suggests that Black males are more successful when they perceive the campus climate as being affirming, diverse, and supportive. For example, in an examination of Black males in California community colleges, Bush and Bush (2010) found that a positive perception of the institution's climate was the strongest predictor of Black males' probability of success in college. Unfortunately, research from Bush (2004) and Wood (2010) illustrate that Black men have tenuous relationships with faculty. Outside class, Black males report that faculty either evade interactions with them or target them for disciplinary action. In fact, Wood noted that these men are more likely to have strong and supportive relationships with advisers, tutors, janitors, and librarians than with faculty.

Implications for Research

Numerous topics relating to the success of Black men in the community college remain unexplored or are in need of further exploration. The five domains model provides context for these needed areas of inquiry. Here, we highlight several research topics that can advance understanding of the Black male experience in the community college. With respect to precollege considerations, researchers should examine how societal normative messages about Black boys and men lead to differential levels of achievement and persistence in community colleges. In this vein, scholars should consider the factors (external to and internal in the institution) that help counter these messages. In addition, scholars may also consider examining differential goals (e.g., personal, academic, career) and how students arrive at these goals.

With respect to the five domains, researchers must explore steps that colleges can take to create institutional climates that foster positive noncognitive outcomes and academic incorporation. Research is also needed to learn what types of social incorporation (e.g., participation in clubs, sports, campus events) lead to positive outcomes for Black men. Moreover, when a negative association between measures of social incorporation and persistence are identified, researchers must investigate why this is occurring. Scholars should also consider investigating promising practices that enable students to leverage environmental factors to facilitate their own success. In addition, we suggest that researchers also examine the interrelationship among domains. For example, scholars can investigate the relationship between campus racial climate and sense of belonging for Black men, and the effect of social involvement on degree utility. In addition, more inquiry is needed to explore the relationship between campus racial climate, sense of belonging, and other noncognitive outcomes for Black men at community colleges. Moreover, studies that examine the intersection of identity (e.g., gender, racial/ethnic, etc.) and achievement for Black males at community colleges are sparse. Finally, inquiry should be directed toward determining the efficacy of various programmatic interventions that have been enacted at community colleges nationally to facilitate student success for Black males in community colleges.

Implications for Practice

Numerous implications for practice can be derived from the five domains model. Findings on the nuanced effects of social domain variables on persistence suggest that college professionals must be cautious in encouraging social integration as a general retention strategy and be more deliberate in the types of involvement that are encouraged. Given the limited research in this area, education professionals (especially counselors) should base recommendations for student involvement and peer-group interaction on experiential knowledge. The model highlights the importance of the noncognitive domain on student outcomes. Often, psychosocial variables are a direct result of institutional contexts that affirm, support, and communicate care or disaffirm, marginalize, and communicate perceptions of inferiority. Education professionals and administrators must focus their efforts on creating positive interactions between students and faculty, developing programs, and revising pedagogical practices to foster positive campus climates.

Also, because faculty play a key role in the success (or lack thereof) of Black males in community colleges, institutions should focus efforts on professional development for faculty to teach faculty to employ culturally relevant pedagogy, interact with Black men in ways that affirm their presence in college, and be mindful of micromessaging. More important, campus administrators committed to equity in education must develop new policies and procedures for evaluating faculty that include their success with student subgroups, such as Black men and other men of color.

Given the importance of environmental factors on college success, colleges must work to mitigate the negative and leverage the positive effects of these variables. This requires a comprehensive intervention approach, including providing scholarships, bus passes, book grants, flexible scheduling, child care, and institutional personnel who are attuned to challenges students face in their out-of-college lives.

Finally, before employing interventions to facilitate the success of Black men, college administrations must engage in inquiry to determine the nature of the interventions needed. The Minority Male Community College Collaborative at San Diego State University has developed an instrument designed to investigate factors influencing the success of men of color in community colleges. This instrument, referred to as the Community College Survey of Men (CCSM), is a needs assessment tool that facilitates benchmarking, performance monitoring, and identifying challenges in need of enhanced attention. The CCSM addresses the primary variables identified within the five domains model. Colleges should use the CCSM or other methods of inquiry (e.g., focus groups, interviews) to be intentional about developing interventions that are sustainable, scalable, and effective. Moreover, Harper and Kuykendall's (2012) eight standards for Black male campus initiatives should guide institutional efforts in designing programs and interventions to facilitate Black male student success.

Notes

1. These data are derived from the 2006 Educational Longitudinal Study (NCES, 2006), which tracks a cohort of students as they make the transition from high school to college. Respondents could mark more than one category and were presented with an expansive range of rationales for delayed enrollment.

2. As an aside, only one peer-reviewed article (to date) has been published on Latino men in the community college (see Vasquez, 2012). Moreover, no articles or other works have been written on Asian American and Native American men in community colleges. These oversights are woeful given the large proportion of these men of color who also enroll in community colleges as their primary entry point into postsecondary education.

References

Bush, E. C. (2004). *Dying on the vine: A look at African American student achievement in California community colleges* (Doctoral dissertation). Available from ProQuest Dissertations and Theses database. (UMI No. 3115606)

Bush, E. C., & Bush. L. (2004). Beware of false promises. *Community College Journal, 74*(5), 36–39.

Bush, E. C., & Bush, L. (2005). Black male achievement and the community college. *Black Issues in Higher Education, 22*(2), 44.

Bush, E. C., & Bush, L. (2010). Calling out the elephant: An examination of African American male achievement in community colleges. *Journal of African American Males in Education, 1*(1), 40–62.

Bush, E. C., Bush, L., & Wilcoxson, D. (2009). One initiative at a time: A look at emerging African American male programs in the California community college system. In H. T. Frierson, W. Pearson Jr., & J. H. Wyche (Eds.), *Black American males in higher education: Diminishing proportions* (pp. 253–270). Bingley, UK: Emerald Group.

Dougherty, K. J., & Kienzl, G. S. (2006). It's not enough to get through the open door. *Teachers College Record, 108*(3), 452–487.

Flowers, L. A. (2006). Effects of attending a 2-year institution on African American males' academic and social integration in the first year of college. *Teachers College Record, 108*(2), 267–286.

Freeman, T. L., & Huggans, M. A. (2009). Persistence of African-American male community college students in engineering. In H. T. Frierson, W. Pearson Jr., & J. H. Wyche (Eds.), *Black American males in higher education: Diminishing proportions* (pp. 229–252). Bingley, UK: Emerald Group.

Glenn, F. S. (2003–2004). The retention of Black male students in Texas public community colleges. *Journal of College Student Retention: Research, Theory, & Practice, 5*(2), 115–133.

Hagedorn, S. L., Maxwell, W., & Hampton, P. (2001–2002). Correlates of retention for African-American males in the community college. *Journal of College Student Retention: Research, Theory, & Practice, 3*(3), 243–263.

Harper, S. R., & Kuykendall, J. A. (2012). Institutional efforts to improve Black male student achievement: A standards-based approach. *Change, 44*(2), 23–29.

Harris, F., III, Palmer, R. T., & Struve, L. E. (2011). "Cool posing" on campus: A qualitative study of masculinities and gender expression among Black men at a private research institution. *Journal of Negro Education, 80*(1), 47–62.

Leach, E. J. (2001). Brother-to-brother: Enhancing the intellectual and personal growth of African-American males. *Leadership Abstracts, 14*(3), 11–14.

Majors, R. G., & Billson, J. M. (1992). *Cool pose: The dilemmas of Black manhood in America*. New York, NY: Lexington Books.

Mason, H. P. (1998). A persistence model for African American male urban community college students. *Community College Journal of Research and Practice, 22*(8), 751–760.

National Center for Education Statistics. (2006). *Rationales for delayed enrollment, by race/ethnicity (with multiple), and gender, for public two-year attendees. Computations with data from the Educational Longitudinal Study, 2002–2006.* Washington, DC: Author.

National Center for Education Statistics. (2009). *Black student enrollment by sector and control, gender 2003. Beginning postsecondary students longitudinal study—PowerStats.* Washington, DC: Author.

National Center for Education Statistics. (2012a). *Delayed enrollment into PSE: Number of years by race/ethnicity (with multiple) and gender, for institution sector (4 with multiple) (public 2-year). Computation by NCES PowerStats, 2007–2008 National Postsecondary Student Aid Study* (NPSAS: 08). Washington, DC: Author.

National Center for Education Statistics (NCES). (2012b). *High school degree type by race/ethnicity (with multiple) and gender, for institution sector (4 with multiple) (public 2-year) and delayed enrollment into PSE: Number of years (X = 0). Computation by NCES PowerStats, 2007–2008 National Postsecondary Student Aid Study* (NPSAS: 08). Washington, DC: Author.

National Center for Education Statistics. (2012c). *Average > 0 delayed enrollment into PSE: Number of years by race/ethnicity (with multiple) and gender, for institution sector (4 with multiple) (public 2-year). Computation by NCES PowerStats, 2007–2008 National Postsecondary Student Aid Study* (NPSAS: 08). Washington, DC: Author.

National Center for Education Statistics. (2012d). *Undergraduate degree program by race/ethnicity (with multiple) and gender, for institution sector (4 with multiple) (public 2-year). Computation by NCES PowerStats, 2007–2008 National Postsecondary Student Aid Study* (NPSAS: 08). Washington, DC: Author.

National Center for Education Statistics. (2012e). *Associate degree type by race/ethnicity (with multiple) and gender, for Institution sector (4 with multiple) (public 2-year) and undergraduate degree program (associate's degree). Computation by NCES PowerStats, 2007–2008 National Postsecondary Student Aid Study* (NPSAS: 08). Washington, DC: Author.

National Center for Education Statistics. (n.d.). *Beginning postsecondary students (BPS).* Retrieved from http://nces.ed.gov/surveys/bps/about.asp

Nevarez, C., & Wood, J. L. (2010). *Community college leadership and administration: Theory, practice and change.* New York, NY: Peter Lang.

Nora, A. & Rendón, L. I. (1990). Determinants of predisposition to transfer among community college students: A structural model. *Research in Higher Education, 31*(3), 235–255.

Perrakis, A. I. (2008). Factors promoting academic success among African American and White male community college students. *New Directions for Community Colleges, 142,* 15–23.

Ray, K., Carly, S. M., & Brown, D. (2009). Power of mentoring African American males in community colleges. In H. T. Frierson, W. Pearson Jr., & J. H. Wyche (Eds.), *Black American males in higher education: Diminishing proportions* (pp. 271–297). Bingley, UK: Emerald Group.

Riley, N. M. (2007). *A steady drop will wear a hole in the rock: Feminism, the John Henry myth and the Black male experience in higher education: A persistence case study* (Doctoral dissertation). Available from ProQuest Dissertations and Theses database. (UMI No. 3291817)

Strayhorn, T. L. (2012). Satisfaction and retention among African American men at two-year community colleges. *Community College Journal of Research and Practice, 36*(5), 358–375.

Vasquez, U. M. (2012). The impact of institutional characteristics on Latino male graduation rates in community colleges. *Annuals of the Next Generation, 3*(1), 1–12.

Wood, J. L. (2010). *African American males in the community college: Towards a model of academic success* (Unpublished Doctoral Dissertation). Arizona State University, Tempe.

Wood, J. L. (2011a, August 5). Developing successful Black male initiatives. *Community College Times*. Retrieved from http://www.communitycollegetimes.com/Pages/Opinions/Developing-successful-black-male-programs-and-initiatives.aspx

Wood, J. L. (2011b, October 13). Falling through the cracks: An early warning system can help Black males on the community college campus. *Diverse Issues in Higher Education, 24*. Retrieved from http://works.bepress.com/cgi/viewcontent.cgi?article=1008&context=jlukewood

Wood, J. L. (2012a). Black males in the community college: Using two national datasets to examine academic and social integration. *Journal of Black Masculinity, 2*(2), 56–88.

Wood, J. L. (2012b). Leaving the two-year college: Predictors of Black male collegian departure. *The Journal of Black Studies, 43*(3), 303–326.

Wood, J. L. (2013). The same . . . but different: Examining background characteristics among Black males in public two year colleges. *Journal of Negro Education, 82*(1), 47–61.

Wood, J. L., & Essien-Wood, I. R. (2012). Capital identity projection: Understanding the psychosocial effects of capitalism on Black male community college students. *Journal of Economic Psychology, 33*(3), 984–995.

Wood, J. L., & Harris, F., III (2012, November). *Examining factors that influence men of color's success in community colleges*. Paper presented at the annual meeting of the Council on Ethnic Participation, Association for the Study of Higher Education, Las Vegas, NV.

Wood, J. L., & Hilton, A. A. (2012a). A meta-synthesis of literature on Black males in the community college: An overview on nearly forty years of policy recommendations. In A. A. Hilton, J. L. Wood, & C. W. Lewis (Eds.), *Black males in postsecondary education: Examining their experiences in diverse institutional contexts* (pp. 5–27). Charlotte, NC: Information Age.

Wood, J. L., & Hilton, A. A. (2012b). Enhancing success in the community college: Recommendations from African American male students. In T. Hicks & A. Pitre (Eds.), *Research studies in higher education: Educating multicultural college students* (pp. 67–83). Lanham, MD: University Press of America.

Wood, J. L., & Hilton, A. A. (2012c). Spirituality and academic success: Perceptions of African American males in the community college. *Religion & Education*,
39(1), 28–47.

Wood, J. L., Hilton, A. A., & Hicks, T. (in press). Motivational factors for academic
success: Perspectives of African American males in the community college. *International Journal of Africana Studies*.

Wood, J. L., Hilton, A. A., & Lewis. C. (2011). Black male collegians in public
two-year colleges: Student perspectives on the effect of employment on academic
success. *NASPA Journal*, *14*(1), 97–110.

Wood, J. L., Nevarez, C., & Hilton, A. A. (2011). Creating a culture of transfer in
the community college. *Making Connections: Interdisciplinary Approaches to Cultural Diversity*, *13*(1), 54–61.

Wood, J. L., & Turner, C. S. V. (2010). Black males and the community college:
Student perspectives on faculty and academic success. *Community College Journal
of Research & Practice*, *35*, 135–151.

Wood, J. L., & Williams, R. C. (2013). Persistence factors for Black males in the
community college: An examination of background, academic, social, and environmental variables. *Spectrum: A Journal on Black Men*, *1*(2), 1–28.

I CAN DO MORE THAN PLAY BALL

Black Male Scholar Athletes

Derrick L. Gragg

T he inauspicious relationship between higher education and intercollegiate athletics has always been a major topic of debate. Throughout its history, intercollegiate athletics has simultaneously served as the consummate pride and the ultimate embarrassment of institutions in this country. From the time athletics was introduced to American institutions of higher learning, its inclusion has been challenged, questioned, and criticized, often with good reason. A major argument against college sports is that if intercollegiate athletics contributes to the overly poor academic performance of its participants, it has no true place in higher education. According to Adler and Adler (1985):

> Most studies of college athletes have found a negative relationship between athletic participation and academic performance. These studies conclude that athletes are unprepared for and uninterested in academics, that they come to college to advance their athletic careers rather than their academic careers; therefore, they have lower grade point averages (GPAs), higher attrition rates, and lower chances of graduating than other students.

During the past 20 years I have been involved in intercollegiate athletics in various capacities. I attended Vanderbilt University as a football student athlete from 1988 to 1992. In 1993 I began my career as an athletic administrator when I became my alma mater's first hands-on academic counselor for student athletes. As a former student athlete and currently an athletic administrator, I am very aware of the negative stereotypes used to describe and label young student athletes, and male African American student-athletes (AASAs) in particular.

Although I am concerned about the welfare and futures of all student athletes who attend American colleges or universities, as an African American, I am particularly concerned about the educational progress of African American males who participate in football and basketball, the two sports that produce the most revenue for all Division I institutions of the National Collegiate Athletic Association (NCAA). According to a study on AASAs, between 2007 and 2010, 2.8% of African American men were full-time degree-seeking undergraduate students but made up 57.1% of college football teams representing the six most highly regarded Division IA (the highest level of college football as recognized by the NCAA) conferences of the Football Bowl Subdivision (FBS) and 64.3% of the men's basketball teams (Harper, Williams, & Blackman, 2013). Further, in many instances, male AASAs make up an even larger percentage of starters (those who are on the field or on the court when a contest commences) or major contributors to their teams. Despite the fact that a large number of African American males participate in Division I football and basketball, graduation rates for these two groups are often much lower than graduation rates of their White male teammates and their female counterparts. Thus, to argue against this trend, I have studied African American football student athletes who actually persisted and graduated from college.

Although a number of current studies and articles emphasize the poor academic performance of African American athletes, AASAs of past years were known for their athletic *and* academic prowess. Throughout the days of Jim Crow, numerous African American male college athletes accomplished impressive feats on the fields and courts of play as well as in the classroom. Despite nearly unbearable conditions, a number of the most outstanding athletes between 1870 and 1890 were African Americans who were often better educated than their White counterparts (Entine, 2000). According to Wiggins (1991), "These men, by whatever standards employed, were an elite group of individuals who approached sport with the utmost seriousness, but unlike many college athletes of the future, always considered sports less important than academic success and educational achievements" (p. 165).

The legendary Paul Robeson, a scholar athlete who attended Rutgers University, entered the university in 1915 and became the epitome of athleticism and scholarship. Robeson is widely considered to have accomplished more athletically and academically than any other AASA past or present. Before his enrollment at Rutgers, Robeson was the top-ranked student in his high school academically, a soloist in the glee club, a member of the debate and drama clubs, and he was an excellent athlete (Wiggins, 1991). Before the Civil War, Rutgers had generally denied admittance to African Americans, allowing only two African Americans to attend the institution before Robeson enrolled (Duberman, 1989). As only the third African American student in Rutgers's history, Robeson had been thoroughly trained by his father to embrace the concept that he should conduct himself in a manner that reflected his race in a positive fashion. According to Yeakey (1973), Robeson once stated:

> [My father] had impressed upon me that when I was out on the football field or in the classroom or anywhere else I wasn't there just on my own. I was the representative of a lot of Negro boys who wanted to play football and wanted to go to college. (p. 491)

While attending the university from 1915 to 1918, Robeson was named All-American in football twice, earning an astonishing twelve varsity letters in four sports (Stewart, 1998). While his athletic prowess was legendary, Robeson's academic and extracurricular achievements were perhaps even more notable. Robeson was one of only four undergraduates (in a class of 80) admitted to the Phi Beta Kappa Society during his junior year at Rutgers (Duberman, 1989). He also won first prize in every speaking competition he entered (Lynch, 1976). When Robeson graduated from Rutgers he was not only a famous athlete, he was also an articulate class valedictorian and a member of the Cap and Skull Society, an honor for seniors (Stewart, 1998). According to Yeakey (1973), "Single-handedly, Paul Robeson seemed to have destroyed the myth of African American physical and athletic inferiority" (p. 495). More important, Robeson's academic success shattered the myth of AASA intellectual inferiority.

Unlike the legendary Paul Robeson, many of today's AASAs achieve academically at much lower levels than their athletic forefathers. Overall, student athletes at many institutions graduate at similar or higher rates than their classmates who make up the general student body; however, this statement does not hold true for male AASAs who participate in the revenue-producing sports programs of football and men's basketball. What is often overshadowed during the quest for athletic glory is the invaluable education one can obtain as a college student athlete. According to Edwards (1984), "By the time many Black student-athletes finish their junior high school sports eligibility and move on to high school, so little has been demanded of them academically that no one any longer even expects anything of them academically" (p. 9).

According to the NCAA (2011), in 2010 the national graduation rate for all student athletes was its highest at 65%, which was two percentage points higher than that of the general student body rate throughout the country. And while the male AASA graduation rate was 12 percentage points higher (50%) than the African American male general student rate (38%), the rate was still 15% lower than the rate for student athletes nationally. Further, in men's basketball and FBS football, the overall rates greatly lag behind the rates of the general male student body and are only three percentage points higher than the general African American male student body rate in basketball and four percentage points higher in football.

Although a minute percentage of student athletes participate on the professional level after college, African American males continue to be programmed from an early age by parents, communities, schools, and universities to pursue athletics while placing less and less emphasis on education. Wiggins (1991) illustrates this point by stating:

> The sad fact is, in short of abolishing college athletics altogether, there seems little chance of finding large numbers of Black scholars, and White scholars for that matter, to grace college playing fields in the manner of yesterday's campus heroes like William Henry Lewis, Howard Drew, and Paul Robeson. The contemporary university's hunger for victories combined with such factors as poor academic training, lack of nurturing support systems, and undue emphasis on sport in America's Black community has virtually guaranteed many Black college athletes will place little emphasis on intellectual pursuits and devote most of their attention to sport in an effort to realize elusive dreams of professional sporting contracts and everlasting glory. (p. 175)

Despite such doom-and-gloom perspectives espoused by Wiggins (1991) and others, many male AASAs overcome poor academic preparation, negativity, stereotypes, and racism, resisting the temptations of leaving college without earning degrees or pursuing wealth on the professional level, and persist as students and graduate from college.

Purpose of the Study

The purpose for conducting this study was to identify the factors that affected academic persistence and graduation rates of male AASAs who participated in the sport of football at Southeastern Conference (SEC) institutions. This study differs from most studies that focus mainly on student athlete academic nonperformance by focusing mostly on the student athletes who successfully navigate the academic processes of higher education and ultimately graduate. Why do some AASAs graduate while others do not? What is it about the individuals who do graduate that separates them from their African American teammates who do not succeed academically? Are there any modern-day Paul Robesons? The primary research question for this study was, What are the main factors that positively affected the academic performance of male AASAs in football who graduated from SEC institutions? The subsidiary research question was, What do football AASAs and student athlete support program (SASP) staff members feel are the main obstacles to AASA graduation?

One only needs to examine the national graduation rates for college student athletes to conclude that football AASAs are in an academic state of crisis. However, this study analyzed the influences on those who succeeded despite the current culture of football AASAs' academic failure. This study is significant because of the lack of research regarding AASA academic success. A total of 23 participants were interviewed, 17 of whom were former football AASAs who competed at one of the six selected SEC institutions. Five of the participants were either current or former SEC SASP staff members. One participant was interviewed twice because he is a former student athlete who competed at one of the SEC institutions and a current SEC SASP staff member.

Summary: Common Themes

The central themes related to academic persistence and graduation that emerged from former student athlete interviews were (a) family member/significant other's influence, such as parents/grandparents, siblings, high school coaches; (b) institutional commitment from coaches, athletic administrators, and SASP staff members; (c) teammate influence or peer acceptance; (d) self-motivation; (e) fraternity influence; and (f) spirituality. The central themes that emerged from SASP staff member interviews were (a) institutional commitment, which includes commitment from athletic staff members, such as athletic directors, student athlete support staff members, coaches, and from campus administrators; (b) family member/significant other's influence; and (c) teammate influence.

Not only did I seek to discover factors that positively affected football AASAs' persistence and graduation, I also sought to determine what participants felt were major deterrents to the academic performance of the athletes who failed to persist academically and graduate from their institutions. Themes that emerged regarding failure to persist included (a) unhealthy team subcultures including ineffective, apathetic, or unsupportive coaches, obstructive teammates, inadequate SASPs and SASP staff members, overwhelming pressure to win; (b) institutional barriers, such as lack of minority presence on campus, negative faculty members; (c) racism, such as conflict with historically White fraternities, stereotypes; (d) lack of positive interaction with campus and community constituents, including lack of interaction with students and faculty, conflicts with historically Black fraternities, lack of social outlets, negative encounters with law enforcement officials; and (e) personal challenges, for example, unrealistic thoughts regarding the National Football League, family culture/background, apathy toward academics, lack of academic ability, negative fraternity influence. The factors that have an effect on football AASAs who obtain their degrees are shown in Figure 12.1.

Recommendations for Practice

This section includes recommendations that should be implemented to help ensure that AASAs persist academically and graduate from college. For institutions whose AASAs have low graduation rates, these recommendations should serve as a foundation for improvement. Additionally, while some institutions graduate a large proportion of their AASAs, the recommendations can help enhance the systems those institutions already have in place.

Revamp study table for student athletes. Study table, or study hall as it is commonly called, is a primary component of most if not all Division I SASP academic monitoring systems. At most Division I universities, student athletes (particularly underclassmen) are required to attend study table for a specified number of hours each week. Study table is theoretically an excellent concept but can also negatively affect student athlete academic progress. The main problem with study table is that most institutions require student athletes to complete the required hours during evenings subsequent to athletically related activities when they are most fatigued. Fatigue (Edwards, 1984) and restricted time for studying (Adler & Adler, 1985) cause many student athletes to give up and cease caring about their academic work. Unable to concentrate and maintain focus, many student athletes view study table as an opportunity to socialize with other student athletes (particularly those of the opposite sex) and teammates, focus on nonacademic matters, or simply sleep through the period.

To take full advantage of study table, institutions should require student athletes to complete as many study table hours during the daytime as possible, particularly during their competitive playing seasons. By completing study table during daytime hours, student athletes should be able to concentrate better because they are less fatigued. Study table hours, if possible, should be completed *before* athletically related activities occur. For example,

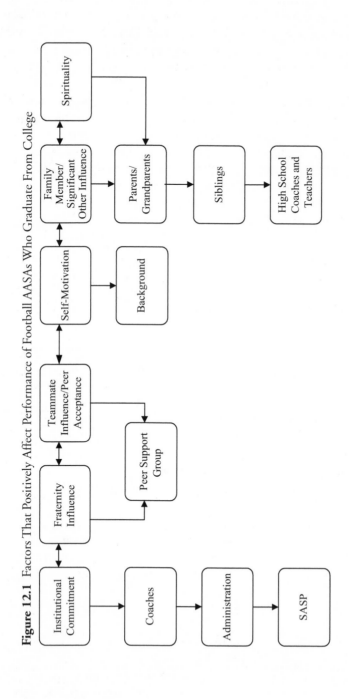

Figure 12.1 Factors That Positively Affect Performance of Football AASAs Who Graduate From College

when I worked as an athletic administrator at Vanderbilt University, all fresh-men football and basketball student athletes were required to attend 7:00 a.m. study table sessions. This system allowed football and basketball student athletes to complete study table hours before they become fatigued and also to complete hours without causing distractions or being distracted by other student athletes.

Provide academic incentives to student athletes. To motivate student athletes academically, coaches should reward those who reach preset aca-demic initiatives (e.g., earning a 3.0 or higher GPA, greatly improving their overall GPAs, earning more than 30 credit hours during an academic year, etc.). For example, upon taking over as head football coach at San José State University several years ago, Fitz Hill, who is now president of Arkansas Baptist College, implemented what he calls the "Operation 3.0 Program." Under this program, football student athletes who earn a 3.0 GPA during a semester are allowed to eat first during team meals and may also get tapped by trainers first for practices and workouts. They are also given T-shirts for their academic accomplishments bearing the phrase Operation 3.0: Mission Accomplished! Hill spoke of the great pride his student athletes took in achieving at least a 3.0 GPA during any given semester. He also spoke of how the T-shirts seemed to help alleviate some of the perceptions and stereotypes that student athletes at his institution face (F. Hill, personal com-munication, March 2, 2003).

Additionally, periodically, coaches should use team-meeting time to recognize academic achievements. I feel that student-athletes who are rec-ognized before their peers will be motivated to continue achieving academi-cally. Hopefully, those who are not recognized before their peers for their academic achievements will be motivated to improve academically.

Encourage AASAs to join historically Black fraternities. Male AASAs should be encouraged to join African American fraternities. Since the 1800s African American groups have provided support for African American stu-dents, especially those who attended predominantly White institutions (PWIs; Kimbrough, 2003). Coaches and athletic administrators should not underestimate the importance of historically Black organizations. Despite the fact that a number of AASA participants of this study who are members of African American fraternities discussed the role their fraternities played in their academic performance while in college, some participants mentioned that coaches often discouraged and even prohibited AASAs from joining fra-ternities. Therefore, coaches should be educated on the merits of African American Greek organizations. I do not think it is an overstatement to say that such organizations are viewed along with churches, barber shops, and athlet-ics as staples in the African American community. Many college students are raised in families where becoming a member of an African American Greek letter organization is very important, particularly if the students' parents, siblings, and other family members belong to these organizations.

Additionally, coaches should know that having AASAs as members of African American fraternities may help alleviate the animosity between fraternities and members of the team. Further, and perhaps more important, African American fraternities can serve as another support system and group for AASAs. Such organizations can enhance the academic performance of AASAs because each organization requires that a prospective member achieve certain GPA requirements to be considered for membership.

Increase the number of African American athletic staff members. Several participants identified the lack of diversity on campus as a major deterrent to football AASA academic performance and graduation. Historically, the number of African American faculty and staff members at PWIs has been extremely low; however, some institutions have made strides to alleviate this problem. Sellers (2000) stresses the need for more African American role models at PWIs. I too feel that AASAs need to encounter and work with administrators and coaches of color they can relate to. African American coaches and athletic administrators can serve as important mentors and role models to AASAs during their college experiences. Thus, institutions should strive to increase the number of African American staff members.

Strongly encourage AASAs to wear proper attire while on campus. Many White faculty members tend to harbor negative stereotypes about African American students' academic ability and potential and view student athletes negatively (Adler & Adler, 1991; Sedlacek & Adams-Gaston, 1992). Therefore, AASAs must find ways to combat the negative stereotypes they face on college campuses rather than behaving in ways that reinforce such stereotypes. Because of their size and the color of their skin, many AASAs are already very noticeable on college campuses and unable to blend into mainstream campus society like many of their White teammates. Wearing proper attire while on campus is one way to combat negative stereotypes regarding African American males. Thus, AASAs should definitely be briefed on proper class and campus attire. SASP staff members and coaches should encourage AASAs to remove earrings, excessive jewelry, baseball caps, hats, do-rags, and bandanas before arriving on campus or in class. These items, especially baseball caps, should definitely not be worn in the classroom. While these items are popular among many young African American males (and some young White males as well), such attire carries a negative stigma. Student athletes must be reminded that many faculty members are from a generation of people who in general may consider such items unacceptable, especially in an academic setting. Reese (2003) states that such attire is a symbol of African

American male defiance that depicts a gangsta-thug image rather than the image of a person who is serious about academics. Reese (2003) asks, "If you have embraced a thug image, how can you blame the system for treating you in the same way that you portray yourself? In other words, if you look like and behave like a thug, people will treat you as a thug" (p. 143). All young African American males should heed these words.

Enable and encourage AASA church attendance. Throughout American history, the African American church has played a prominent role in African American communities across the country. Hence, many African Americans are raised in homes where God and spirituality are of utmost importance. Several football AASA participants supported this assertion by mentioning the significant role spirituality and the church played in their academic persistence and graduation.

During my years as an undergraduate football student athlete, it was often difficult for me and other African American teammates to attend church services because we had mandatory workout sessions on Sundays at 1:00 p.m. To enable football student athletes to attend church services, head coaches who require workouts or practice on Sundays should set later times for those activities. Since the NCAA mandates that student athletes be given a day off each week with no mandatory athletically related activities (e.g., mandatory practice, workout sessions, film sessions, etc.), coaches may want to consider designating Sundays as the days student athletes rest, attend church services, and recuperate.

Increase interaction with law enforcement officials. Athletic department staff members and coaches should take several steps to help alleviate negative interaction between AASAs and law enforcement officials. First, athletic department administrators should hold training sessions on how to behave when encountering law enforcement officials. AASAs should be encouraged to treat law enforcement officers with respect and refrain from arguing or antagonizing them when interacting with them in social settings or if pulled over for traffic infractions. Second, local law enforcement officials should be invited to team meetings during preseason training to meet and greet new and returning football student athletes. Football coaches I have worked with have done a good job of inviting law enforcement officials, including Federal Bureau of Investigation agents, to conduct presentations that educate their student athletes on the risks they may face. Coaches should continue to seek ways for their student athletes to interact positively with law enforcement officials.

Increase interaction with faculty members. Sparent (1989) suggests that communication between faculty and student athletes may help some student athletes become more well-rounded students. Astin (1993) adds that student retention is positively associated with high levels of student involvement with faculty. Therefore, AASAs should be encouraged to interact more often with their faculty members.

Additionally, a football AASA participant mentioned that AASAs should seek to interact frequently with African American faculty members. Even if AASAs do not take classes offered by African American faculty members, they should find ways to interact with them in other settings. Since faculty members are sometimes invited to travel with football squads for games at other universities, SASP staff members can help increase AASA interaction with African American faculty members by inviting the faculty members to travel with the teams. Even though their interaction on such trips is minimal, the trips can serve as an opportunity to at least introduce the AASAs to African American faculty members they can connect with on other occasions.

Avoid off-the-field problems and any peers who do not. Today, student athletes and college athletic programs face unprecedented scrutiny. Embarrassing situations involving student athletes have occurred at many institutions during the past few years; thus, AASAs should avoid all signs of trouble and anyone, including teammates and close friends who behave inappropriately. They should also avoid anyone who jeopardizes their personal safety, scholarship, and reputation. AASAs should keep in mind that young African American males are six times more likely to be incarcerated than Whites who commit similar crimes. Also, race significantly affects the probability that a person will be convicted and sentenced for a crime (Reese, 2003).

Conclusion

Today, the African American male can be described as an endangered species in our society. Unfortunately, more African American men are incarcerated across the country than enrolled in colleges. African American males are also more susceptible to violence and premature death than males of other ethnic backgrounds. Traditionally, athletics has provided many African American males who may not have otherwise attended college with an opportunity to further educate themselves. By studying the football AASAs who graduated from college, I hoped to gather information that may be useful to other AASAs who are following in the footsteps of those who have gone before them. While I have worked with and continue to work with AASAs who lack direction, motivation to succeed academically, and viable role models, I have also worked with many dynamic, intelligent, goal-oriented AASAs. Despite the fact that male AASAs graduate at lower rates than other Division I student athletes, findings from this study reveal that it is certainly possible for Division I AASAs to persist academically and graduate. Modern-day Paul Robesons do indeed exist. Many can do more than just play ball.

References

Adler, P., & Adler, P. (1985). From idealism to pragmatic detachment: The academic performance of college athletes. *Sociology of Education, 58*, 241–250.

Adler, P., & Adler, P. (1991). *Backboards and blackboards: College athletes and role engulfment.* New York, NY: Columbia University Press.

Astin, A. W. (1993). *What matters in college? Four critical years revisited.* San Francisco, CA: Jossey-Bass.

Duberman, M. (1989). *Paul Robeson.* New York, NY: The New Press.

Edwards, H. (1984). The collegiate arms race: Origins and implications of the "Rule 48" controversy. *Journal of Sport and Social Issues, 8*(1), 4–22.

Entine, J. (2000). *Taboo: Why Black athletes dominate sports and why we are afraid to talk about it.* New York, NY: PublicAffairs.

Harper, S., Williams, C., & Blackman, H. (2013). *Black male student-athletes and racial inequities in NCAA Division I college sports.* Philadelphia: University of Pennsylvania, Center for the Study of Race and Equity and Education.

Kimbrough, W. (2003). *Black Greek 101: The culture, customs, and challenges of Black Greek fraternities and sororities.* Madison Teaneck: New Jersey. Farleigh Dickinson University Press.

Lynch, A. R. (1976). Paul Robeson: His dreams know no frontiers. *The Journal of Negro Education, 45*(3), 225–234.

National Collegiate Athletic Association. (2011). *Trends in graduation success rates and federal graduation rates at NCAA Division 1 institutions.* Retrieved from http://www.ncaa.org

Reese, R. (2003). *American paradox: Young Black men.* Durham, NC: Carolina Academic Press.

Sedlacek, W., & Adams-Gaston, J. (1992). Predicting the academic success of student-athletes using SAT and noncognitive variables. *Journal of Counseling & Development, 70*(6), 724–727.

Sellers, R. (2000). African-American student-athletes: Opportunity or exploitation? In D. Brooks & R. Althouse, (Eds.), *Racism in college athletics: The African-American Athlete's experience* (2nd ed., pp. 133–154). Morgantown, WV: Fitness Information Technology.

Sparent, M. E. (1989). The student-athlete in the classroom: The impact of developmental issues on college athletes' academic motivation and performance. *Research & Teaching in Developmental Education, 5*(2), 7–16.

Stewart, J. C. (1998). *Paul Robeson: Artist and citizen.* New Brunswick, NJ: Rutgers University Press.

Wiggins, D. K. (1991). Prized performers, but frequently overlooked students: The involvement of Black athletes in intercollegiate sports on predominantly White campuses, 1890–1972. *Research Quarterly for Exercise and Sport, 62*(2), 164–177.

Yeakey, L. H. (1973). A student without peer: The undergraduate college years of Paul Robeson. *The Journal of Negro Education, 42*(4), 489–503.

I AIN'T NO PUNK

A Framework for Black Gay Male Students' Belonging

Terrell L. Strayhorn

In February 2009, President Barack Obama announced to a joint session of Congress, "America will once again have the highest proportion of college graduates in the world [by 2020]." Currently, the United States ranks 12th in the world in terms of educational attainment, far behind countries like Korea and Canada. President Obama's public pronouncement of the country's college degree completion goal has been revised and restated by others over time. All sources converge on the goal of restoring the United States' status as the world leader in educational attainment by increasing the proportion of 25- to 34-year-olds who hold an associate's degree or higher to 55% by the year 2025.

National data are helpful for placing the country's college completion goal in context. Consider that today, 41.1% of individuals 25- to 34-years-old have earned an associate's degree or higher. However, a very different picture emerges when data are disaggregated by race and ethnicity. Although 69.1% of Asians have earned an associate's degree or higher, only 48.7% of Whites, 12.2% of Latinos, and 29.4% of Blacks have done so (National Center for Education Statistics, 2012). Rates can be appallingly lower when studying racial or ethnic subgroups, such as low-income Latinos, first-generation Native Americans to attend college, or Black men who have the lowest college degree completion rates among both sexes and all racial and ethnic groups. Two thirds of all Black men who enter college leave before completing their degree (Strayhorn & Terrell, 2010).

A number of policy agencies have estimated what national college degree completion goals mean in more practical terms. A report by the National Center for Higher Education Management Systems (Kelly, 2010) estimates that 8.2 million more college degrees are needed to close the attainment gap by 2025; in short, that's increasing U.S. degree production by 4.2% annually. Estimates vary among organizations based on the use of different methods, assumptions, and age cohorts. For example, a report by Excelencia in Education and the National Center for Public Policy in Higher Education (2000) estimates the need for 13.3 million more degrees by 2025. No matter the variance, it's clear that a fairly large number of additional degrees are needed to meet our national goals for college degree completion and to increase the country's global competitiveness. To get there, we will need to draw on all pools of available talent and strengthen the educational pipeline for all students including those who may face the most significant challenges in higher education such as Black men.

The condition of education for Black men is reflected in the titles of articles, books, and reports. For instance, Ronald Roach (2001) asked a poignant question in his article titled, "Where Are the Black Men on Campus?" Kunjufu's (1986) *Countering the Conspiracy to Destroy Black Boys* is a classic, while Anne Arnette Ferguson's (2000) *Bad Boys* illuminates the ways schools and educators manufacture "bad boys," who are disproportionately Black, through inequitable disciplinary practices that condition some young men to penal-like environments marked by surveillance of (mis)behavior and punishment. A couple of years later, Michael Cuyjet (2006), professor at the University of Louisville, edited a volume titled *African American Men in College*, which he opened by reflecting on a commencement ceremony at the institution where he was employed in which thousands of degrees were awarded but not a single one to a Black male. In light of these stubbornly persistent trends, the National Urban League (2007) devoted its *State of Black America* to painting a portrait of Black males in society. On almost every indicator of sociopolitical and economic success, Black males were lowest performing, significantly disadvantaged, or virtually absent.

Despite fairly consistent radicalized patterns in indicators of Black males' situation in American society, there are important nuances in the Black male portrait. Not all Black men are the same, and by extension, neither are their challenges and successes. Consider Black gay men who represent a nearly missing or invisible subpopulation in the research literature. What's known about lesbian, gay, bisexual, and transgendered (LGBT) people in society focuses almost exclusively on early work that attempted to explain the cause of homosexuality (e.g., Ellis, 1901), often concluding it was a "diagnostic category of mental illness" (Gibson, Schlosser, &

Brock-Murray, 2006, p. 33); on reports that emphasize rates of sexually transmitted diseases among LGBT groups; and studies that try to explain the process individuals go through to understand their gay identity (Cass, 1984; D'Augelli, 1994). For instance, Cass suggested that gay identity development is a six-stage process, moving from *identity confusion* to *identity synthesis* through four other phases (i.e., identity comparison, identity tolerance, identity acceptance, identity pride). Still, much of this literature is based on predominantly White samples from the 1970s, 1980s, and 1990s, with little to no attention paid to the contemporary experiences of LGBT people of color.

Scholars of color have directed much-needed attention to the experiences of LGBT people of color in larger society as well as in college. For instance, Icard and Nurius (1996) found that recognizing and publicly acknowledging one's own homosexuality can be seriously traumatizing, especially for gay people of color who often find themselves rejected or marginalized by members of their own race—the very people and resources they need to productively cope with life challenges. In terms of college students, I and my students (Strayhorn, 2013a, 2013b; Strayhorn, Blakewood, & DeVita, 2008, 2010; Strayhorn & Scott, 2012) have conducted several studies on Black, Latino, and Asian gay male collegians. For instance, Strayhorn and colleagues (2010) found that most of the Black gay male undergraduates who participated in the study reported being kicked out of their parents' home, dismissed by family members or siblings, alienated or socially isolated by peers in campus clubs and organizations, or rejected by church members when they disclosed their sexual orientation to others.

Because peers, faculty, and internally derived commitments play an important role in the success of Black gay men in college, I thought it useful to identify or develop a theoretical framework that accounted for the role of such agents in college students' adjustment, transition, and success, especially the extent to which they felt accepted, protected, and valued by others in an organization or social system, which is the essence of sense of belonging (Strayhorn, 2012). As Bazarsky and Sanlo (2011) rightly concluded, "Regardless and inclusive of sexual and gender identity, all students, faculty, and staff deserve to feel they belong" (p. 138).

However, sense of belonging in college had not yet been framed as a theoretical model or framework consisting of distinct concepts. I settled on developing such a frame for at least three reasons. First, most of my work with gay men of color emphasized the role that belonging played in their academic experiences—from interacting meaningfully with others on campus to coming out to others who were significant in their lives. Second, sense of belonging had potential for theoretical expansion and, in my opinion, could be empirically tested using new and existing scales that tapped aspects of learning environments and interpersonal relations. Last, sense of belonging—as I understood it initially—provided constructs for talking about students' lived experiences and social realities in ways that illuminated what might otherwise go hidden or undiscussed, or were far too complex to discuss. With these objectives in mind, I developed the sense of belonging framework that many of my studies and a book is based on (Strayhorn, 2012).

Framework: Sense of Belonging in College

As I've said elsewhere, "*sense of belonging* is one term with many meanings" (emphasis added; Strayhorn, 2012, p. 8). Vast differences exist in the terms or labels attached to this phenomenon, ranging from *belonging* to *membership*, from *relatedness* to *community*, to name a few. Similarly, a number of different definitions have been published in the literature. Consider the following:

1. Sense of belonging refers to "a feeling that members matter to one another and to the group, and a shared faith that members' needs will be met through their commitment to be together" (Osterman, 2000, p. 324).
2. Sense of belonging refers to "students' sense of being accepted, valued, included, and encouraged by others (teachers and peers) in the academic classroom setting and of feeling oneself to be an important part of the life and activity of the class [or educational environment]." (Goodenow, 1993, p. 25)

In my previous work, I have defined sense of belonging as students' perceived social support on campus, a feeling of connectedness, or that one is important to others, in consonance with understandings rendered by previous scholars. For instance, I analyzed survey data from 289 Latino and 300 White students as a way of predicting *sense of belonging* in college, which was operationally defined as their perceived sense of integration on campus (Strayhorn et al., 2008). I explained that a "sense of belonging reflects the social support that students perceive on campus; it is a feeling of connectedness, that one is important to others, that one matters" (p. 305). And, like Hurtado and Carter (1997), I suggested that sense of belonging may be particularly important for students who perceive themselves as marginal to campus life, such as Latino students and Black gay men.

Sense of belonging is framed as a basic human need and motivation, sufficient to influence behavior. In this way, it is not only an important aspect of college student life but relevant to life for all of us, although it seems to take on heightened importance for college students, given where they are generally in their personal identity development (i.e., identity exploration, vulnerable to peer influence) and in educational contexts where they are predisposed to feeling marginalized or excluded. In my book (Strayhorn, 2012), I outline seven core elements of sense of belonging and explain each in the context of existing literature. The core elements of college students' sense of belonging are

1. Sense of belonging is a basic human need.
2. Sense of belonging is a fundamental motive, sufficient to drive human behavior.
3. Sense of belonging takes on heightened importance (a) in certain contexts, such as being a newcomer to an otherwise established group; (b) at certain times, such as (late) adolescence when individuals begin to consider who they are (or wish to be), with whom they belong, and where they intend to invest their time and energies; and (c) among certain populations, especially those that are marginalized or inclined to feel that way in a given context
4. Sense of belonging is related to, and seemingly a consequence of, mattering.
5. Social identities intersect and affect college students' sense of belonging.
6. Sense of belonging engenders other positive outcomes.
7. Sense of belonging must be satisfied on a continual basis and likely change as circumstances, conditions, and contexts change.

Along with lengthy descriptions of the core elements, I also offer a visual depiction of the framework (see Figure 13.1). The model situates belonging as a fundamental need, alongside physiological needs, safety, esteem, and self-actualization. College students enter various spaces and contexts during the college years, sometimes on campus and sometimes off campus, where their fundamental needs emerge in a sort of hierarchy depending on the salience of various identities to their experiences in such settings. Gratification of physiological needs permits emergence of other (and higher) social motives or goals such as the need to belong. The emergence of that need in college drives students' behaviors and perceptions. Some students whet their appetite to belong through deep, meaningful involvement in clubs and organizations, others by establishing mutually rewarding relationships or friendships with others on campus, or by learning the values and norms of the profession they aspire to, which socializes them to bona fide membership. Of course, not all students engage in educationally purposeful or prosocial behaviors to satisfy their need to belong—far too many resort to antisocial,

Figure 13.1 A Hypothesized Model of College Students' Sense of Belonging.

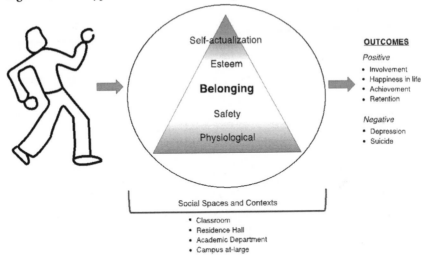

Note. From *College Students' Sense of Belonging: A Key to Educational Success*, p. 25, by T. L. Strayhorn, 2012, New York, NY: Routledge. Copyright by Taylor & Francis. Reprinted with permission.

unhealthy, or risky behaviors such as joining a gang, consuming too much alcohol, or using illegal drugs and substances to fit in, gain membership, or stand out from others around them.

At least two other important aspects of the model deserve mention. First, sense of belonging takes on heightened importance in certain spaces and contexts, at certain times, and under certain conditions for particular populations. This is reflected in Figure 13.1 by "Social Spaces and Contexts" near the base of the circle. Although the model includes a single section for spaces and contexts marked off by a bracketed line under the larger circle, notice that the words *spaces* and *contexts* are plural—students typically navigate, negotiate, and traverse multiple spaces during their college career. In each of these spaces their fundamental needs emerge, rising and falling over time in terms of salience and driving their behaviors and motivations as originally hypothesized. Two-dimensional figures hardly capture the form and nature of three-dimensional phenomena. Still, readers are encouraged to try envisioning an individual student working in a number of circles and arenas (as shown in Figure 13.1) at different times in his or her college career.

Second, I intentionally included all of Maslow's (1954) theorized needs in the hypothesized model of college students' sense of belonging. Maslow explained that human needs are not completely independent of each other or other motives. For example, physiological needs give rise to all sorts of other needs. "The person who thinks he or she is hungry may actually be seeking more for comfort, or dependence, than for vitamins or proteins" (Maslow, p. 16). Similar theories hold true for college students. The student who may be striving for esteem or confidence may find that what he or she really needs is safety or belonging. And there may be times when students—say, Black gay male collegians—are working to establish a sense of belonging through involvement in clubs or organizations (e.g., gospel choir, LGBT student group), but out of nowhere the threat of danger is triggered by a stimulus in the environment (e.g., a homophobic slur, antigay sermon), and therefore they regress to more basic safety needs.

The final model is useful for future practice and research, in my opinion. College student educators might employ the model in their work with students, especially when thinking about their motivations for behaving in certain ways. A separate line of inquiry focuses on sense of belonging and its association with outcomes in higher education; to date, college students' sense of belonging has been linked to academic success (Walton & Cohen, 2007), students' plans to stay in college (Berger, 1997), and retention (Jacoby & Garland, 2004). Researchers might also continue to test the validity of the model by applying it to diverse student samples under different conditions at different times. To that end, I use the model in the next section to highlight the ways it applies to data from a national study of gay men of color (Strayhorn, 2012).

Use of the Framework

Since I was interested in explaining how the model was used in my previous research, I drew upon data from my national study (Strayhorn, 2012) of gay male collegians of color at predominantly White institutions (PWIs) and historically Black colleges and universities (HBCUs) in the United States. The study employed a constructivist qualitative approach, which is congruent with my own epistemic beliefs about the very nature of knowledge as well as my positioning as a researcher. In short, data were collected via semistructured, in-depth, one-on-one interviews with willing participants.

Participants were recruited in a number of ways over several years. Initially, members of my research team and I worked with presidents of gay student alliances on each participating campus to identify and recruit a pool of prospective participants. Individuals who met the sampling criteria were contacted by the president of the student group, who relayed information about the study to them and encouraged them to share their e-mail address with our team. Over time, additional steps were taken to recruit participants. For instance, some participants were recruited through online gay networking sites and Web advertisements. On average, interviews lasted about 90 minutes; all interviews were digitally recorded and transcribed by a professional. For more information about the study, see Strayhorn (2012).

Sense of belonging applies to Black gay male collegians included in my national study (Strayhorn, 2012) of gay men of color in several ways; here I illustrate how belonging applies to this population using verbatim quotes and survey data (where possible) from respondents in the study. First, recall that the first core element of the model suggests that sense of belonging is a basic human need. Black gay men in my studies alluded to how important belonging or connectedness or acceptance by others was to them as racial or ethnic and sexual minorities in college. Many described how their urge to "be out and live out" motivated their decision to attend college in hopes of finding social communities where they could be out as gay, engage in LGBT activities (e.g., dating, attending gay clubs), and find a sense of belonging among others who share their expectations and experiences. Indeed, all people want to belong, all students want to belong in educational contexts, and striving to belong is a basic human need that emerges naturally, just like the need for air, food, and safety.

In response to their yearning to belong, Black gay male collegians have affective, behavioral, and psychological reactions. Consider Dracula (a pseudonym), a second-year Black gay male student at a large public PWI in the southeastern region of the country, whose following comments echo the sentiments of others:

> I didn't really think about what I was going to do in college. . . . I mean do, like how I was going to be involved. I thought mostly about my major and my career that I was going to pursue after I graduated. But I definitely knew that I wanted to put away the facade. I didn't want to keep that up anymore because I did it in high school for my family and friends. In college, I had decided that I was going to be me, you know . . . like not queeny, but me. So when I got here I stayed away from people who would make me act like I'm straight and looked for people who were like me or who I thought liked me for who I was. It was not easy but it made me get involved in like the gay student organization on campus and I even attended a few events on campus like National Coming Out Day and stuff.

Dracula's comments reflect the spirit of what other participants said. A desire to belong emerged—ascended to importance—when some Black gay men entered college. To satisfy their need to belong, many became involved in campus clubs and organizations or activities off campus to find others who shared their expectations, experiences, and identities. Their words clearly demonstrate how sense of belonging is a fundamental motive, sufficient to drive Black gay male collegians' behaviors.

Embedded in Dracula's comments and those from others (such as Desmond in Strayhorn, 2012) is the sense that belonging takes on a heightened importance (a) in certain contexts, (b) at certain times, and (c) among certain populations, especially those that are marginalized or inclined to feel that way in education contexts. While belonging is a basic human need that can be satisfied by an individual's home ecology (e.g., parents or guardians, siblings) from birth to adolescence, new or different belonging needs can emerge for students who enter college environments that can be dramatically different from their cultures of origin; such is the case for many Black gay male collegians. So, as Desmond, a 19-year-old psychology and public relations double major, plainly explained, the need to belong can take on heightened importance when some Black gay men enter college, after years of passing as straight or concealing their sexual orientation from friends and family.

> I guess . . . it's like I came here expecting college to be this life-changing experience—and it was or it is. I expected to get away from [my hometown] where I would be around more open-minded people and felt free to be myself. But I don't really feel like I fit in here. I mean, I do in some places but then it's like really homophobic too. Well, for starters, the people here are not necessarily more open-minded. (p. 44)

Another core element of the model relates to comments like those from Dracula, Desmond, and Joseph, a graduating senior majoring in sociology and sexuality studies, that is, that social identities intersect and simultaneously affect Black gay male collegians' sense of belonging in college. For instance, Dracula talked about how he found a community or friendship group among White LGBT students on campus; hanging out with friends, going to gay clubs, and attending gay pride events facilitated his sense of belonging in college. As he spent time with White LGBT friends, shared memories about their times together, and came to understand them (and vice versa), he felt connected to others on campus and felt cared about and special, and thus his need to belong was satisfied. Table 13.1 presents the proportion of gay men of color, across all studies, who reported engagement in various activities as a way of satisfying their need to belong.

However, like so many other Black gay men in the study, Dracula and others assume multiple social identities at once—that is, they are at once Black, gay, male collegians from various socioeconomic strata, geographic locations, and religious affiliations, to name a few. These multiple social identities intersect in unpredictable ways and simultaneously affect Black gay male collegians' need to belong and the ways they might satisfy such needs. For instance, Dracula and Desmond gave lengthy accounts of how their need

TABLE 13.1
The Belonging Activities of Gay Men of Color

Category/Activity	Percent Sample Reporting Yes
Involvement in salient communities	
Ethnic nightclubs	48
Gay nightclubs	41
Gay pride event(s)	77
Ethnic student organization(s)	62
LGBT student organization(s)	35
Spirituality and religion	
Prayer	66
Church attendance	34
Yoga or related expression	14
Journaling	25
Relationships	
Fictive kin	55
Monogamous dating	41
"Hooking up"	31

Note. LGBT = Lesbian, Gay, Bisexual, and Transgender. From *College Students' Sense of Belonging: A Key to Educational Success for All Students*, p. 45, by T. L. Strayhorn, 2012, New York, NY: Routledge. Copyright by Taylor & Francis. Reprinted with permission.

to belong was satisfied among White LGBT friends until issues of race, class, or gender came up through racial jokes, costly outings, and male-bashing sessions by lesbian friends (Strayhorn, 2012). In those instances, social identities that seemed less relevant or obvious become important, and previously established feelings of belonging can be reduced to alienation and isolation.

As I explained in the previous section, sense of belonging engenders other positive outcomes such as academic success, plans to stay in college, and retention (e.g., Walton & Cohen, 2007). Countless examples abound in my national study of gay men of color generally and Black gay male collegians specifically (see Strayhorn, 2012). For instance, Black gay men have said how finding a sense of belonging in college nurtured their college and professional aspirations above and beyond what they initially expected. Many went to college worrying if they would make friends, fit in among other LGBT students, or even find same-sex partners suitable for dating. By making friends, sharing interests in common with other LGBT students, and dating same-sex partners, some Black gay men felt more confident in their academic abilities, were convinced that college was for them (and thus aspired to graduate school), and reported feeling better about themselves (i.e., esteem) and their future (i.e., happiness). Sorting student interviews and demographic data into two groups—one group in which the preponderance of evidence suggests the students feel as if they belong in college, the other in which they do not—lends additional support to this conclusion. The grade point average for the "belonging group" was 3.32, while for the "alienated group," it was 2.74 (unpublished analysis of prior data). Indeed, sense of belonging engenders other positive outcomes for Black gay men in college.

Finally, the last core element of the model applies to Black gay men in college too. Sense of belonging must be satisfied on a continual basis, and it likely changes as circumstances, conditions, and contexts change. For this point, I draw upon a few participants as illustrative examples. Recall that Dracula and Desmond talked about how their need to belong was satisfied until issues of race, class, or gender came up in casual conversations or unfiltered joking (Strayhorn, 2012). Conversations and insensitive jokes of this kind served as stimuli in the environment that interrupted existing feelings of belonging and acceptance, introduced or reintroduced the need to belong, and initiated strivings to belong under new circumstances, conditions, or contexts. As another example, Jamon, a Black gay male at an HBCU in the northeast region of the country, spoke in detail about how his need to belong was satisfied in college through his peers and boyfriend until he attended chapel one day and the campus minister delivered an antigay, offensive sermon that assumed homosexuality as unforgivable sin. Once the context changed (i.e., he went to chapel), conditions changed (i.e., campus minister condemned homosexuality), and circumstances changed (i.e., his boyfriend was stressed and hurt), so too did his sense of belonging, his need for safety and protection, and his ability to negotiate that setting. With little to say and few options in mind, Jamon walked out of chapel service to avoid further psychological and emotional damage (Strayhorn, 2012). It's important to note that some Black gay men do more than leave chapel, they drop out of college altogether in similar situations.

This section clearly demonstrates that the sense of belonging model and each of its core elements apply to this subpopulation of Black male collegians. By understanding their precollege histories, demographic backgrounds, social identities, emergent psychological needs, and whether and how these needs rise and fall in ascendancy over time in various contexts and settings, college student educators can work more effectively with Black gay male collegians, assist them during difficult transitions, and offer data-based advice about how to find a sense of belonging in college, which is a key to educational success for all students.

Recommendations for Research

Information presented in this chapter has many implications for future research. For instance, themes identified in the previous section lend persuasive support to the model outlined in my larger work (Strayhorn, 2012). Future researchers might continue this line of work, advancing theory in a number of directions. One way to do this is to test and retest the sense of belonging model on other LGBT subpopulations such as Latino gay men, Asian lesbians, or Native Americans who identify as free spirits. While this chapter demonstrates the utility of qualitative studies on LGBT students of color, future researchers might extend what's presented in Table 13.1 by surveying similar samples to assess how often participants disclose their sexual orientation to others, the timing of identity disclosure, the frequency of their involvement with same-race LGBT peers, and levels of satisfaction with college, to name a few. Using a blend of descriptive and multivariate statistics, researchers can measure the correlation between gay males' college involvement and their subjective evaluation of academic life.

Also consistent with the model described in this chapter, Black gay male collegians articulated skillfully how the threat of danger, perceived or realized, caused them to regress from higher needs (e.g., belonging, esteem) to more basic physiological and safety needs (recall Jamon's story). This lends credible support to the proposed model and suggests that it may be applicable to other gay students of color who may perceive themselves as marginal to campus life, although this latter point awaits empirical testing. Future research might be designed to test the timing and duration of such regressions and to assess the impact of regression on identity development across multiple dimensions of self, including race or ethnicity, sexual orientation, and religious affiliation, among others.

A significant number of Black gay men in my studies (Strayhorn, 2013a, 2013b; Strayhorn & Tillman-Kelly, 2013) reported losing contact or communication with biological parents (or guardians) and siblings as a result of disclosing their sexual orientation. As a result, they stressed the important roles that friendships and family-like relationships with fictive kin played on their success in college. *Fictive kin* are individuals who are not related by blood but by imaginary ties of choice; these individuals accept the affection and duties of real kin. Depending on the participant and his situation, fictive kin served as major socializing agents and pillars of support many Black gay men relied on. The scope of my work to date, however, has not included specific attention to how such relationships are formed, maintained, and nurtured over time; this represents a promising direction for future research. Learning more about how such relationships are formed, established, and maintained may yield helpful insights that can be used to bring other caregivers, counselors, and allies (e.g., pastors) into familial-like relations with Black gay male collegians.

Recommendations for Practice

This chapter may prove useful to a number of groups. For instance, parents and guardians of Black gay men might consider this information when sorting through their own issues about sexual orientation. I continue to be dismayed by the large number of men in my studies who have been cut off, ostracized, or rejected by their parents, guardians, siblings, or cultural supports (e.g., church, pastors) as a result of disclosing their sexual orientation. To date, 100% of Black gay men who have participated in my studies report contemplating suicide or seriously attempting suicide, at least once, as a result of such rejection (Strayhorn & Tillman-Kelly, 2013). And while I can't stop this from happening entirely, I can call attention to it through chapters like the present, national keynote addresses, and through my own advocacy. I hope that parents, counselors, pastors, parishioners, and educators will remember a phrase hailed by the Human Rights Campaign—Love conquers hate—and keep it in mind when working with Black gay men, listening to their testimonies, and advising them about overcoming challenges.

Counselors and psychologists might find this information helpful when working with students and clients. What I provide here is a description of a theoretical model that describes the core elements of a sense of belonging in college, illuminates the needs of Black gay male collegians to belong, how they attempt to satisfy that need, and what happens when their need to belong is satisfied even if only partially. As I have mentioned elsewhere (Strayhorn, 2012), until the need to belong is gratified, all behaviors and responses should be interpreted as the individuals attempt to whet that appetite to fulfill higher order needs such as esteem and self-actualization. College student educators should consider this information when advising Black gay men through LGBT student groups, coaching Black gay men through conversations with their parents, and mentoring Black gay men through programs that may fail to acknowledge all their social identities and the ways they intersect.

Conclusion

The model not only applies to the subpopulation of Black gay men in college, but it relates to improving the condition of education for Black males, which was described in the opening section of this chapter. By helping some Black males, such as gay men, find a sense of belonging in college, we can nurture their academic self-efficacy and effectively raise their degree aspirations, thereby significantly increasing the odds that they will stay in college, earn good grades, and complete their college degree within a reasonable time. Helping Black gay males complete their college degree contributes to achieving the nation's 55 by '25 completion goal, which, in time will help restore the United States to its standing as a global leader in educational attainment. Anything less is unacceptable for a democratic nation committed to education for all its students.

References

Bazarsky, D., & Sanlo, R. (2011). LGBT student, faculty, and staff: Past, present, and future directions. In L. M. Stulberg & S. L. Weinberg (Eds.), *Diversity in American higher education: Toward a more comprehensive approach* (pp. 128–141). New York, NY: Routledge.

Berger, J. B. (1997). Students' sense of community in residence halls, social integration, and first-year persistence. *Journal of College Student Development, 38*(5), 441–452.

Cass, V. C. (1984). Homosexuality identity formation: Testing a theoretical model. *The Journal of Sex Research, 20*(2), 143–167.

Cuyjet, M. J., & Associates (Eds.). (2006). *African American men in college.* San Francisco, CA: Jossey-Bass.

D'Augelli, A. R. (1994). Identity development and sexual orientation: Toward a model of lesbian, gay, and bisexual development. In E. J. Trickett, R. J. Watts, & D. Birman (Eds.), *Human diversity: Perspectives on people in context* (pp. 312–333). San Francisco, CA: Jossey-Bass.

Ellis, H. (1901). *Studies in the psychology of sex, volume 2: Sexual inversion.* Philadelphia, PA: F. A. Davis.

Ferguson, A. A. (2000). *Bad boys: Public schools in the making of Black male masculinity.* Ann Arbor: University of Michigan Press.

Gibson, D. D., Schlosser, L. Z., & Brock-Murray, R. D. (2006). Identity management strategies among lesbians of African ancestry: A pilot study. *Journal of LGBT Issues in Counseling, 1*(4), 31–57.

Goodenow, C. (1993). Classroom belonging among early adolescent students: Relationships to motivation and achievement. *Journal of Early Adolescents, 13*(1), 21–43.

Hurtado, S., & Carter, D. F. (1997). Effects of college transition and perceptions of campus racial climate on Latino college students' sense of belonging. *Sociology of Education, 70*(4), 324–345.

Icard, L. D., & Nurius, P. S. (1996). Loss of self in coming out: Special risks for African American gays and lesbians. *Journal of Loss and Trauma, 1*(1), 29–47.

Jacoby, B., & Garland, J. (2004). Strategies for enhancing commuter student success. *Journal of College Student Retention: Research, Theory, & Practice, 6*(1), 61–79.

Kelly, (2010). *Closing the college attainment gap between the U.S. and most educated countries, and the contributions to be made by the states.* Boulder, CO: National Center for Higher Education Management Systems.

Kunjufu, J. (1986). *Countering the conspiracy to destroy Black boys.* Chicago, IL: African American Images.

Maslow, A. H. (1954). *Motivation and personality.* New York, NY: Harper & Row.

National Center for Education Statistics. (2012). *The condition of education 2012* (NCES Report No. 2012-081). Washington, DC: Author.

National Center for Public Policy and Higher Education. (2000). *Measuring up 2000*. Washington, DC: Author.

National Urban League. (2007). *The state of Black America 2007: Portrait of the Black male*. New York, NY: Beckham.

Obama, B. H. (2009). *Remarks of President Barack Obama: As prepared for delivery to Joint Session of Congress*. Retrieved August 15, 2009, from http://www.whitehouse.gov/the_press_office/remarks-of-president-barack-obama-address-to-joint-session-of-congress/

Osterman, K. F. (2000). Students' need for belonging in the school community. *Review of Educational Research, 70*(3), 323–367.

Roach, R. (2001). Where are the Black men on campus? *Black Issues in Higher Education, 18*(6), 18–24.

Strayhorn, T. L. (2008). Sentido de pertenencia: A hierarchical analysis predicting sense of belonging among Latino college students. *Journal of Hispanic Higher Education, 7*(4), 301–320.

Strayhorn, T. L. (2012). *College students' sense of belonging: A key to educational success*. New York, NY: Routledge.

Strayhorn, T. L. (2013a). And their own received them not: Black gay male undergraduates' experiences with White racism, Black homophobia. In M. C. Brown II, T. E. Dancy III, & J. E. Davis (Eds.), *Educating African American males: Contexts for consideration, possibilities for practice* (pp. 105–119). New York, NY: Peter Lang.

Strayhorn, T. L. (2013b). Coming out, fitting in: Interrogating the social experiences of Black gay males at White colleges. In T. E. Dancy III, & M. C. Brown II (Eds.), *African American males and education: Researching the convergence of race and identity* (pp. 151–170). Charlotte, NC: Information Age.

Strayhorn, T. L., Blakewood, A. M., & DeVita, J. M. (2008). Factors affecting the college choice of African American gay male undergraduates: Implications for retention. *NASPA Journal, 11*(1), 88–108.

Strayhorn, T. L., Blakewood, A. M., & DeVita, J. M. (2010). Triple threat: Challenges and supports of Black gay men at predominantly White campuses. In T. L. Strayhorn & M. C. Terrell (Eds.), *The evolving challenges of Black college students: New insights for policy, practice and research* (pp. 85–104). Sterling, VA: Stylus.

Strayhorn, T. L., & Scott, J. A. (2012). Coming out of the dark: Black gay men's experiences at historically Black colleges and universities. In R. T. Palmer & J. L. Wood (Eds.), *Black men in college: Implications for HBCUs and beyond* (pp. 26–40). New York, NY: Routledge.

Strayhorn, T. L., & Terrell, M. C. (Eds.). (2010). *The evolving challenges of Black college students: New insights for policy, practice, and research*. Sterling, VA: Stylus.

Strayhorn, T. L., & Tillman-Kelly, D. L. (2013). When and where race and sexuality collide with other social locations: Studying the intersectional lives of Black gay men in college. In T. L. Strayhorn (Ed.), *Living at the Intersections: Social identities and Black collegians* (pp. 237–257). Charlotte, NC: Information Age.

Walton, G. M., & Cohen, G. L. (2007). A question of belonging: Race, social fit, and achievement. *Journal of Personality and Social Psychology, 92*(1), 82–96.

AFTERWORD

R esearch that not only explores the condition of Black males in education but also provides practical solutions for educators, student affairs professionals, and policymakers is more critical than ever before because of the changing racial demography of the United States. According to the U.S. Census Bureau (2012), racial minorities (e.g., Blacks, Latinos/Latinas, Asian Americans, and Native Americans) are projected to become the new majority while concomitantly the White population is expected to decline. Given this reality, it is particularly important that scholars produce meaningful research to improve the educational outcomes among students of color in general and Black males specifically.

While research on how to improve educational outcomes of Black women is critical, research of this nature on Black males is particularly salient for the myriad of reasons researchers have described in this book. This book makes a meaningful contribution to the scholarship on Black males in the P–20 education pipeline because of its unique approach in addressing ways to increase college access and the success of this population. Another unique feature of this book is that it provides a seamless integration of the educational experiences of Black males in K–12 and higher education contexts.

A subsequent feature that makes this volume particularly compelling is that it does not treat Black males as homogeneous. Rather, many of the book's contributors recognize the diversity that exists among Black males in various educational settings. This is important because as my colleague J. Luke Wood and I argued in our book, *Black Men in College: Implications for HBCUs and Beyond* (New York, NY: Routledge, 2012), research must avoid homogenous depictions of Black males in postsecondary education. Instead, we argued that intersectionalities must be addressed with respect to a range of student characteristics. Being cognizant of the in-group differences among Black male populations will enhance insight and lead to better practices to improve outcomes for this population throughout the education pipeline.

The theme of this book is consistent with Robert Frost's (1988) poem *The Road Not Taken* in which Frost metaphorically reflects on a divergent road. While he could have traveled down the seemingly easy road, he took the road less traveled, which ultimately engendered a more fruitful and rewarding experience. Having taken the road less traveled in my research, I understand the enormous benefits that faculty, administrators, student affairs professionals, and policymakers can gain from such a decision. Specifically, while many researchers focused on examining the experience of Black males in predominantly White institutions, I sought to provide insight into the experiences of Black males at historically Black colleges and universities. This work was critical because primarily all that was known about Black males enrolled in historically Black colleges and universities was that they experienced a more supportive campus climate compared with their counterparts in predominantly White institutions.

Congruent with the theme of *The Road Not Taken*, each chapter of this book concludes with a framework or model, which is an effective way to bridge the gap between theory and practice. By including these frameworks or models, K–12 educators and administrators as well as higher education faculty, student affairs professionals, administrators, and policymakers have a template that they can use in their capacities to make tremendous inroads in increasing educational outcomes for Black males throughout the educational pipeline. Providing a model or framework is a meaningful way not merely to discuss the problems facing Black males in education but also to provide some practicality regarding how stakeholders might think about addressing these issues.

This timely book joins important work being done on Black males in the higher education and K–12 contexts by noted scholars, such as M. Christopher Brown, Michael J. Cuyjet, T. Elon Dancy II, James Earl Davis, Donna Y. Ford, Tarek C. Grantham, Shaun R. Harper, Jerlando Jackson, James L. Moore III, Pedro Noguera, Terrell L. Strayhorn, and J. Luke Wood, to name a few. Collectively, the chapters in the book serve as a much-needed and important resource on how to advance the success of Black males in education. Indeed, this book is a must-read, and more work of this nature is necessary to have a meaningful impact on Black males as they matriculate through various educational contexts.

Robert T. Palmer
Assistant Professor of Student Affairs
Department of Student Affairs Administration
State University of New York at Binghamton

References

Frost, R. (1988). The road not taken. In R. Ellman & R. O'Clair (Eds.), *The Norton anthology of modern poetry* (2nd ed., p. 247). New York, NY: Norton.

U.S. Census Bureau. (2012). *Most children younger than age 1 are minorities, Census Bureau reports*. Retrieved from http://www.census.gov/newsroom/releases/archives/population/cb12-90.html

CONTRIBUTORS

Quaylan Allen is assistant professor in the College of Educational Studies at Chapman University and serves on the editorial board of *Urban Education*. His research addresses educational equity by critically examining the implications of social and educational policy and practice on culturally diverse populations. In particular, his research centers on three interrelated areas. The first focuses on Black male educational outcomes and the construction and performance of Black masculinities in school. The second focuses on the educational prospects of the Black middle class, and the third focuses on the development and use of participant visual methodologies with Black male youths. His latest study was a school-based visual ethnography examining the implications of school policy and teacher practice on Black middle-class male high school achievement and middle-class social reproduction.

Stanford O. Amos is the founder and chief executive officer of S.O.S. Consulting. He is an advocate for education reform (including advanced placement/gifted classes for underrepresented students and increasing the number of Black male teachers and administrators). Stanford is a published poet and an entrepreneur with over 25 years of experience as a human resources professional, facilitator, mediator, public speaker, and corporate trainer. He is a graduate of Mississippi Valley State University, a U.S. Air Force veteran, and single father who is on a mission to save our sons and daughters.

Jerell Blakeley is a master's student at Rutgers University in the Graduate School of Education; he is concentrating in the social and philosophical foundations of education. He has a BA in history with a minor in political science from Howard University. While pursuing his master's degree, Blakeley was awarded the Harold and Reba Martin-Eagleton Fellowship of Politics and Government. Blakeley currently serves as a social studies teacher in New Jersey and as an educational specialist for the Upward Bound program at Mercer County Community College. Blakeley also serves on the boards of the Children's Home Society of New Jersey, UIH Family Partners of New Jersey, the Mercer County Workforce Investment Board, and as director of educational activities for the Zeta Iota Lambda chapter of Alpha Phi Alpha fraternity.

Fred A. Bonner II is the Samuel DeWitt Proctor Endowed Chair in Education at the Graduate School of Education at Rutgers University and an esteemed expert in the field of diversity in education. Prior to joining Rutgers, he was professor of higher education administration and dean of faculties at Texas A & M University–College Station. He earned a BA in chemistry from the University of North Texas, an MSEd in curriculum and instruction from Baylor University, and an EdD in higher education administration and college teaching from the University of Arkansas. Bonner has been the recipient of numerous awards, including the American Association for higher education Black Caucus Dissertation Award and the Educational Leadership, Counseling and Foundation's Dissertation of the Year Award from the University of Arkansas College of Education. His work has been featured nationally and internationally.

Eric M. Bridges is associate professor of psychology at Clayton State University. His research agenda investigates health and racial identity among African American males and how African traditional spiritual systems can be used as healing modalities for people of African descent. He serves on the editorial boards for the *Journal of African American Males in Education* and *PsycCRITIQUES*.

T. Elon Dancy II is associate professor of higher education at the University of Oklahoma in Norman, where he also holds joint appointments in African and African American studies, women's and gender studies, and the Center for Social Justice. His research agenda investigates sociocognitive outcomes among college students, particularly at the intersections of race, gender, and culture. His 50 publications include four books, including *The Brother Code: Manhood and Masculinity Among African American Males in College* (Charlotte, NC: Information Age, 2012) and *Educating African American Males: Contexts for Consideration, Possibilities for Practice* (New York, NY: Peter Lang, 2013). He has received funding from the National Science Foundation for his work on males of color, gender identity, and achievement in science, technology, engineering, and mathematics. Dancy's honors and awards include recognition as one of the nation's top emerging scholars by the publication *Diverse: Issues in Higher Education* in 2014.

Alonzo M. Flowers III is an assistant professor in the Department of Educational Leadership, Counseling, and Foundations at the University of New Orleans. Dr. Flowers specializes in educational issues including poverty and academic giftedness of African American males, STEM education, diversity, and college student transition and development. Dr. Flowers's research focuses on the academic experiences of academically gifted African American and Latino students in the STEM disciplines, particularly engineering, mathematics, and science. He has completed 35 peer-reviewed conference presentations since 2005. This includes several national presentations at the Association for the Study of Higher Education and Texas Association for the Gifted and Talented state conference. Recently, he was selected to be the keynote speaker at the first annual Texas African American Males in College Achievement & Success Symposium in Austin, Texas, where he discussed Giftedness at a Crossroads for African American Male College Students in STEM.

Lamont A. Flowers is the Distinguished Professor of Educational Leadership and the executive director of the Charles H. Houston Center for the Study of the Black Experience in Education in the Eugene T. Moore School of Education at Clemson University. Dr. Flowers received a bachelor's degree in accounting from Virginia Commonwealth University. He also received a master's degree in social studies education and a doctoral degree in higher education from the University of Iowa. Additionally, he received a master's degree in industrial statistics from the University of South Carolina.

Lawrence O. Flowers is an assistant professor of microbiology in the Department of Biological Sciences at Fayetteville State University in Fayetteville, North Carolina. He received a bachelor of science in biology from Virginia Commonwealth University in Richmond, Virginia and a master of science in science education and a master's of science in biology from the University of Iowa in Iowa City, Iowa. Dr. Flowers received his doctorate in microbiology and cell science from the University of Florida in Gainesville, Florida. After obtaining his doctorate, Dr. Flowers served as a postdoctoral research associate in the Department of Immunology at Duke University in Durham, North Carolina. He has published several scientific research articles in the following scientific journals: *Journal of Immunology, Oncogene, Biochemistry,* and *The Journal of Experimental Medicine.* Dr. Flowers is also a member of several national professional organizations including the National Science Teachers Association (NSTA) and the American Society for Microbiology (ASM).

Donna Y. Ford is professor of education and human development at Vanderbilt University. She is the 2013 Harvie Branscomb Distinguished Professor and holds a joint appointment in the Department of Special Education and the Department of Teaching and Learning. Ford earned her doctor of philosophy degree in urban education (educational psychology). Ford conducts research primarily in gifted education and multicultural/urban education. Specifically, her work focuses on the achievement gap, recruiting and retaining culturally different students in gifted education, multicultural curriculum and instruction, culturally competent teacher training and development, African American identity, and African American family involvement. She consults with school districts and educational and legal organizations on such topics as gifted education underrepresentation and advanced placement, multicultural/urban education and counseling, and closing the achievement gap. She is the author or coauthor of several books that address these areas of scholarship. Ford has written over 150 articles and book chapters, and conducted thousands of presentations and workshops in schools, colleges and universities, and communities. Her work has been recognized by many organizations.

Derrick L. Gragg was named University of Tulsa's vice president and director of athletics on March 20, 2013. Before arriving at Tulsa, Gragg spent seven years as the director of athletics at Eastern Michigan University. Gragg's experience covers 20 years in progressively advanced roles at the universities of Arkansas, Michigan, Missouri, and Vanderbilt. A former collegiate football wide receiver, Gragg lettered four years at Vanderbilt while earning his bachelor's degree in human development, which he received in 1992. He earned his master's degree in sports administration from Wayne State University in 1999. Gragg received his doctorate in higher education administration from the University of Arkansas in May 2004 and has also taught several college courses during the past years. A native of Huntsville, Alabama, Gragg was inducted into the Huntsville-Madison County Athletic Hall of Fame in 2010. He is a member of the National Association of Collegiate Directors of Athletics and the Black Coaches and Administrators organization.

Tarek C. Grantham is an associate professor in the Department of Educational Psychology at the University of Georgia, and he has served as coordinator in the Gifted and Creative Education Program, where he teaches primarily in the Diversity and Equity Strand. Grantham's research addresses underserved ethnic minority students, particularly Black males, in advanced programs. He has coedited two books: *Gifted and Advanced Black Students in School: An Anthology of Critical Works* (Waco, TX: Prufrock Press, 2011), and *Young, Triumphant, and Black: Overcoming the Tyranny of Segregated Minds in Desegregated Schools* (Waco, TX: Prufrock Press, 2013). Grantham serves as the convention program chair for the Special Populations Network of the National Association for Gifted Children. He also serves as a board member for the Council for Exceptional Children, Talented and Gifted Division, and he is cochair of its Parent, Community, and Diversity Committee. Grantham received the 2012 Mary M. Frasier Excellence and Equity Award from the Georgia Association for Gifted Children for outstanding achievement in practices that promote equitable identification procedures or the provision of high-quality services to gifted students from underrepresented groups. Grantham is the fortunate husband of a wonderful wife, Kimberly D. Grantham, senior lecturer in marketing at the University of Georgia, and he is the proud father of three children, Kurali, Copeland, and Jovi.

Frank Harris III is an associate professor of postsecondary education and codirector of the Minority Male Community College Collaborative at San Diego State University. His research is broadly focused on student development and student success in postsecondary education and explores questions related to the social construction of gender and race on college campuses, college men and masculinities, and racial and ethnic disparities in college student outcomes. Harris's scholarship has been published in leading journals for education research and practice, including the *Journal of College Student Development, Journal of Men's Studies, Journal of Student Affairs Research and Practice, Qualitative Research*, and *Journal of Negro Education*. He is coeditor of *College Men and Masculinities: Theory, Research, and Implications for Practice* (San Francisco, CA: Jossey-Bass, 2010). Before joining the faculty at San Diego State, Harris worked as a student affairs educator and college administrator in the areas of student affairs administration, student crisis support and advocacy, new student orientation programs, multicultural student affairs, academic advising, and enrollment services. Harris earned a bachelor's degree in communication studies from Loyola Marymount University, a master's degree in speech communication from California State University Northridge, and an EdD in higher education from the University of Southern California.

Thomas P. Hébert is professor of gifted and talented education in the College of Education at the University of South Carolina. Hébert has more than a decade of K–12 classroom experience working with gifted students and 20 years in higher education training graduate students and educators in gifted education. He has also conducted research for the National Research Center on the Gifted and Talented. He served on the board of directors of the National Association for Gifted Children and the Association for the Gifted of the Council for Exceptional Children. He has provided consulting services internationally in Italy, Taiwan, Paraguay, Peru, Mexico, Hong Kong, and Ghana. His research interests include gifted culturally diverse students, social and emotional development of gifted students, and problems faced by gifted young men. He has published widely, including over 100 refereed journal articles, book chapters, and scholarly reports. He is the author of the award-winning text *Understanding the Social and Emotional Lives of Gifted Students* (Waco,

TX: Prufrock Press, 2011). Hébert has received numerous research and teaching awards including the 2000 Early Scholar Award from the National Association for Gifted Children and the 2012 Distinguished Alumni Award from the Neag School of Education at the University of Connecticut.

Christopher O. Johnson is a doctoral candidate in the Department of Educational Psychology (Applied Cognition and Development Program) at the University of Georgia, and he has taught and cotaught in the undergraduate introductory teaching and learning educator preparation foundations courses. His research interests focus on motivation, racial identity, and gifted Black males. At the University of Georgia, Johnson's scholarly achievements include the Dean's Award for International Study, Kappa Delta Pi International Honor Society Inductee, and the Southern Regional Education Board Doctoral Scholar Fellowship. Johnson was selected as a participant for the Asa G. Hilliard III and Barbara A. Sizemore Research Institute on African Americans and Education sponsored by the American Educational Research Association's Research Focus on Black Education Special Interest Group. He has served on the search committee for the university's College of Education dean's position, and as a member of the Public Policy Committee for the Association of Black Psychologists. Upon completion of his degree, Johnson plans to pursue a faculty position in higher education, conducting research and teaching on diversity and equity issues.

Tim King is founder, president, and chief executive officer of Urban Prep Academies, a nonprofit organization operating a network of public college/ preparatory boys' schools in Chicago (including the nation's first all-male charter high school) and related programs aimed at promoting college success. All (100%) of Urban Prep graduates—African American males and mostly from low-income families—have been admitted to four-year colleges or universities. King also serves as an adjunct lecturer at Northwestern University and has published articles in the *Journal of Negro Education, Chronicle of Higher Education, Chicago Tribune, Chicago Sun Times,* and *Huffington Post.* King was named ABC's *World News's* Person of the Week, *Chicago* magazine's Chicagoan of the Year, *People* magazine's Hero of the Year, and was listed in *Ebony* magazine's Power 100 list. He was featured on *Good Morning America,* the *Oprah Winfrey Show,* USA Network's *Characters Unite* series, and he was recognized by presidents Barack Obama and Bill Clinton for his work with youths. King has completed postgraduate work in Kenya and Italy, holds the doctorate honoris causa from the Adler School, and received his bachelor of science in foreign service and juris doctor degrees from Georgetown University.

L. Trenton Marsh is a doctoral student at New York University's Stein-hardt School in the teaching and learning department. He is concentrating in urban education and social psychology. He has a BS in business adminis-tration with a double major in marketing and enterprise management from American University. He earned his MA in education with a concentration in human resource development from George Washington University. Marsh is also an author and public speaker on education, specifically on academic and professional excellence. His book *From 1.0 to 4.0* (Bloomington, IN: Traf-ford, 2008) highlights the strategies he used to make the transition from a struggling high school student to a successful student leader and academi-cian. Marsh is a founding member of CommitMEN, a virtual think tank that provides scholarship and guidance to African American men from high school through college.

Ebony O. McGee is an assistant professor of diversity and urban schooling at Vanderbilt University's Peabody College and a member of Scientific Careers Research and Development Group at Northwestern University. She received her BS in electrical engineering from North Carolina Agricultural and Tech-nical State University, her MS in industrial engineering from the New Jersey Institute of Technology, her PhD in mathematics education from the Uni-versity of Illinois at Chicago, and she was a National Academy of Education/ Spencer Foundation Postdoctoral Fellow and a National Science Foundation Postdoctoral Fellow. As a former electrical engineer, she is concerned with science, technology, engineering, and mathematics (STEM) learning and participation among marginalized students of color. Her research focuses on the role of racialized biases in educational and career attainment, resiliency, mathematics identity and identity development in high-achieving marginal-ized students of color in STEM fields.

Sharon Michael-Chadwell is campus college chair in the College of Edu-cation in the University of Phoenix as well as an associate professor with Liberty University's School of Education. She received an MA in human resources development, an MBA from Webster University, and completed her EdD in educational leadership from the University of Phoenix. She has over 30 years of experience in education working in the K–12 and higher education sectors. Michael-Chadwell's research focus is on race and minor-ity student achievement; race and teacher or administrator development; and educational policy and student achievement. She has presented her research on factors related to the underrepresentation of African Americans and Hispanics in gifted and talented programs at state, national, and inter-national levels and has completed articles and book chapters focusing on this topic.

H. Richard Milner IV is the Helen Faison Professor of Urban Education, professor of education, professor of Africana Studies, and professor of social work as well as director of the Center for Urban Education at the University of Pittsburgh. His research, teaching, and policy interests center on urban education, teacher education, African American literature, and the sociology of education. Professor Milner's work has appeared in numerous journals, and he has published five books. His latest book, *Start Where You Are But Don't Stay There: Understanding Diversity, Opportunity Gaps, and Teaching in Today's Classrooms* (Cambridge, MA: Harvard Education Press, 2010), has been recognized with two awards: the 2012 American Association of Colleges for Teacher Education Outstanding Book Award and the 2011 American Educational Studies Association Critics' Choice Book Award. In 2006 Milner received an Early Career Award from the Committee on Scholars of Color in Education of the American Educational Research Association. Currently, he is editor in chief of *Urban Education* and coeditor of *The Handbook of Urban Education* with Kofi Lomotey (New York, NY: Routledge, 2014).

James L. Moore III is an associate provost in the Office of Diversity and Inclusion, where he also serves as the inaugural director of the Todd Anthony Bell National Resource Center on the African American Male at The Ohio State University. Additionally, Dr. Moore is the EHE Distinguished Professor of Urban Education in the College of Education and Human Ecology. Dr. Moore has a nationally and internationally recognized research agenda that focuses on school counseling, gifted education, urban education, higher education, multicultural education/counseling, and STEM education. He recently coedited two books with Dr. Chance W. Lewis of the University of North Carolina at Charlotte: *African American Students in Urban Schools: Critical Issues and Solutions for Achievement* (New York, NY: Peter Lang, 2012) and *African American Male Students in PreK–12 Schools: Informing Research, Policy, and Practice* (Bingley, UK: Emerald Group, 2014). Further, Dr. Moore has published over 100 publications, obtained over $8 million in grants, contracts, and gifts, and given over 200 scholarly presentations and lectures throughout the United States and other parts of the world.

Rev. Otis Moss III is the senior pastor of Trinity United Church of Christ in Chicago, IL. A leading progressive Christian activist and cultural critic, Moss is a jazz-influenced pastor with a hip-hop vibe. He is committed to the gospel of Jesus Christ, rooted in love and justice, and is inspired by the works of Zora Neale Hurston, August Wilson, and Howard Thurman. His creative Bible-based messages have inspired young and old alike. His intergenerational preaching gift has made Moss a popular speaker on college campuses and at conferences and churches across the globe. Moss is author of *Redemption in a Red Light District*; coauthor of *The Gospel Re-Mix: How to Reach the Hip-Hop Generation*; and is coauthor with his father, Rev. Otis Moss Jr., of *Preach! The Power and Purpose Behind Our Praise*. His sermons, articles, and poetry have appeared in publications and blog sites such as *Huffington Post*; *Urban Cusp*; The Root; *Power in the Pulpit II: America's Most Effective Preachers*; *Joy to the World: Sermons From America's Pulpit*; *Sound the Trumpet: Messages of Hope for Black Men* (Valley Forge, PA: Judson Press, 2009); *The Audacity of Faith: Christian Leaders Reflect on the Election of Barack Obama*; *Sojourners Magazine*; and *The African American Pulpit Journal*; and his book of sermons, *The Gospel According to the Wiz: And Other Sermons from Cinema* (Cleveland, OH: Pilgrim, 2013). A native of Cleveland, Ohio, Moss is an honors graduate of Morehouse College and Yale Divinity School, and has a doctor of ministry degree from Chicago Theological Seminary.

Robert T. Palmer is assistant professor of student affairs administration at the State University of New York at Binghamton. Palmer's work has been published in national refereed journals, and he has authored or coauthored well over 80 academic publications. In 2009 the American College Personnel Association's (ACPA's) Standing Committee for Men recognized his excellent research on Black men with its Outstanding Research Award. In 2011 Palmer was named an ACPA Emerging Scholar, and in 2012 he received the Carlos J. Vallejo Award of Emerging Scholarship from the American Education Research Association. Furthermore, in 2012 he received the Association for the Study of Higher Education Mildred García Junior Exemplary Scholarship Award.

Angie C. Roberts-Dixon was born in the Caribbean and raised as a Caribbean American. She has been committed to the education of minority students for more than 20 years. Roberts-Dixon has worked with youths across the United States from New York City to Walla Walla, Washington. Her research has focused on issues of diversity in countries such as Guyana, Kenya, and Thailand. As a school psychologist, she believes that the key to students' embracing a multicultural perspective involves creating centers of learning where they can interact, form friendships, and grow through discovery. Roberts-Dixon is founder of the nonprofit organization Enterprising Women, and her current work focuses on helping young women discover and build on their strengths through identifying with other women of the world.

Terrell L. Strayhorn is associate professor of higher education in the College of Education and Human Ecology (EHE) at The Ohio State University (OSU), where he also serves as director of the Center for Inclusion, Diversity and Academic Success (IDEAS), EHE chief diversity officer, faculty research associate in the Kirwan Institute for the Study of Race and Ethnicity, and senior research associate in the Todd A. Bell National Resource Center for African American Males. He also holds faculty appointments in OSU's Departments of African American and African Studies, engineering education, and sexuality studies (as a courtesy). Strayhorn maintains an active and highly visible research agenda focusing on major policy issues in education: student access and achievement, equity and diversity, impact of college on students, and student learning and development. Specifically, his research and teaching interests center on two major foci: assessing student learning and development outcomes and the ways college affects students, and identifying and understanding factors that enable or inhibit the success of historically underrepresented and misrepresented populations in education, with a particular accent on issues of race, class, and gender and how they affect the experiences of racial and ethnic minorities, college men, economically disadvantaged individuals, and marginalized groups in postsecondary education. Strayhorn is author or lead editor of seven books, including *College Students' Sense of Belonging: A Key to Educational Success* (New York, NY: Routledge, 2012), *Living at the Intersections* (Charlotte, NC: Information Age, 2013), and *Theoretical Frameworks in College Student Research* (Lanham, MD: Rowman & Littlefield, 2013).

Gilman Whiting is an associate professor of African American and diaspora studies and director of the Scholar Identity Institute. He received his PhD from Purdue University. Whiting teaches courses on the African American diaspora, Black issues in education; Black masculinity; race, sport, and American culture; Blacks in the military; and qualitative research methods. His areas of interest and research include special needs populations (gifted, at-risk learners), developing scholar identities, education reform, welfare reform, young Black fathers and fatherhood initiatives, and health, fitness, and nutrition in the Black community. He is the author of more than 40 scholarly publications relating to minority populations, especially males, special education, and teacher education in *Council for Exceptional Children, Urban Education, Roeper Review, Willamette Journal: Special on African American Studies, Gifted Education Press Quarterly, Journal for Secondary Gifted Education, Gifted Child Today,* and the *Midwestern Educational Research Journal.* He is editor of "On Manliness: Black American Masculinities," *AmeriQuests* (2008).

J. Luke Wood is assistant professor of administration, rehabilitation, and postsecondary Education at San Diego State University. Wood is codirector of the Minority Male Community College Collaborative, chair of the Multicultural and Multiethnic Education special interest group of the American Educational Research Association, and chair-elect for the Council on Ethnic Participation for the Association for the Study of Higher Education. He is also the founding editor of the *Journal of African American Males in Education*. Wood's research focuses on factors affecting the success of Black (and other minority) male students in community colleges. In particular, his research examines contributors (e.g., social, psychological, academic, environmental, institutional) to positive outcomes (e.g., persistence, achievement, attainment, transfer, labor market outcomes) for these men. Wood has written nearly 70 pieces for publication, including two coauthored textbooks, four edited books, and more than 30 peer-reviewed journal articles.

fighting, 143, 145
financial obstacles, 126, 181
Fire in the Ashes: Twenty-Five Years Among the Poorest Children in America (Kozol), 99
five domains
  academic domain, 180
  for community college, 178–81
  institutional domain, 181
  noncognitive domain, 179–80
  social domain, 179
Flowers, Alonzo M., 5–6, 125, 129
Flowers, Lamont, 6
Flowers, Lawrence, 6
Football Bowl Subdivision (FBS), 189
Ford, Donna Y., 54, 64, 67, 70, 91, 110, 115, 132
FP. *See* fatherhood program
Frasier, Mary, 55, 110
Frasier's Talent Assessment Profile (F-TAP), 55
fraternities, 148, 194, 195–96
friendships. *See* peers
frientoring, 153
Fries-Britt, S., 114
"From At Risk to At Promise: Developing Scholar Identities Among Black Males" (Whiting), 91
Frost, Robert, 6–7, 215–16
Fryer, Roland, 96
F-TAP. *See* Frasier's Talent Assessment Profile
full-time enrollment, persistence and, 180

Gamson, Z. F., 149
Garibaldi, A., 144
gay, lesbian, bisexual, and transgendered (GLBT), 6
  belonging for, 200–213
  GPA for, 210
  in HBCUs, 206
  Latino Americans as, 211

practice recommendations for, 212
  in PWIs, 206
  research recommendations for, 211–12
GEMS. *See* gifted ethnic minority students
gender roles, 146, 147
generalizability, 118
Gifted Black Males: Understanding and Decreasing Barriers to Achievement and Identity (Whiting), 92
Gifted Child Today, 91
gifted ethnic minority students (GEMS), 46–52
  underrepresentation of, 46
giftedness
  achievement gap and, 63
  advocacy for, 62, 70
  core attributes of, 55, 58
  creativity in, 58, 81–82, 114
  definitions for, 53, 127
  extended family and, 82–83
  family and, 80, 112–13, 119
  HBCUs and, 109–20
  identification of, 64–66, 70
  intelligence test scores and, 66, 68
  mentoring for, 86
  nonrecognition of, 66
  P–12 and, 111–13
  P–16 and, 110
  peers and, 112–13, 115–16, 118–19
  postsecondary education and, 113–18
  PWIs and, 109–20
  rural poverty and, 75–87
  self-identity and, 83–85
  SIM and, 129
  STEM and, 125–36
  stereotypes for, 66
  student integration model and, 128–29
  triarchic theory of intelligence and, 127–28

Also available from Stylus

Men of Color in Higher Education
New Foundations for Developing Models for Success
Edited by Ronald A. Williams
With LeManuel Lee Bitsói, Edmund T. Gordon, Shaun R. Harper, Victor B. Sáenz, and Robert T. Teranishi
Foreword by Freeman A. Hrabowski III

"*Men of Color in Higher Education* embraces asset-based models like the one developed at UMBC—and it holds practitioners accountable for being precise about what we mean when we talk about improving student success and providing better support for students of color. Whether examining the outcomes of Asian and Pacific Islander or African American students, the authors make a compelling case for nuance and precision. Not only must colleges and universities carefully examine student outcomes by gender and race, but they must go further in disaggregating data.

Perhaps the most powerful promise presented by *Men of Color in Higher Education* is that if we can help our most vulnerable students succeed, we can ensure that all students experience the type of education that is at the heart of the American dream."

—Freeman A. Hrabowski III,
President, University of Maryland, Baltimore County

This book brings together five of today's leading scholars concerned with the condition of males of color in higher education—LeManuel Lee Bitsói, Edmund T. Gordon, Shaun R. Harper, Victor B. Sáenz and Robert T. Teranishi—who collaborated closely through of a series of conversations convened by the College Board to diagnose the common factors impeding the success of underrepresented males, and identify the particular barriers and cultural issues pertaining to the racial and ethnic groups they examine.

This book advances the critical priorities of increasing enrollments and completion rates among college men of color, and of graduating well-developed men with strong, conflict-free gender identities.

For practitioners who work with these populations, it offers insights and signposts to create successful programs; for researchers, it offers a set of new directions for analysis; and for policymakers, it offers new ways of thinking about how policy and funding mechanisms ought to be reconsidered to be more effective in responding this issue.

22883 Quicksilver Drive
Sterling, VA 20166-2102

Subscribe to our e-mail alerts: www.Styluspub.com